THE EYE THAT IS LANGUAGE

Harriet Pollack, Series Editor

THE EYE THAT IS LANGUAGE

A Transatlantic View of Eudora Welty

Danièle Pitavy-Souques

Edited with a Preface by Pearl Amelia McHaney

University Press of Mississippi / Jackson

The University Press of Mississippi is the scholarly publishing agency of
the Mississippi Institutions of Higher Learning: Alcorn State University,
Delta State University, Jackson State University, Mississippi State University,
Mississippi University for Women, Mississippi Valley State University,
University of Mississippi, and University of Southern Mississippi.

www.upress.state.ms.us
The University Press of Mississippi is a member
of the Association of University Presses.

Any discriminatory or derogatory language or hate speech regarding race,
ethnicity, religion, sex, gender, class, national origin, age, or disability that
has been retained or appears in elided form is in no way an endorsement
of the use of such language outside a scholarly context.

Quotations from the work by Eudora Welty are used with permission
of Eudora Welty, LLC, with the cooperation of the Mississippi Department
of Archives and History and Massie & McQuilkin Literary Agents.

Copyright © 2022 by University Press of Mississippi
All rights reserved

First printing 2022
∞

Library of Congress Cataloging-in-Publication Data

Names: Pitavy-Souques, Danièle, author. | McHaney, Pearl Amelia, editor.
Title: The eye that is language : a transatlantic view of Eudora Welty /
Danièle Pitavy-Souques, edited with a preface by Pearl Amelia McHaney.
Other titles: Critical perspectives on Eudora Welty.
Description: Jackson : University Press of Mississippi, 2022. |
Series: Critical perspectives on Eudora Welty | Includes bibliographical
references and index.
Identifiers: LCCN 2021057684 (print) | LCCN 2021057685 (ebook) |
ISBN 978-1-4968-4058-5 (hardback) | ISBN 978-1-4968-4059-2
(trade paperback) | ISBN 978-1-4968-4061-5 (epub) |
ISBN 978-1-4968-4060-8 (epub) | ISBN 978-1-4968-4063-9 (pdf) |
ISBN 978-1-4968-4062-2 (pdf)
Subjects: LCSH: Welty, Eudora, 1909–2001—Criticism and interpretation. |
Women authors, American—Criticism and interpretation. |
Mississippi—Women authors—Criticism and interpretation. | BISAC:
LITERARY CRITICISM / Women Authors | LITERARY CRITICISM /
Modern / 20th Century
Classification: LCC PS3545.E6 Z843 2022 (print) | LCC PS3545.E6 (ebook) |
DDC 813/.52—dc23/eng/20220208
LC record available at https://lccn.loc.gov/2021057684
LC ebook record available at https://lccn.loc.gov/2021057685

British Library Cataloging-in-Publication Data available

CONTENTS

Preface vii
Acknowledgments xiii
The Eye That Is Language: An Introduction 3
Chapter 1. Technique as Myth:
  The Structure of *The Golden Apples* (1979) 7
Chapter 2. A Blazing Butterfly:
  The Modernity of Eudora Welty (1987) 17
Chapter 3. A Rereading of Eudora Welty's
  "Flowers for Marjorie" (2018) 36
Chapter 4. Of Human, Animal, and Celestial Bodies
  in Welty's "Circe" (2005) 46
Chapter 5. "The Fictional Eye": Eudora Welty's Retranslation
  of the South (2000) 57
Chapter 6. Private and Political Thoughts in *One Writer's
  Beginnings* (2001) 75
Chapter 7. Eudora Welty and the Merlin Principle:
  Aspects of Story-Telling in *The Golden Apples*—
  "The Whole World Knows" and "Sir Rabbit" (2009) 90
Chapter 8. "The Inspired Child of [Her] Times":
  Eudora Welty as a Twentieth-Century Artist (2010) 107
Chapter 9. "Moments of Truth": Eudora Welty's Humanism (2014) . . . 127
Afterword by François Pitavy 143
Notes 145
Works Cited 153
Additional Publications by Danièle Pitavy-Souques 163
Index 165

PREFACE

"This is really a love affair, and how can one write about such things without feeling at once shy and eager?" This was Danièle Pitavy-Souques's response when asked about her first becoming acquainted with Eudora Welty and her work, the question itself a nod to John Keats's sonnet "Upon First Looking into Chapman's Homer." Danièle, who shall always be regarded as a powerhouse of Eudora Welty studies, thereafter, explained why reading Welty's work, meeting, and knowing her had been "the passion" of her life, "something of the heart, and something of the soul after being first something of the mind."[1]

Danièle Pitavy-Souques published two books on Welty's work, *La mort de Méduse: L'art de la nouvelle chez Eudora Welty* (*The Death of Medusa: The Art of the Story by Eudora Welty*, 1991) and *Eudora Welty: Les sortilège du conteur* (*Eudora Welty: The Witchcraft of Storytelling*, 1999), and dozens of essays. She convened conferences and earned French, American, and international awards for Welty and herself. Prior to her death in 2019, Danièle planned this collection of eight of her essays on Welty published between 1979 and 2014, composed a new essay on Welty's short story "Flowers for Marjorie," and wrote her introduction, "The Eye That Is Language." It is an honor to assist in the realization of Danièle's intentions to provide a volume of her Welty essays in English for both confirmed and new readers of Eudora Welty's fiction, nonfiction, and photographs.

Danièle organized and hosted the The Southernness of Eudora Welty conference at the University of Burgundy, Dijon, France, in 1992. She and Géraldine Chouard planned the Eudora Welty: The Poetics of the Body conference in cooperation with the Faulkner Foundation at the University of Rennes, France, a decade later, in 2002. She made many visits to the United States, including celebrations of Welty's eighty-fifth (1994) and ninetieth (1999) birthdays at Lemuria Books in Jackson, Mississippi, and the Eudora Welty Society and Millsaps College "Mississippi Home Ties: A Eudora Welty Conference" (1997), also in Jackson. During the centennial year of Welty's birth, 2009, Danièle participated in multiple celebrations and conferences in the United States, France, and Italy.

It is doubtful that the French Americanists would have ever read Eudora Welty's work were it not for Danièle's vigorous studies and leadership. *The Golden Apples* was on the 1992 French *Agrégation de Lettres Classique*, a national competitive exam for all who wish to become teachers at the secondary or university level, so Welty's masterpiece, her story cycle, was studied throughout France. The following year, 1993, when Danièle prompted the University of Burgundy to award Welty her first honorary degree from outside the United States, Danièle explained that it was an appropriate award "because of some deep affinities between the South and Burgundy, because of the confluence of two imaginations, lofty and exacting, paradoxically aware of the extreme beauty of the sensuous world as well as of the exigencies of the spiritual world, up to that very spirit of resistance that marks their histories."[2]

In 1996, Danièle and former Mississippi governor and Welty's friend William Winter presided over ceremonies at the Old Capitol Building in Jackson to present Welty with the French Chevalier de la Légion d'honneur. The occasion afforded Danièle an opportunity to explain what made Welty unique.

> First, she distanced her fiction from the dominant Southern themes of history, guilt, and painful racial issues. Instead, she regarded "that which all non-artists call 'form' as content, as 'the matter itself'" as Nietzsche puts it. She thus renewed the problematics of writing about injustice, prejudice, extreme poverty. Southern violence is there, but it is to be found in her technique, in her constant search for new ways of telling a story, in her endless experimenting with new narrative modes that tend towards abstraction. She was echoing in this the contemporary trend in the pictorial arts and inventing postmodernism. In this way, she liberated Southern fiction, from William Faulkner included, and broke fresh new paths that made it possible for younger Southern writers to write.
>
> Then, her fiction is Protean, since it displays an infinite variety of moods, styles, and themes. And this comes from her magnificent baroque imagination. What you might call Southern gothic or Southern grotesque in her work partakes of that more universal mode of apprehending life and the work of art, something which privileges the singular and the fleeting moment, which presents life as dissolving instants, ever changing appearances, and endless plays on reflections. The baroque is also theatricality, what sees the spectacle, stages it, then laughs at it. It inspires the magnificent comedy, parody, burlesque, and music hall spirit that pervade all Welty's fiction.

Finally, like all great women writers, Eudora Welty has a cosmic view of life and the world. Her characters are all simple, ordinary people. Her plots belong to our average experience, yet, beneath it all, she sees those great battles fought by mankind against time and death and fate. She sees that other dimension, what she calls the holiness of life, something that was strongly brought to her when she visited Europe. In front of the capitols of the cathedral of Autun in Burgundy, for instance, she saw what she had been doing all along in her fiction, that unique combination so characteristic of Romanesque art, between the familiar and the spiritual, that medieval tension between the given experience and the revealed. What transported her there was what another woman artist, the Canadian painter Emily Carr, felt before Haida totem poles: "The power that I felt was not the thing itself, but in some tremendous force behind it, that the carver had believed in" (*Klee Wyck* 36). Likewise in *One Writer's Beginning*, Eudora Welty writes, "It was later, when I was able to travel farther, that the presence of holiness and mystery seemed, as far as my vision was able to see, to descend into the windows of Chartres, the stone peasant figures in the capitals of Autun." (877)[3]

These perspectives suggest the powerful visions articulated in Danièle's essays collected here. Drawing from her life experiences, her deep study of visual arts, her transatlantic travels, and her keen sensibility for beauty of all kinds, Danièle reads Welty's fiction, memoir, and photographs in new ways.

In 2002, Danièle received two awards: the French government recognized Danièle with this same honor that Welty had received, the Chevalier de la Légion d'honneur, and the Eudora Welty Society presented her with the Phoenix Award for her significant contributions to Welty studies. The Légion d'honneur recognizes "those who have distinguished themselves in some artistic or literary field,"[4] and, for Danièle, this includes not only her contributions to Welty studies, but also her investigations of other United States writers including Willa Cather, Kate Chopin, Ellen Douglas, William Faulkner, Kaye Gibbons, Josephine Humphreys, and Elizabeth Spencer, as well as Canadian writers and artists Margaret Atwood, Emily Carr, Leon Rooke, and Alice Munro and the founding and directing of the Eudora Welty Center for the Study of Northern American Women Writers at the University of Burgundy. The award also significantly commends Danièle for her work with the French Association of University Women and the International Federation of University Women (now Graduate Women International) for which she served as vice-president and the international coordinator for France and on many committees for empowering women.

In her comments upon receiving the Légion d'honneur, Danièle cited two statements of particular importance that also serve our understanding of her perspective in reading Welty. First is a sentence near the end of Margaret Atwood's 1972 novel *Surfacing*: "*This, above all, to refuse to be a victim,*" and second is a line by Milton pondering how he should write given his blindness: "And that one talent which is death to hide."⁵ Danièle claimed these as

> rules by which to live and think. Foremost, never to give up when confronted with trials and difficulties, something which my father taught me, when in the hands of the Gestapo he refused to speak, and later, when he died in a concentration camp comforting his fellow prisoners. Secondly, to be convinced that each one of us has a talent, however humble, which we must develop and put to the service of others. Thirdly, to refuse to be sorry for oneself, because from the moment we try to find self-excuses, we lose our humanity and shut ourselves within sterile grievance. Three rules, simple and not original, which help us to live.⁶

Following her father's example of justice and her mother's model as a graduate of the École Normale Supérieure de Sèvres, Danièle was first a teacher in a lycée (a secondary school for those wishing to continue to university studies) before beginning her tenure as professor in the Department of English at the University of Burgundy, France. In 1993 she received a Fulbright research grant, and from 1996 to 2009, she was the director of the Center for Canadian Studies at the University of Burgundy from which she retired in 2017.

The nine essays selected by Danièle and gathered here are testament to both Danièle's and Welty's visions. *The Eye That Is Language: A Transatlantic View of Eudora Welty* is an integration of Danièle's assessments of Welty's work, written in English over the past thirty-odd years. Included are her seminal essays "Technique as Myth: The Structure of *The Golden Apples*" (1979, reprinted in 1983 and 1986) and "A Blazing Butterfly: The Modernity of Eudora Welty" (1987). Essays written between 2000–2009 as well as the previously unpublished "Re-reading of 'Flowers for Marjorie'" (2014) often challenge previous readings of Welty's prose and photography and are presented in the broad context of artistic, political, and philosophical currents. They include "'The Fictional Eye': Eudora Welty's Retranslation of the South" (2000), "Private and Political Thoughts in *One Writer's Beginnings*" (2001); "Of Human, Animal, and Celestial Bodies in Welty's 'Circe'" (2005); "Eudora Welty and the Merlin Principle: Aspects of Story-Telling in *The Golden*

Apples—'The Whole World Knows' and "Sir Rabbit'" (2009). The last two essays, "'The Inspired Child of [Her] Times': Eudora Welty as a Twentieth-Century Artist" (2010) and "'Moments of Truth': Eudora Welty's Humanism" (2014, an assessment of Welty's innovations with the long-form works *Losing Battles*, *The Optimist's Daughter*, and *One Writer's Beginnings*) range widely across Welty's canon, demonstrating that Welty remains one of the most daring and important writers of the twentieth century who has significant import in the twenty-first century as well.

Seminal passages from Welty's work applied to varying themes recur in Danièle's essays. Lorenzo Dow's meditation on Love and Separateness and Virgie Rainey's comprehension of the three moments of Perseus slaying Medusa are touchstones for Danièle as are themes of vaunting and mirroring, murder and rebirth, dystopia and death. She impresses upon readers that "the forces of death—the artist's great theme," are explored throughout Welty's writing (86). Danièle reveals Welty's use of mirrors and masks to deconstruct the confluent existence of love and hate, order and chaos, utopia and dystopia. She reads "Livvie" first as a "complex rewriting of slavery" and elsewhere in terms of a concentration camp (61, 119). The watermelon scene in *Losing Battles* is "the simulacrum of a ritualized execution" (131); Ran Maclain's wife, Jinny Love, is an "avatar of the flapper Daisy Buchanan" of *The Great Gatsby* (99). Danièle reminds us of Welty's courage, her "leap in the dark" to forge new techniques, to write of the fascination of and toward death.[7] In her writing, Welty responds to painters Beckmann, Kandinsky, Matisse, Mondrian, Picasso, Pollock; to sculptors Brancusi, Cellini, and Maillol; to the dynamic liquid blackness of cinema, of directors Buñuel and Bergman in particular.

The Eye That Is Language: A Transatlantic View of Eudora Welty offers readers and scholars a global perspective of Welty's achievements. The readings emanate from Danièle's European education; her sophisticated understanding of theories of shamanism, modernism, and postmodernism, and artistic and literary movements abroad, especially surrealism and abstract expressionism; and her passion for the literary achievement of women of genius. Thus, Danièle's essays in *The Eye That Is Language* explain Welty's techniques of using new narrative modes that move Welty's work beyond Southern myths and mysteries into a global perspective of humanity. Her essays reveal and explain Welty's brilliance for employing the particular to discover the universal.

In her concluding remarks upon receiving the *Légion d'honneur*, Danièle said, "What I admired and tracked in Eudora Welty's fiction was her major concern with language, her way of fictionalizing or dramatizing a concern that reduced plot and characters to nothing but brilliant language constructions. She was both ahead of her time and in deep 'resonance' with it."[8]

Pearl Amelia McHaney

ACKNOWLEDGMENTS

Certainly, the most important acknowledgment is of Eudora Welty and Danièle Pitavy-Souques. They met several times, had numerous conversations, and shared an appreciation for the importance of art for understanding human relationships. Danièle and I also worked together in the preliminary planning of this collection of her essays, although it did not come to fruition in her lifetime. I am extremely grateful that François Pitavy has encouraged the project and granted permission for the publishing of these essays.

The following essays have seen earlier publication and are reprinted with permission: "Technique as Myth: The Structure of *The Golden Apples*," *Eudora Welty: Critical Essays*, edited by Peggy Whitman Prenshaw, UP of Mississippi, 1979 (259–68); "A Blazing Butterfly: The Modernity of Eudora Welty," *Mississippi Quarterly*, vol. 39, no. 4 (1986) and reprinted in *Welty: A Life in Literature*, edited by Albert J. Devlin, UP of Mississippi, 1987 (113–38); "'The Fictional Eye': Eudora Welty's Retranslation of the South," *South Atlantic Review*, vol. 65, no. 4, 2000 (90–113); "Private and Political Thoughts in *One Writer's Beginnings*," *Eudora Welty and Politics: Did the Writer Crusade?*, edited by Harriet Pollack and Suzanne Marrs, Louisiana State UP, 2001 (203–21); "Of Human, Animal, and Celestial Bodies in Welty's 'Circe,'" *Eudora Welty and The Poetics of the Body*, Ètudes Faulknériennes, edited by Géraldine Chouard and Danièle Pitavy-Souques, PUR, 2005 (167–73); "Eudora Welty and the Merlin Principle: Aspects of Story-Telling in *The Golden Apples*—'The Whole World Knows' and 'Sir Rabbit,'" *Mississippi Quarterly: Eudora Welty Centennial Supplement*, April 2009 (101–23); "'The Inspired Child of [Her] Times': Eudora Welty as a Twentieth-Century Artist," *Eudora Welty Review*, vol. 2, 2010 (69–92); and "'Moments of Truth': Eudora Welty's Humanism," *Eudora Welty Review*, vol. 6, 2014 (9–26).

I am indebted also to James A. Jordan, Sarah Gilbreath Ford, Harriet Pollack, Katie Keene, Mary Heath, Caroline O'Connor, Forrest Galey, Mary Alice White, and Eudora Welty LLC, Deborah Miller, and my dearest friend and husband Tom McHaney. Each has contributed to my joy as I edited this collection of essays.

THE EYE THAT IS LANGUAGE

THE EYE THAT IS LANGUAGE

An Introduction

> The mystery lies in the use of language to express human life.
> —EUDORA WELTY "WORDS INTO FICTION" (137)

The singular fiction of Eudora Welty continues to inspire with awe and admiration her readers all over the world. Her work belongs to those resisting texts whose depth, width, and beauty are fully grasped after much meditation and rereading. Each new critical approach partially lifts the veil that hides the endless complexity and richness of Welty's vision of life. There have been and will be many more penetrating readings of the meaning of her fiction, but what intrigued me from the first and what I wanted to explore specifically was the way those stories were written, what made them so resisting, so full of hidden meaning that a new critical approach, founded on narrative technique, could help identify and make easier to grasp and fully admire. It is something distantly related to what Welty wrote about shape: "Shape is something felt. It is the form of the work that you feel to be under way as you write and as you read. At the end, instead of farewell, it tells over the whole, as a whole, to the reader's memory" ("Words" 143).

We remember Welty's repeated concern with narrative technique: "It is of course the *way* of writing that gives a story . . . its whole distinction and glory," "something learned, by dint of the story's challenge and the work that rises to meet it" as well as her poetically stated magisterial explanation of her work with the story "No Place for You, My Love" ("How I Write" 242, "Writing and Analyzing a Story" 775). In this volume, some of the essays I have written over the years on the fiction of Eudora Welty are collected under a title inspired by the great Canadian writer Rudy Wiebe, about whom I have taught and lectured, who constantly reflected on the link between writing and seeing. By what necessary imaginary figure does the writer Eudora

Welty envision her art? Her answer is fictionalized rather than plainly stated: The figure of Perseus defiantly holding the head of the Medusa, which his undaunted courage had slain with the help of a mirror. An engraving has hung, and still hangs, in Welty's study of Benvenuto Cellini's powerful statue of Perseus in Florence.[1] A remarkably strong representation of the art of writing for a writer who has endlessly explored the many-faceted aspects, passions, and feelings of the myth: celebrating endless curiosity of the Other behind a mask, mastery of the technical tool of the mirror-shield, showing undaunted courage in the facing and denouncing of evil. For Welty's fiction, with unusually strong and complex texts that require close reading to apprehend their richness and endless narrative experimentation, belongs to those works that open the mind and enlarge the heart.

Eudora Welty entered the literary scene with *A Curtain of Green and Other Stories* in 1941, her first collection of short stories, whose title was chosen by John Woodburn, Welty's editor at Doubleday (Kreyling 63). The remarkably complex title story, which *The Southern Review* published in 1938 saying that "they were very impressed" with it, deserves a few words in this introduction as, in a way, it dramatizes some of the most innovative ideas of the young writer, then in her late twenties, ideas that would feed her entire fiction (Kreyling 20). This founding text can be read as Welty's masterly first attempt to fictionalize both the figure and the territory of the artist.

With the garden of Mrs. Larkin, a desperate young widow whose young husband was killed by a falling tree as he arrived home, Welty creates a space that transcends an ordinary overgrown garden in Mississippi. She invests it with metaphorical significance as she transforms it into a stage for a dramatic psychic recovery, which is in fact a shamanic experience as the plot suggests with the succession of traditional elements: chaos, trance, sacrifice, and cure. Centered on the mediation between human beings and the spirits of nature, that spiritual practice from indigenous animist cultures was well known among avant-garde artists on both sides of the Atlantic: surrealist writers in France and experimental painters and creators in the United States who participated in the general spiritual debate of the times shared in particular by the distinguished thinkers whom Welty was seeing in New York, George William Russell (A. E.) and his son Diarmuid Russell especially.

"A Curtain of Green" is written on the tension between the necessary setting in the reality of the Southern experience—the exuberant overgrown natural space in the South—and the aesthetic necessity to transcend the visible in order to say the invisible, which recent scientific and anthropological discoveries had stressed. With the dramatic form of a spiritual revelation, the story fictionalizes the process of literary creation with the artist's dual territory: a physical landscape and a human experience, from the realistic observation of the everyday world to the intimation of a superior truth, which it is the artist's role to show.

The artist's territory is first presented as a natural space emblematic of the South; entangled with vegetation and surrounded with houses and people, this is Welty's own territory, which her fiction will represent in its varied geographical and historical aspects. Work in a Southern garden is comparable to an ordinary writer's own work. Inspired by the life he sees around, with characters, emotions, death and murderous instincts, his role is to select and reject, like a gardener cutting and separating an excess of vegetation. But Mrs. Larkin, buried in her grief and blind to the others, is blamed by everybody for refusing to conform. The transgressive quality of this text is to write the garden as the triumphant metaphor for the writer's illumination when he *sees* at last what he is aiming at. His subject will be forever to write about feelings and emotions. The ordinary landscape is transfigured into the place of revelation; it becomes the matrix of creativity when Mrs. Larkin is finally restored to a full human life. At last, she is able to come out of the prison where her grief had locked her, indifferent to the others and to the common plight of mankind.

With the current phenomenon of stasis before the long-expected daily rain comes the seminal metaphor inspired by the shamanism of a finger parting the hedge to communicate with Mrs. Larkin lost in grief: "She felt all at once terrified, as though her loneliness had been pointed out by some outside force whose finger parted the hedge. She drew her hand for an instant to her breast. An obscure fluttering there frightened her, as though the force babbled to her" (133).[2] The finger reintroduces Mrs. Larkin to the world of the living and at last opens her mind, later her heart, to the presence of the others: she literally sees her gardener for the first time as she observes the black face lost in a private dream. "Then as if it had swelled and broken over a daily levee, tenderness tore and spun through her sagging body" (135).

The final invention of a finger parting the hedge to (re)introduce the leading character of the story to the people, with their lives and feelings, whom she had ignored for so long confirms the exemplarity of this early story and proves how the young writer was that early much advanced in her reflection on writing. In this respect "A Curtain of Green" as title story of the first collection proves the penetrating insight of John Woodburn, an insight corroborated by Eudora Welty herself when she expanded the metaphor to present her dedication to writing after recalling that she had begun as a photographer during her work as a junior publicity agent for the WPA:

> In my own case, a fuller awareness of what I needed to find out about people and their lives had to be sought for through another way, through writing stories. But away off one day up in Tishomingo County, I knew this anyway: that my wish, indeed my continuing passion, would be not to point the finger in judgment but to part a curtain, that invisible shadow that falls between people, the veil of indifference to each other's presence, each other's wonder, each other's human plight. ("One Time, One Place" 354–55)

Chapter 1

TECHNIQUE AS MYTH

The Structure of *The Golden Apples* (1979)

> Tu remarquas, on n'écrit pas, lumineusement, sur champ obscur, l'alphabet des astres, seul, ainsi s'inique, ébauché ou interrompu; l'homme poursuit noir sur blanc.[1]
> —MALLARMÉ

Because Eudora Welty herself has suggested that *The Golden Apples* was more than just another collection of short stories,[2] the structural unity of the book has puzzled critics over the years. Nearly all the articles dealing with *The Golden Apples* as a whole tackle the problem and attempt to solve it by establishing close parallels between (mostly) Greek mythology and the various characters and incidents in the book.[3] Whether they underline the recurrent myths that can be traced in the different stories or organize all mythical allusions into echoes and leitmotiv that weave a symphonic web in the book, these critical approaches remain at the surface of the work. No doubt, the task is not easy, perhaps chiefly because of the looseness of the book. It is composed of seven stories, each a brilliant experiment in technique, and of several different myths—Celtic as well as Greek—collected under a title that seems to introduce yet another myth. The very multiplicity of these mythic readings and the lack of a strong unifying device, such as one finds in *Ulysses*, have marred all attempts at finding a satisfactory structure. Could not then a different approach be used that would do full justice not only to this complex work but to the artist herself who of her generation is perhaps the most deeply aware of her art?

Content cannot be dissociated from form; the text should be analyzed as a whole. Indeed, its narrative functioning deserves the closest attention since it alone shows the author's intentions. Just as important is the examination of any infraction of the norms established by the work itself, as these infractions help evaluate the aesthetic success of the book and give clues that indicate the presence of a less obvious narrative system. The study of the structure of *The Golden Apples* should thus be based on the narration as well as the fiction and take into account the apparent infractions of its narrative code. Only through such study can one perceive the essential function of myth in the book, thence the deeper meaning of Welty's work.

In *The Golden Apples*, Welty very deliberately used what T. S. Eliot called "the mythical method" in his 1923 *Dial* review of *Ulysses*: "It is simply a way of controlling, of ordering, of giving a shape and a significance to the immense panorama of futility and anarchy which is contemporary history. It is a method already adumbrated by Mr. Yeats, and of the need for which I believe Mr. Yeats to have been the first contemporary to be conscious. It is a method for which the horoscope is auspicious" (177–78). Myth here is technique, imposed on the world of action, shaping our perception and reaction to it. Eliot's comment is further relevant because he gives credit to Yeats for adumbrating this technique and also mentions the horoscopes. Both are directly related to the technique used in *The Golden Apples*. That Eudora Welty intended to experiment with the mythical method in a sustained and deliberate way is indicated by the genesis of her work. The first story of the cycle, "June Recital," was originally called "The Golden Apples"[4] and appeared in *Harper's Bazaar* under this title, partly inspired by "The Song of Wandering Aengus." Yeats's poem was extensively quoted in the first version. This nucleus story was thus under the double parentage of Yeats and Greek myth. Later, it was renamed, and the mythical title was transferred to designate the collection as a whole—a unique instance in Welty's work, for the three other collections bear the name of one story. As she worked on the various stories of *The Golden Apples*, she realized, as she said, she was "writing about the same people" ("'The Interior'" 43).

The futility of decoding the characters and events of the book according to a strict mythological system becomes evident from the first story. The warning is there, in the title itself, which functions as a signal to indicate a reality beyond the events in the story. "Shower of Gold" heralds the birth of Perseus to any cultivated reader. But on what level? If we remain on the purely factual level, we read in the story nothing more than the birth of the MacLain twins, Randall and Eugene, not the clandestine birth of an only son. And the "quotation" in the text is scant; the word *gold* is not even mentioned: "She looked like more than only the news had come over her. It was like a shower of something had struck her, like she'd been caught out in something bright" (322). Moreover, this title appears as an infraction of the functioning of the story, which rests entirely on the "truth" of King MacLain's visit to his wife on Halloween. Indeed, this title has nothing to do with the fiction if we except the incomplete allusion. (It functions, of course, as a mythical clue of King MacLain, whom we are thus invited to see as the modern counterpart of Zeus. But this belongs to the surface level of the book; story after story, we are told of the amorous exploits of the character.) We must therefore look elsewhere for the function of the title, beyond the single short story, considering this first piece of narrative as part of a whole, and see whether other allusions to Perseus occur in the book.

The hero reappears, again without being named, in the fourth story, "Moon Lake." The parallel is explicit enough never to have left critics in doubt as to the equation of Loch Morrison's bringing Easter back to life after she has fallen into the lake with Perseus's rescuing Andromeda from the sea monster. The reference is quite precise, developed at length and confirmed, so to speak, by the vision of Loch, alone and enjoying his triumph outside his tent as Perseus did after his first victory. But here again, Perseus and Andromeda and their love affair have no part in the plot of the story. What is most impressive is the strong sexual coloration of the life-saving process. We are once more aware that the significance of this episode is on a second level of reality.

Finally, Perseus's slaying Medusa is the object of Virgie Rainey's long meditation in "The Wanderers." The meditation functions no more directly in this narrative than in the other two stories. It should be noted, however, that Virgie's interpretation is rather unorthodox and shakes the commonly accepted views of the myth:

> Miss Eckhart had had among the pictures from Europe on her walls a certain threatening one. It hung over the dictionary, dark as the book. It showed Perseus with the head of the Medusa. "The same thing as Siegfried and the Dragon," Miss Eckhart had occasionally said, as if explaining second-best. [...] [Virgie] saw the stroke of the sword in three moments, not one. In the three was the damnation—no, only the secret, unhurting because not caring in itself—beyond the beauty and the sword's stroke and the terror lay their existence in time—far out and endless, a constellation which the heart could read over many a night." (554, 554–55)

At this stage, we can draw two conclusions. The myth of Perseus is undoubtedly present in *The Golden Apples*, and Welty's use of this myth is highly deliberate, creative. There is another technical difficulty to solve before examining more closely the function of the myth of Perseus: the title of the collection itself.

The quest for the golden apples is very distantly linked to the myth of Perseus—some late accretions, which critics bent on finding thematic unity have hunted for and made the most of. But generally speaking, no one connects Perseus with the golden apples (though he is Heracles's ancestor). Since the title "Shower of Gold" functions symbolically, we may infer that the only other title with a mythical connotation, the general title of the collection, functions in the same way: it would thus refer not to a definite search but to *any* search. The text corroborates this hypothesis. The title "Golden Apples" was first given to "June Recital," which originally included the full last stanza of Yeats's poem, with the reference to "The silver apples of the moon,/The golden apples of the sun" (Welty, "The Golden Apples" 320; Yeats 150). When Eudora Welty revised the story, she eliminated the too explicit lines, favoring indirectness to pedantry, the more refined method of distant allusion to a labored exercise in name dropping. In fact, she kept the spirit rather than the letter of the poem. And what quest had Yeats in mind? Several times he pointed out the duality in the myth and legends about those who live in the waters and can take any shape like "the little silver trout" which became "a glimmering girl": "The people of the waters have been in all ages beautiful and changeable and lascivious, or beautiful and wise and lonely, for water is everywhere the signature of the fruitfulness of the body and of the fruitfulness of dreams" (Yeats 149, 802).[5]

Indeed, the search for the apples provides a loose thematic link between the different short stories. By their Greek and Celtic parentage, the golden fruit represent the artist's attempt at showing the universality of myth—human desire and longing, at bringing about a new awareness of the fundamental ambivalence of man through a comparison between several worlds.[6] The brilliant fabric of mythological names and echoes that adorns the surface of the text functions in this same way. Welty's use of this technical device is quite original; it is not coincidence or influence but technique. She uses mythology as deliberate "quotations" from Yeats, Joyce, or T. S. Eliot, with the resulting effect of implying that she is writing about universal passions as eternal as *art* and the created world itself. (Another way of doing it is to project what takes place on earth into the stars and constellations, whose names are derived from the myth, what T. S. Eliot implied when he mentioned the horoscope.) This effect of quotation is a means of guaranteeing the truth of her fiction, just as, paradoxically, this truth is warranted at the other end, the realistic end, by the list of the characters printed at the beginning of the book. What is more, these highly sophisticated literary "quotations" are a means of suggesting that literature is itself the endless repetition of the same stories. Welty's attitude becomes reflexive, just as literature, she seems to suggest, is a mirror. She questions her art in the very moment she is creating it. Somehow, those "quotations" are the play within the play, contesting the story and the genre while functioning within it. They constitute the mirror that Welty holds to her fiction. Perseus does nothing else: the writer *is* Perseus. To the point here is Reynolds Price's superb definition of the artist—not unconnected with *The Golden Apples*, it seems, as it appears in an essay significantly entitled "Dodging Apples": "The central myth of the artist is surely no Narcissus but Perseus—with the artist in all roles, Perseus, and Medusa and the mirror-shield" (8). Here, brilliantly summed up, are indeed the elements of the myth—Perseus, Medusa, and the mirror-shield.

The center of this trinity is fascination—Medusa's deadly gaze, or rather fascination defeated, overcome by another gaze—Perseus's in the mirror. At the mythic as well as the symbolic level, fascination means death. At the level of human relations, it refers to that spell, that *abus de pouvoir* [abuse of power] by which we tend to objectify the Other, to make him lose his identity and become a thing, an object. In his phenomenological study of gaze in *L'Etre et le Néant*,[7] Sartre was perhaps the first to show that fascination is central to the problem of the gaze and to the relation of one being to another. Nearly every form of meaningful relation to the Other derives from fascination. Prestige likewise reverses the relation of subject-object. It forces the admirer to lose his identity and wish to identify with the object of his admiration. Emptied of his substance, drained of his blood, the contemplator dies, so to speak. There is also the reverse form of fascination, shame, which is self-loathing. Sartre concludes at the end of his chapter on gaze that, beyond the irreconcilable duality of our relation to the Other, there is the body, apprehended as the purely contingent presence of the Other. This apprehension is a particular type of nausea. We can see how seduction and the wish to possess the body of the Other are, eventually, another form of fascination with one's own death, what Sartre calls the obscene. That the myth has strong sexual connotation is evident when we look at its development. Originally, Gorgo was an ugly creature with hissing snakes as hair; she later became a once beautiful woman turned ugly by Hera's jealousy; at the Hellenistic period, she was simply a beautiful young maid whose gaze was deadly.

All the complexity of feelings based on fascination, tearing man between attraction and repulsion, loving and loathing, fulfillment and destruction inform the treatment of human relations in *The Golden Apples*. There is the fascination for an unworthy type—King MacLain, a rascal who brazenly defies all the social and moral conventions in "Shower of Gold" and "The

Wanderers." The nausea linked to the flesh and the self as experienced in sex is central to "Sir Rabbit" and "The Whole World Knows." Death also provides a perilous allure in "Moon Lake." In the more complex stories, the theme of fascination shapes with infinite subtlety the projection of the self onto the idealized alter-ego, as in "Music from Spain" and "June Recital," which present the most devastating picture of feelings related to this theme.

Perseus is not a "culture hero" in the sense Prometheus and Heracles are culture heroes, that is, the saviors of mankind, the transgressors, the "transformers" who by their heroic action help civilization progress. Perseus's victory is of a more private kind and concerns the terrors of the soul and the agony of the heart rather than the ordering of chaos.

Even if to the painters Perseus must have been the triumphant hero ("The vaunting was what she remembered, that lifted arm," *The Golden Apples* 554), even if Loch's victory over death swells him with too much pride in the eyes of Nina Carmichael and Jinny Love, Perseus in *The Golden Apples* is above all that most complex character who alone was able to conceive the full horror of Medusa since he overcame it: "Because Virgie saw things in their time, like hearing them—and perhaps because she must believe in the Medusa equally with Perseus—she saw the stroke of the sword in three moments, not one" (554–55). Those three moments in one represent the utmost fascination and the awareness of it; somehow it is the fascination of the artist himself, as André Malraux, before Price, suggested in the preface he wrote for the French translation of William Faulkner's *Sanctuary* in 1932: "The deepest fascination, the artist's, draws its strength from its being both the horror and the possibility to conceive it" (9). To this fascination, Welty gives a personal coloring: "Cutting off the Medusa's head was the heroic act, perhaps, that made visible a horror in life, that was at once the horror in love, Virgie thought—the separateness" (554). Perseus stands for the fascinated become fascinator, the slaying of Medusa for the lover who could grasp the full essence of his beloved only by killing her. The severed head is not only the visible sign of that permanent scandal—death; it is also the visible sign of that other scandal—the destructive power of love, any form of love (of fascination). For it is the essence of fascination, the utmost form of gaze, to become annihilated in the very accomplishment of the transgression it implies. This failed epiphany Welty calls "separateness." In "A Still Moment" Lorenzo Dow, the watcher, and Audubon, seer and voyeur, slayer and lover, knew already that fascination is a knowledge and a love that contains in itself the death of all knowledge and love.

The agony of separateness is what most married characters in *The Golden Apples* experience. Whether it be an unfaithful husband ("Shower of Gold"), an unfaithful wife ("The Whole World Knows"), or an inadequate spouse ("Sir Rabbit," "Music from Spain," Mrs. Morrison in "June Recital"), they all feel the unbreachable gulf between what they dream or hope for and the reality that makes their lives. In "The Wanderers," Virgie Rainey's long chain of lovers shows that she too has not been able to find fulfillment in love. Just as excruciating can be the loneliness of thwarted affection, whether born of unrequited devotion—a maternal love transfer, Miss Eckhart's feelings for Virgie Rainey in "June Recital"—or the result of death, the scandalous distress of the orphaned child ("Moon Lake"), or the hundred smaller sorrows daily experienced.

The third constituent of the myth, the mirror, points to the fascination of Perseus—his awareness of horror and its fascination for him. The place of desire, the mirror becomes the door to death. A reflection, it is the sign of the near identity of opposites: "Virgie never saw it differently, never doubted that all the opposites on earth were close together, love close to hate, living to dying; but of them all, hope and despair were the closest blood—unrecognizable one from the other sometimes, making moments double upon themselves, and in the doubling double again, amending but never taking back" (546).

This endless doubling upon oneself is fascination—again. And this is true not only of "moments," but of the short stories themselves as structures. They are built on this endless reflection, which doubles and doubles again. There are two parts or two movements in each story that are based on the ambiguity between a real experience and a dreamed one, between asserted reality and hypothetical reality. (Interestingly, some of Virginia Woolf's finest stories, like those of Welty, follow this pattern).[8] In "The Wanderers," the axis is "the feeling of the double coming-back," as Virgie Rainy experiences it (or the double departure, which is just its reverse, its reflection in the mirror) (545). Starting from that evident dichotomy, Eudora Welty elaborates on a most sophisticated play on reflections. Two examples will illustrate the technique and stress the duality in the composition of the book itself, since it rests on two major trends, a comic one based on the celebration of the word—the art of telling—and a tragic one based on vision—the fascination of the *spectacle*.

This reflection at times functions as the proof of the authenticity of the object, as in "Shower of Gold." The narrative problem here is the "truth" of King's visit on Halloween. In the first part, Mrs. Rainey draws a portrait of King MacLain, a rogue pursuing his amorous career all over the South, and through her, we hear the adoring voice of the community. In the second part, she tells at length how he was seen at the door of his house on a surprise visit to his wife, how he thought better of it when circled by his two young sons disguised for the day, and ran away once more. But these facts cannot be proved. Apparently, part 2 illustrates the gossips told in part 1 and corroborates them. However, a close study of the narration shows that it is just the reverse: the legend surrounding King MacLain is what makes the aborted visit credible—in the narrative system of the story.

With a more refined composition, based on the alternating voices of Loch Morrison and his sister Cassie, "June Recital" sends back and forth a series of reflections that contribute to the most scathing criticism of human relations in society. The overall effect is that of the play within the play since for each witness, the *spectacle* he sees constitutes the epitome of his vision—a reflected microcosm of his world. To this mirror-effect within each narrative, a more subtle one is added, which provides the structural link between the two parts. The grey, dull picture of what seems the preparation for a celebration is followed by the brilliantly colored images of the celebration itself—the recital. We hesitate over the true nature of what we see (which is the reflection? which is the object?), and a new awareness of the tragedy of human relations is born as the second mirror-effect begins to dawn on us. Until we realize we should superimpose the two scenes so as to see the complete picture, we do not fully apprehend the structure—hence the subject of "June Recital." In Loch's narrative, Miss Eckhart's lavish decoration of her studio with "maypole ribbons of newspaper and tissue paper" reads like a black-and-white snapshot of the June recital narrated in Cassie's part, its negative rather (342). The relation between the two scenes provides the key to the understanding of the story; in spite of appearances, they are very much alike. Just as we see a proliferation of stage properties in part 1, part 2 presents a proliferation of visual elements to the prejudice of musical ones. The empty stage in part 1 represents a distortion of the spectacle, produced for its sole end without any audience, just as the June recital deprived of its musical end is similarly distorted. The finality of both spectacles is elsewhere. For that one night in the year, the ladies of Morgana cooperate with Miss Eckhart to celebrate themselves, in the end, under the pretense of honoring their daughters. Staged by a narcissistic town enamored of its own image, the brilliantly colorful recital derives its deceptive splendor from success and power. It represents the supreme illusion of the town contemplating its social achievement therein. In the other scene, stripped of its false appearances, the studio looks what it is really—an empty stage for a demented puppet. Likewise, Miss Eckhart's loneliness is made visible together with the destructive effect of her love for Virgie; she has been drained of her vital flux by the dazzled gaze she gave her idol-pupil. Thus, the two scenes function like Medusa's head and its reflection in the mirror. The reflected head loses its power to fascinate because it is deprived of the deadly glamour. Vulnerability becomes apparent with the emptiness that fascination implies. The reflection is "truer" than the object and cannot be dissociated from it. When superimposed, the two pictures give an image in relief, so to speak, suggesting the depth of the tragedy of human relations behind the brilliant surface.

The three elements of the myth of Perseus thus correspond to the major themes and techniques of the book: they are present in every story, and each element functions in the same way as it does in the myth. This structure suggests three organizing principles: all the short stories have a plot based on fascination, they are all constructed with a mirror-effect, and the theme of separateness runs throughout the volume. In other words, the narratives that constitute *The Golden Apples* are dramatizations of the functioning of the myth of Perseus—the essential theme of the book, which was discussed at the beginning of this analysis. *The Golden Apples* illustrates what Jean Ricardou called a "theorem" in his study of the critical problems of the Nouveau Roman: "Great narratives can be recognized in that the story they tell is nothing but the dramatization of their own functioning" (178).

The Golden Apples can be read at the ordinary level of dramatic action. It offers then the picture of a microcosm with its passions and frustrations, hate and prejudice, heroes and scapegoats. At a more significant level, it is concerned with the kinds of awareness various minds have of death, which it is man's fate to fear, fight, and fool as much and as long as he can. As the protean figure of Death makes his insidious way into every passion, great or small, that seethes in the heart of man, there are thousands of encounters before the final destruction. Man's dignity or heroism is this endless fight against death and all forms of evil, which are forms of death. For this, he has "the pure wish to live" (545). He has love or art: Miss Eckhart "had hung the picture on the wall for herself. She had absorbed the hero and the victim and then, stoutly, could sit down to the piano with all Beethoven ahead of her. With her hate, with her love, and with the small gnawing feelings that ate them, she offered Virgie her Beethoven" (555).

The myth of Perseus is central to Welty's thought from "A Curtain of Green" to *The Optimist's Daughter*. Only in *The Golden Apples*, of which she said that "in a way [it] is closest to my heart of all my books," has she fully developed it ("'The Interior'" 42). The mythic method, which she uses again in *Losing Battles* though quite differently, leaves the fight endless and somewhat unresolved except by art. "In Virgie's reach of memory a melody softly lifted, lifted of itself. Every time Perseus struck off the Medusa's head, there was the beat of time, and the melody. Endless the Medusa, and Perseus endless" (555). Pursuing her own ceaseless war with time and death, the artist comes to a different compromise in a more classical novel like *The Optimist's Daughter*. The answer is no longer determined by the fixed revolutions of the heavenly bodies, but it is inscribed in human time and relies on that best of man's weapons, memory. A crucible in which man's heart and spirit are purified of desire and remorse, memory becomes the privileged place where the patterns of our lives—any lives—are written and disclosed to the artist, whose creative vision can thus dominate chaos. In *The Golden Apples*, the stars are not alone in transcending time in their eternal movement; so do myths, becoming as fixed in their revolving through centuries and cultures as the constellations which bear their names. And so does the work of art, which first explores the depth of the human heart and then stands in black letters against the white page. Gaining immortality, the work of art thus gives the reverse picture of the luminous stars against the black sky, as Mallarmé once wrote: "You noticed, one does not write with light on a dark background; the alphabet of the stars, alone, is marked in this way, uncompleted or interrupted; man pursues black against white" (370).

Chapter 2

A BLAZING BUTTERFLY

The Modernity of Eudora Welty (1987)[1]

> He dreams that he is a great blazing butterfly stitching up
> a net; which doesn't make sense.
> —EUDORA WELTY "OLD MR MARBLEHALL" (118)

> Vous moquez-vous de nous, Monsieur, avec une parielle histoire?
> Est-ce qu'il n'y a pas, Madame, une espèce de tulle qu'on
> apelle du tulle illusion?
> —BARBEY D'AURÉVILLY *LES DIABOLIQUES*[2]

To the late-twentieth-century reader, Eudora Welty appears an adventurer of the mind. A spirit of challenge, of pure exhilaration, lifts the fiction of a writer who taught her readers how to "creep out on the shimmering bridge of the tree," and whose figure of the artist in its protean garb is the wanderer, defiant and heroic, brave and vain—Loch Morrison, the young rebel, hanging upside down in the hackberry tree to see better, thus re-establishing the truth through his subversive vision; or Miss Eckhart, the foreign musician, devoured by a passion for her life work, her own art; or else, Perseus the mythic hero ("June Recital" 382). These examples are all taken from *The Golden Apples* (1949), that central book in Eudora Welty's work.

In "The Wanderers," Virgie Rainey meditates upon an engraving of "Perseus with the head of the Medusa" that hung above the piano in Miss Eckhart's studio: "The vaunting way what she remembered" (554). Nearly thirty years later, writing in praise of two American writers with whom she feels some spiritual kinship—Willa Cather and Mark Twain—Eudora Welty emphatically dwells on the same word, "vaunt":

Who can move best but the inspired child of his times? Whose story should better be told than that of the youth who has contrived to cut loose from ties and go flinging himself might and main, in every bit of his daring, in joy of life not to be denied, to vaunt himself in the love of vaunting, in the marvelous curiosity to find out everything, over the preposterous length and breadth of an opening new world, and in so doing to be one with it? ("The House of Willa Cather" 51–52)

The term is more ambiguous than it seems. Applied to Perseus, "vaunt" expresses the legitimate pride of the slayer of Medusa; to Twain and Cather, it links creative joy to ostentatious victory. And indeed, evidence of her secret fascination with appearances runs throughout Welty's work. She creates characters who delight in flaunting and shocking, from Virgie Rainey with her daredevil behavior and dress, to the "middle-aged lady" in "The Bride of the Innisfallen," who parades in a striped raincoat; or those who adore staging their response to life's drama, such as Fay dressed in glistening black satin, playing the part of the disconsolate widow in *The Optimist's Daughter*, or the narrator so magnificently building up a stage for *Losing Battles* in the first few pages. The very excess of such scenes betrays the ambiguity of Welty's feelings, the sense of ridicule that makes her laugh at the gesture while she cannot help admiring it. Etymology throws some light; the allied terms "vaunt" and "vain" are both stamped with vacuity, their common Latin origin meaning "empty" or "hollow." We come close to vainglory, at least to the idea of taking excess pride, when a more modest attitude is required.

To grasp the complex connotation of "vaunt" for Welty, consider how she uses the word "vain" in a later work, *The Optimist's Daughter*. When Laurel McKelva comes upon a photograph of her dead mother, she remembers Becky's pride in the blouse she wears in the picture: "'The most beautiful blouse I ever owned in my life—I made it. Cloth from Mother's own spinning, and dyed a deep, rich, American Beauty color with pokeberries,' her mother had said with the gravity in which she spoke of 'up home.' 'I'll never have anything to wear that to me is as satisfactory as that blouse.' How *darling* and *vain* she was when she was *young*! Laurel thought now" (966, italics added). The association "young-vain" is that of Perseus himself, and here "darling" softens the blame and asserts the right to glory. As for the garment itself, it is the symbol for the undaunted pioneering spirit that defied every obstacle that nature put in its way. Reflexively, Eudora Welty's praise of Twain and Cather comes to mean the celebration of two writers who wrote of America's challenge to the wilderness—not mere recorders but adventurers, too, in the fresh province of Western literature. But behind the very necessity and nobleness of the conquest looms its costly aftermath, as Clement Musgrove, the cotton planter in *The Robber Bridegroom*, suspects. The reverse side of the success story weighs heavily and deserves examination. Just as, figuratively speaking, on his return journey, the triumphant Perseus wore the mask of the slain Medusa, which he put on the better to be seen—not the other way around—so Welty's fiction also explores the inside of the mask, examines the figure observing the Other: Perseus behind the face of Medusa watching reflexively this arrogant, vaunting, other self that moves behind a mask. The artist is both performer and audience, watched and watching. Hence those paired characters that people her fiction, one of whom acts—often with bravado and ostentation—while the other watches. And in this onlooker's gaze (character, narrator, or the writer herself), there passes the awareness of the futility of it all, the weariness and restlessness that Eudora Welty inscribed at the very beginning of her work in a brilliant story whose trope is a key, that of the title, which functions in many ways as trope for her entire fiction. In "The Key," the stance that she gives to the red-haired man reveals a writer singularly ahead of her time: "In his eyes, all at once wild and searching, there was certainly, besides the simple compassion in his regard, a look both restless and weary, very much used to the comic. You could see that he despised and saw the uselessness of the thing he had done" (47).

To complete this imaginary figure by which Welty's fiction can be represented, I should add the other two elements of the myth: the mirror-shield and the Medusa, with corresponding mirror effects in the writing, and fascination and death as themes. We know how those elements, which have always been present in serious fiction, became tropes of the modernist novel, the fiction of James, Conrad, Joyce, or Virginia Woolf.

I choose to single out Perseus because he stands for "the inspired child of his times," what could be called *modernity*, and with this word we are sent traveling down the twentieth century. Although influenced by and heir to the aesthetic principles of the great modernist writers like all other writers in the twentieth century, Eudora Welty has a much more advanced and complex position than her moment in time would lead one to expect. As early as the mid-1930s, alone and brave, she was already displaying that new spirit and experimenting with techniques that have since become accepted as postmodernist. I will not make her a postmodernist, though, for several reasons, perhaps the chief one being that she never fails to achieve, in William Gass's phrase, "the full responsive reach of [her] readers" (73).

The word "modernity" was first used by the nineteenth-century French poet Charles Baudelaire, who in many respects was one of the founding fathers of modern thinking (and a great admirer of another Southerner,

Edgar Allan Poe). "Modernity," Baudelaire wrote, "is what is transitory, fugitive and contingent—one half of art, whose other half is the eternal and immutable"; as a corollary, he insisted on "the dual composition of the Beautiful though it is experienced as one" ("De l'heroïsme" 194).[3]

To Baudelaire, modernity meant even more receptiveness to the new ideas of one's time and immersion in one's own present, a spirit of challenge, the desire to question the "given" for the truly innovative artist is he who tries to capture and represent in his work what he perceives as a new *rapport* of the human mind with the created world. This involves altering known modes of representation since any new questioning of the reality of things and the way the self perceives its position in the universe necessarily affects mimesis. For instance, Baudelaire admired Eugène Delacroix because, alone in his time, he opposed the prevalent realism of such official painters as David or Ingres and was already trying new techniques to express the slowly emerging tendency toward abstraction. To the rendering of surface reality, Delacroix preferred the suggestion of the hidden truth; to the realistic painting of a brawny sinewy arm, the suggestion of *tension* produced by a new use of color and shadow. Moreover, those "brilliant modern discoveries," which somehow acknowledged the inadequacy of painting to represent, resulted in a pervasive *mood of melancholy*, that "most remarkable quality which truly signals Delacroix as *the* nineteenth-century painter" (Baudelaire, "Eugène Delacroix" 114–15). While writing this, Baudelaire was quite aware of the near impossibility of the artistic endeavor: a mood is perhaps the closest that an artist can come to modernity.

There are many moods in Eudora Welty, as Ruth Vande Kieft brilliantly stressed many years ago. Earlier, Robert Penn Warren had taught us how to read this serious fiction: "The items of fiction (scene, action, character, etc.) are presented not as document but as comment, not as a report but as a thing made, not as history but as idea" (257). Rather than develop this symbolic aspect of Welty's writing, a "method ... similar to the method of much modern poetry," I want to examine, first, how Welty's challenge to mimesis expresses a radical fracture of the self, then, how in the organization of experience she moves further away from modernist writers by favoring a conceptual mode of thinking that leads toward abstraction and structure rather than pattern (Warren 257).

The theory of representation—a word I prefer to mimesis because the Aristotelian term does not imply possible negation—rests on the human faculties of recollection and imagination. Whereas recollection dominated narrative literature in the eighteenth and nineteenth centuries, imagination rules in the twentieth. There has been, in Suzi Gablik's words, "a gradual shift in art from iconic modes of representation (which are essentially figurative and are linked to immediate perceptual experience, where the image closely resembles the concrete objects to which it refers) towards non-representational, non-mimetic modes which are conceptual in organization" (qtd. in Hassan 113). Here Gablik follows Jean Piaget, who writes: "The object only exists ... in its relations with the subject and, if the mind always advances more toward the conquest of things, this is because it organizes experience more and more actively, instead of mimicking, from without, a ready-made reality" (qtd. in Hassan 113). At the same time, Sartre posits irreality in his theory of the imagination. His phenomenological psychology leads him to reject the three classical theories of associationism, continuity between the different modes of knowledge (i.e., between image and idea), and strict separation of image from idea, a disjunction that takes the image of a thing and dismisses its fallacy.[4] Conversely, Sartre says, the image is "a certain type of consciousness. The image is an act, not a thing. The image is awareness of something" (*L'imaginaire* 232). He thus states the dissociation between the faculty of producing images and the world of reality and then goes further when he postulates as a prerequisite for the image "the possibility to posit irreality" ("la possiblilité de poser une thèse d'irréalité") (232). For Sartre, the negative action is constituent of the image ("l'acte négatif est constituif de l'image") (*L'imagination* 162).

Such theories throw needed light on the more experimental side of Welty's fiction, that side which the generous, inspired tone of her criticism tends to blur. Welty herself, in her work, is far more daring than her literary tastes would have us believe. As early as her first collection, *A Curtain of Green* (1941), she showed her preoccupation with uncertainty. Not the modernist sense of ambiguity or the technical device of a variety of narrators each telling or recreating the truth, nor the Chekhovian juxtaposition of events or delayed exposure—rather what Ruth Vande Kieft has called "The Mysteries of Eudora Welty" (25). These mysteries lead Welty to explore the borderline situations, the reversals, shifts, and crossings of borders; to attempt to submerge the frame, "to render problematical what is, as it were, inside a text and what is outside it," as Tanner says of postmodernist writers (25). Or she twists the narrative and lets in new narrative possibilities as in "Death of a Traveling Salesman," "Powerhouse," "A Piece of News," or "Flowers for Marjorie," one of the more accomplished stories in this respect. However, "A Memory" is most daring as an instance of Welty's exploration—it belongs to those remarkable stories in *A Curtain of Green* that are metaphors, stories whose form is the dramatization of their meaning. "A Memory" is about representation and the process of seeing and writing. Or it is a story about "the familiar and its ghostly other," as Regis Durand puts it (73). Durand also quotes a paper entitled "On Aspects of the Familiar World," in which Walter Abish uses the idea of the familiar and its representations to make a distinction between fictional modes: "The need to see the world *familiarly* is a result of a preoccupation with the 'self' rather than with the world. The 'familiar' is to be equated with 'self' preoccupation" (qtd. in Durand 73).[5] This preoccupation with the self, supreme in a self-centered world, is what we find in the modernist novel, in James or Proust. When Proust describe the experience of the madeleine, he is dealing with an "Effet de Réel," as Barthes says; in other words, he is representing "reality," trying to see the world familiarly. The reader who has had a similar experience will identify with Marcel and be reassured in the belief they both belong to the same world, share the same reality. Proust's fiction represents the self trying to come to terms with the world.

On the other hand, a postmodernist text, according to Walter Abish, "must disavow a self-centered world in which the self continues to reign supreme," for it is essentially "a novel of disfamiliarization, a novel that has ceased to concern itself with the mapping of the 'familiar' world, for to do so would compel the characters to adopt a perception of the everyday predicated on an unquestioning affirmation of the function and role of the 'self' in society, as rigidly governed by the 'reality principle' and as subsumed by the logic of everyday existence as we are" (qtd. in Durand 74).

Let us look closely at "A Memory." We have a first "picture" or "representation" of reality, but what do we see? Certainly not a realistic painting or even a "virtually pastoral"[6] one:

> The water shone like *steel*, motionless except for the feathery curl behind a distant swimmer. From my position I was looking at a rectangle brightly lit, actually *glaring* at me, with sun, sand, water, a little pavilion, a few solitary people in *fixed* attitudes, and *around* it all a border of dark rounded oak trees, like the engraved thunderclouds *surrounding* illustrations in the Bible. Ever since I had begun taking painting lessons, I had made small frames with my fingers, to look out at everything.
> ... I was at an age when I formed a judgment upon every person and every event which came under my eye, although I was easily frightened. (92, italics added)

What is shown here is not reality as it is experienced directly in everyday life, but a *conventional representation of a public park*, a descriptive discourse acknowledged by a group at a given time. At the same time, *this description is extremely hostile*, as the words "steel," "glaring," and "thunderclouds" imply. Third, *this picture is framed*, and framed by the Bible, so to speak.

The first picture, which the young girl sees in her innocence, will be shattered soon. In other words, Eudora Welty rejects it, and she does so for reasons that seem to me very much postmodernist. First, we are confronted with a general suspicion of the myth of reality, that is, "the consensual discourse describing the official representation of the world in a given cultural community at a given time" (Couturier 5). Then, the picture raises the problem of frames and framing. This the young girl learned when she began taking painting lessons as part of the conventional way of dealing with representation. A frame is a way of delimiting her subject, of imposing restraint and cutting out all that might crop up unexpectedly. In this context, especially with the reference to the thunderclouds in the Bible, the frame represents the law, the repressive law of Jehovah. When writing about the "problematic of judicial framing and the jurisdiction of frames," Jacques Derrida refers to "all organized narration" as "a matter for the police," that is, subjected to some kind of law, which, in a written work, may be simply "language," not this or that discourse, but language itself (Derrida, qtd. in Tanner 22). Barthes speaks too for the "fascism" of language: "Fascism is not the power to prevent from saying but the power to force to say" ("Lecture" 5). In "A Memory" the picture is "dictated" for the child, who in placing and judging people is somehow "framed" herself, that is, held in a false position by the oppressive prejudice of her parents that makes her feel guilty when she asserts her rights to see and know. Breaking frames is also what the story is about, which is as old as the novel, and it is one of the first things that Welty as a user of language learned. Heidegger envisioned the possibility of inverting this "relation of dominance": "Man acts as though he were the shaper and master of language, while in fact language remains the master of man. When this relation of dominance gets inverted, man hits upon strange maneuvers. Language becomes the means for expression" (*Poetry* 213). Eudora Welty expresses much the same view in her beautiful essay "Words into Fiction": "We start from scratch, and words don't" (134). And just as Heidegger hopes for "strange maneuvers," Welty speaks of a "leap in the dark" or, in a superb image that reflects Heidegger's proposition, "in the boat" (*Being* 154): "it was not so much that they drifted, as that in the presence of a boat the world drifted, forgot. The dreamed-about changed places with the dreamer" ("Words" 134; "Moon Lake" 433–34).

The third reason is linked to the deceiving quality of language—or vision. This picture is traditionally modernist for in it "the need to see the world *familiarly* is a result of the preoccupation with the self rather than with the world" (qtd. in Durand 73). The narrator of "A Memory" says nothing else:

> To watch everything about me I regarded grimly and possessively as a *need*. All through this summer I had lain on the sand beside the small lake, with my hands squared over my eyes, finger tips touching, looking out by this device to see everything: which appeared as a kind of projection. It did not matter to me what I looked at; from any observation I would conclude that a secret of life had been nearly revealed to me—.... (92–93)

Framing and the need to see the world familiarly combine and represent the efforts of the self to master the world. The young girl feels such control because she can produce at will the memory of a brief encounter with a young boy, her first love: "I still would not care to say which was more *real*—the dream I could make blossom at will, or the sight of the bathers. I am presenting them, you see, only as simultaneous" (94, italics added). At this first stage, otherness is defined as the not-self, the "world." Here the not-self is what is most familiar, the world she inhabits, the "real" society. "The paradox," Regis Durand remarks, "is that the familiar world is most familiar to us when it is least seen as it is, for what it is, but simply as the need of the self to see things familiarly: the real world treated familiarly" (74). Modernist writers stop at this point, showing the self (as Walter Abish says), "Forever striving to reach an agreement with the desirable otherness" (qtd. in Durand 74). Welty goes a step further, not only investigating the familiar, but also *looking at it for what it is*. We should perhaps bear in mind Freud's definition of the "uncanny" or *Unheimlich*: "The 'uncanny' is that class of terrifying which leads back to something long known to us, once very familiar" (123–24).

The second picture presented in "A Memory" is one of violence and distortion as the child sees "a group of loud, squirming, ill-assorted people who seemed thrown together only by the most confused accident, and who seemed driven by foolish intent to insult each other, all of which they enjoyed with a hilarity which astonished my heart" (94). The pleasantly controlled circle of the first picture becomes "wobbly ellipses" as the little boys chase each other (86). The trim white pavilion is replaced by the shapeless mound of sand built around the ugly woman. This is a painful initiation into the contingency of life as it is: in order to be true, the artist must be able to see all the violence and rage and ugliness that is part of life. But it is more than that for in the culminating point of "A Memory," the little girl has a true vision of death. All of the images referring to the woman point to a petrified landscape. "Fat hung upon her upper arms like an arrested earthslide on a hill," her legs looked like "shadowed bulwarks," and when she pulled down the front of her bathing suit to empty out the "mashed and folded sand," the child "felt a peak of horror, as though her breasts themselves had turned to sand" (95, 97). This petrified landscape is the intrusion into the narrative of the face of the Medusa, the swoon into which the narrator falls, a sort of death. In "A Memory" the only escape from this "framed" condition seems to be through death; in other stories it will be through diffusion or dispersal, as in "Old Mr Marblehall."

We see how petrification functions here as a strange maneuver by which Welty indicates that the girl's experience is not one of appropriation, as all her preceding ones were, but of disavowal. More important, it is one of intensification, an intensification of the radical otherness of the Other, a recognition of the difference, of the unaccountable. But this disavowal, which is precisely the word used by Walter Abish, has a more complex meaning than just negation; it is, in a Freudian sense, something that involves the negation of the reality of a perception, usually a traumatic one, and it concerns itself with *the presence of an absence*. It is, as Freud has shown, the principle behind the cleavage of the self. Yet, in "A Memory" this deconstructive gesture is confronted by a very strong impulse to reestablish order, unity: "I tried to withdraw to my most inner dream, that of touching the wrist of the boy I loved on the stair; I felt the shudder of my wish shaking the darkness like leaves where I had closed my eyes; I felt the heavy weight of sweetness which always accompanied this memory; but the memory itself did not come to me" (97). This world, the familiar world, is still present in a way, the same and not quite the same; but since the new experience is that of an *absence*, there is a fracture: "I did not know, any longer, the meaning of my happiness; it held me unexplained" (97).

The third picture is that of the devastated beach. The narrator confesses: "For the object which met my eye, the small worn white pavilion, I felt pity suddenly overtake me, and I burst into tears" (97). Those very tears are what Serge Leclaire, in *Rompre les charmes*, has called "the compulsion to referentiality," the illusions and displacements that the self creates to conceal the fracture, to uphold the fiction of a narcissistic whole, of an interior space (241). But we see how very precarious this new picture is, how pitiful our poor attempts at creating images are. It seems our lot in the end to accept the cleavage of the self, for what is the "other" but the revelation of the nonidentity of self to self. This is the lesson taught in "A Still Moment."

In this story, which belongs to the second collection (*The Wide Net*, 1943), Welty pursues her reflection on a representation—a reflection on the visible as it is affected by the presence of an absence. The obvious figure of the artist is Audubon, naturalist and painter. But the other two characters—Murrell, the murderer devoured by a dream of domination and the will to wrench the secret of life from his dying victims, and Lorenzo Dow, the preacher convinced in his teleological vision of the world that his fate is to save all souls—stand for the artist's darker selves or tempters. Their passion is the artist's, and so is their awareness of "the object," the white heron, perceived by Murrell as a projection of himself, by Lorenzo as a part of God's creation, and by Audubon as a thing of beauty to be painted.

Just as the artist is seen in three, so is the creative process. In the first stage, there must be a deep immersion in the sensible world, which prevails over the world of ideas, and an intimate knowledge of its workings. We note Welty's (or Perseus's) joy in the created world because it holds wonder, but this does not mean that evil of all manner is not forever present, as "A Still Moment" reveals. The mirror surface of the story functions very much like one of those mirrors used by painters after the fashion of Claude Lorrain, framing and reflecting what is not seen directly—control and direction in technique. In the second stage, the artist must accomplish some form of severance; he must acknowledge the inevitable fracture, which is symbolized in "A Still Moment" by the killing of the heron. The third stage is that of representation. It states the impossibility of drawing from memory and restoring to wholeness an instant's vision of absolute beauty. Instead, the artist will reconstruct that vision through fragments, which is a deconstructive gesture: "[Audubon] knew that the best he could make would be, after it was apart from his hand, a dead thing and not a live thing, never the essence, only a sum of parts; and that it would always meet with a stranger's sight, and never be one with the beauty in any other man's head in the world" (239). The artist faced with the impossibility of representing pure essence has become a cliché, as Welty, the avid reader of Virginia Woolf's fiction and diaries, knows all too well. But I think Welty departs from her modernist predecessors when she shows how representation involves a fracture, a construction that amounts to deconstruction ("never the essence, only a sum of parts"), and, still more pointedly, when she acknowledges the presence of an absence through the symbolism of the dead bird used to represent a live one. I would even suggest that "separateness" in this context—that of Lorenzo's dismay—means "an endeavor to dispose of causality," in Claude Richard's phrase (86). Let me quote again that well known passage in "A Still Moment":

> He could understand God's giving Separateness first and then giving Love to follow and heal in its wonder; but God had reversed this, and given Love first and then Separateness, as though it did not matter to Him which came first. Perhaps it was that God never counted the moments of Time; Lorenzo did that, among his tasks of love. Time

did not occur to God. Therefore—did He even know of it? How to explain Time and Separateness back to God, Who had never thought of them, Who could let the whole world come to grief in a scattering moment? (239)

If time no longer ordains, the whole logically organized sequence of a narrative no longer matters. And indeed, the text is about a "still moment." Moreover, as the necessities of likeness or unlikeness disappear, representation may move further away from the original object. It becomes, in effect, a reflection on the distorting power of absence over presence, an absence that is a sort of echo but not the thing itself. This is the crux of Audubon's method; to represent a bird alive, the painter must kill it.

This experience of "otherness" in the familiar occurs again in *The Golden Apples*. "Moon Lake" is a story about the Other (whether he be a boy for the girls, a grownup, or an orphan for Nina and Jinny Love), a story about disavowing a self-centered world, with a lesson similar to that of "A Memory." To discover the Other is to acknowledge one's own mortality, to become aware of the other side of the mirror, of the self.

The story begins with an exploration of differences, which, in our need to see the world familiarly, we tend to categorize. This is deeply ironic since the camp at Moon Lake was intended to abolish all differences, especially between the orphans and the respectable little girls of Morgana, but it has only succeeded in making them more bitterly felt. Nina's initiation consists in renouncing her own system of differentiation to acknowledge true "separateness." Her first intimation of the presence of the Other *as presence* comes of a denial, when she realizes that Easter will not return or acknowledge her gaze—that is to say, when Easter refuses to be *seen*, possessed by Nina; in other words, when Nina's need to see the world familiarly fails. For although Nina has already "placed" the orphans, it is not without ambiguity—as the "not answerable" already hints with disquieting otherness: "The reason orphans were the way they were lay first in nobody's watching them, Nina thought. . . . They, they were not answerable. Even on being watched, Easter remained not answerable to a soul on earth. Nobody cared! And so, in this beatific state something came out of *her*" (425). Then, for the first time, Nina is able to enter Easter's mind and know what she thinks after they have played together in the boat. To signify this development in the narration (told from Nina's point of view), all "as if" and "it seemed" constructions are dropped; we have pure affirmative sentences, as the following modulation suggests: "A dragonfly flew about their heads. Easter only waited in her end of the boat, not *seeming* to care about the disappointment either. If this was their ship, she was their figurehead, turned on its back, sky-facing. She wouldn't be their passenger" (429, italics added). For the first time, the voice we hear is no longer Nina's but Easter's.

The next step occurs through writing when Nina becomes capable of seeing herself as an object, just as she has seen Easter as the Other. She writes side by side "Nina," then "Easter." The fine point made later about the spelling of Easter's name is that this *Other* is totally unaccountable, not "wholly calculable" as Henry James said (160). It lives its own life and escapes our power of naming it; this is why *Easter* can spell her name *Esther*, which is at least a real name, not a nickname, and can proudly say in a world defying all laws of causation—that new world which Welty's fiction ceaselessly explores—"I let myself name myself" (430).

I will not insist upon Nina's education as a writer, which implies the experience of death and, ultimately, becoming the Other. Yet, I wish to make one more point in this exploration of the unfamiliar: somehow, Easter's proud declaration brings us close to "A Still Moment." The reflexive pronoun becomes warped on the way back. "I let myself name myself" does not describe the same/identical, that is, what Nina expected—Easter. Instead, there rises from the depth of time the Other—Esther. Duration and time are challenged as Nina is brought face to face with the mirror of writing: it reflects the person whom we call, but his true character is never spelled correctly. Instead of the foundling, the biblical heroine faces Nina. The silvering is now *before* the mirror, not behind, thus turning it into a medal (a coin). What is sent back to Nina is no longer her own image but that of other women unknown to her: "Easter's eyes ... were neither brown nor green nor cat; they had something of metal, flat ancient metal, so that you could not see into them. Nina's grandfather had possessed a box of coins from Greece and Rome. Easter's eyes could have come from Greece or Rome that day" (418–19).

The fine quality of Welty's writing comes from this dual texture. Beneath the apparently familiar world—shall we say realistic?—spreads the huge territory of the never quite known or mapped, the wholly elusive. Here I mean more than the unconscious, which has always been explored by writers; I mean the very questioning of the possibilities of the human mind to conceive and represent the world. In work after work, Welty tries to represent the functioning of the human mind, to evoke the duality between an extreme susceptibility to the sensuousness of the created world and the desire to grasp it and show it through figures. This abstracting tendency in her fiction I would now like to examine in relation to the way she constructs her own stories. This will be a discussion of structure as opposed to pattern.

In the modernist aesthetic of the early part of the twentieth century, the formal and symbolic resources of the novel were emphasized; "form," "pattern," and "myth" were of paramount importance. Traces of this can be seen in *The Wide Net* but we see in a later story such as "Circe" (1955) how Welty has decisively broken new paths. Let me quote from both a postmodern writer and a postmodern critic to make my point. John Hawkes writes in 1965: "I began to write fiction on the assumption that the true enemies of the novel were plot, character, setting, and theme, and having once abandoned these familiar ways of thinking about fiction, totality of vision or structure was really all that remained. And structure—verbal and psychological coherence—is still my largest concern as a writer" (qtd. in Scholes 68–69).

And Robert Scholes in 1967: "Fabulation, then, means a return to a more verbal kind of fiction. It also means a return to a more fictional kind. By this I mean a less realistic and more artistic kind of narrative: more shapely, more evocative, more concerned with ideas and ideals, less concerned with things" (12). This could be compared with what Welty writes in "Words into Fiction," where we note her essential preoccupation with form, the "totality of vision and structure":

> The novel or story ended, shape must have made its own impression on the reader, so that he feels that some *design* in life (by which I mean esthetic pattern, not purpose) has just been discovered there. And this pattern, shape, form that emerges for you then, a reader at the end of the book, may do the greatest thing that fiction does: it may move you. And however you have been moved by the parts, this still has to happen from the *whole* before you know what indeed you have met with in that book. (144, italics added)

The important words, of course, are *design* and *whole*. In this deep awareness of form, what matters is the ultimate shape of the finished work, the concern for the *figures* that graphically represent the written work, just as a building is represented by the blueprint of an architect. In this can be traced Welty's surest right to innovation. Claude Simon in *Les Géorgiques*, his 1981 novel, points out this fictional mode and insists on the fact that to read the blueprint correctly one must be aware of the code; otherwise, the design is indecipherable. This is somewhat akin to Welty's story of the caves in "Words into Fiction" (136–37). We need an interpretation.

The difficulty of her work comes from the fact that Eudora Welty used those codes at a time when few could decipher them. The reading of more avant-garde fiction has since taught the public how to look for another representation beneath or behind the story, how to seize, hidden in the visible broken pattern, a more secret pattern. Out of the wide range of figures by which this fiction reveals itself, I will select two, equally beautiful, although the more daring and brilliant may well be the earlier one. Both show, however, the extremely lucid and original way in which Eudora Welty deals with the South—I mean "Old Mr Marblehall" and "Kin."

"Old Mr Marblehall" is a story about the imposture of writing; it shows the creation, the "fabrication," of a character and its limitations. Once again, the surface is deceptive; the apparent subject of the narration is a picture of the decadent society of the Old South, the South seen as myth, if you prefer, and consequently reduced to staging with sets and costumes. In reality, the story shows what Genette argues in *Figures III* about the *recit*, the narrative, which is related both to the story as story and to the act of telling a story. In other words, "Old Mr Marblehall" stages the specificity of the literary act, the questioning of the very nature of poetical invention and what happens at the moment invention becomes a narrative. In large measures, Eudora Welty's innovative art rests upon this constant shifting towards narration: the *telling* of the story as opposed to the story proper. In "Old Mr Marblehall," the story is always shown as something elusive, uncertain, in great danger of complete dissolution. Along with this postmodernist tendency to destroy all certainties and reduce the story to its mere constituent parts, we have another well-known trope, constant in Welty's fiction, which I shall call "narrative reversal." Apparently, we shift from what is seen to what is written, but this is pure illusion for it is just the reverse.

To create her character, Eudora Welty raises the two basic questions at the same time: How do we define a character? How do we give him a fictional existence? For this, she relies entirely on a stylistic device often adopted by later writers (William Gass, for instance), that of stylization or the use of stereotypes. It enables her to satirize a number of clichés about the South, to expose hypocritical attitudes, and to insure the active critical participation of her reader. This discourse, founded on a number of infallible and reiterated signs, aims at producing all the marks of what is conventionally as the Old South, *including its reverse*. The two possible dangers of stylization, imitation and parody (i.e., excessive admiration for one's model or harsh criticism), are brilliantly avoided. This results in Eudora Welty's inimitable tone—her unique voice—which transmutes into poetry the displacement inherent in parody. No labored effects, rather arabesques and flights of the imagination. Writing becomes "a great blazing butterfly" ("Old Mr Marblehall" 97).

Character as it appears in the twentieth-century English novel is defined by family, house, and social life. In "Old Mr Marblehall," Welty plays on doubles that are not quite identical in order to deconstruct such traditional conception of character. Thus, instead of drawing a portrait of Mr Marblehall as a Southern gentleman, she paints a full-scale portrait of Mrs Marblehall as a Southern gentlewoman—hyperbolic if not hysterical. The reality of the couple is denied by the deliberately Balzacian effect of the portrait, doubled by the poor histrionic origins of the husband on another level and also by the fabricated existence of their child whose portrait is a series of collages from nineteenth- and twentieth-century writers. For Mr Marblehall's other more common family, Welty follows the same process in the reverse. The whole story, then, is based on the deconstruction of the characters; by stressing their unimportance and artificiality, Welty presents them as *literary constructions*. The signifier becomes the signified, form becomes matter. Poor insignificant Mr Marblehall, unnoticed by his fellow citizens, comes to nothing, or rather to that illusion that the story represents. That Welty changed old Mr Grenada into old Mr Marblehall and the town of Brewster into Natchez corroborates her wish to satirize at the same time the artificiality and anachronism of any literature about the Old South and its myth *and* the traditional way of creating character. She inaugurates here a new kind of character without past existence, which heralds the heroes of the *nouveau roman*.

Duly provided with a stylized mansion, ancestors, and a wife, Mr Marblehall still lacks what would make him exist: a life. This is the narrative problem that is presented when we read that Mr Marblehall, in his desire to catch up with time, or the others, is a bigamist. To insert oneself into the flow of time by claiming a past, a present, and a future, and to force the town's attention, is to accede to existence. But this existence is kept doubtful throughout the story:

> Nobody cares. Not an inhabitant of Natchez, Mississippi, cares if he is deceived by old Mr Marblehall. Neither does anyone care that Mr Marblehall has finally caught on, he thinks, to what people are supposed to do. This is it: they endure something inwardly—for a time secretly; they establish a past, a memory; thus they store up life. He has done this; most remarkably, he has even multiplied his life by deception; and plunging deeper and deeper he speculates upon some glorious finish, a great explosion of revelations . . . the future. (117–18)

It all amounts to a matter of vision and vision is what founds the dialects used in "Old Mr Marblehall": *to see and to show on the narrative level, to show oneself and (not) be seen on the narrated level*. The injunction to "Watch" is the key word of the text; added in the revised version, it centers the whole story on the creative act that takes place between the puppeteer and his audience (111). This injunction is obviously addressed by Mr Marblehall to the other characters in the narrative. The positive exchange in the first case becomes negative or null in the second. If we look at the last scene, when old Mr Marblehall imagines he is discovered by his second son, we are warned that it *cannot happen,* for the *whole* passage is based on the sum of all the different signs attached to his different lives. This scene is purely fictitious in the narrative with no other reality than the writing to give it existence. The text, then, can be read as a kind of staging of Welty's *ars poetica*: writing is a matter for illusion; it begets it while it feeds on it. "Old Mr Marblehall" fictionalizes the process of writing; it is the imposture of narration.

"Kin" also deals with imposture: what a fraud a family portrait is. Here the structure is based upon the principle of the play within a play. André Gide noted this device in his *Journals*, in reference to the famous Van Eyck painting *The Wedding of the Arnolfini* (17). In it, the guests, that is to say, the witnesses, those who testify to the truth of the event, are not shown directly but as reflections in a mirror. In "Kin," Welty also uses the device of a mirror to represent opposition, but the shift is no longer in space as with the Arnolfini (the witnesses standing where we stand, so to speak) but in time. The mirror does not reflect directly a part of the scene that is presented to the spectator or reader, but the fragment of another scene, of which it constitutes the only material proof, thus putting the first picture into perspective. The beauty of the story comes from the perfect adequacy of the medium for the subject: one must look at the portrait of the great-grandmother in order to understand the meaning of a story about people coming to have their picture taken. "Kin" treats the myth of the Old South after the manner of Monet or Vuillard: only fragments on the shimmering surface. Certainly, Eudora Welty satirizes the nostalgia, but at the same time, she celebrates the South, whose essence remains immortal because it is steeped in vivid sensations.

"Kin" is a comedy whose obvious target is Sister Anne, vulgar, money-grabbing, without scruples or delicacy, who relinquishes her duties to the dying Uncle Felix and desecrates the house by letting an itinerant photographer use it. Her gain will be her own picture taken for free.

Two objects form the critical distance, the portrait of Great-Grandmother Jerrold and the stereoscope. By a narrative perversity, the point of view is Dicey's, who, like Laurel McKelva of *The Optimist's Daughter*, is the Southerner gone North who comes back home to visit. The aptness of her remarks is such that we believe her—we are, in fact, in great danger of being taken in by Dicey's lively, charming speech. The extreme impressionistic—and postmodern—fragmentation of the narration, the intermingling of the present and the past, hides the counterpoint, which we see only at the end of the story. In "Old Mr Marblehall," the Southern way of life was doubled; here it is tripled as it would be in a series of mirrors endlessly reflecting the same picture, producing an effect of closure. Thus, three versions of Southern life are presented almost identically (Welty uses the same words). They consist of a present positive image (Dicey revisiting the South), a negative one (Sister Anne), and a much earlier one (the heroic past of the family). The function of the first scene is to establish, *en transparence*, that conventional code by which we can appreciate the structure. For all its beauty and polished appearance, this society is essentially racist, materialistic, frivolous, and irresponsible. But these flaws, so deeply engrained in Southern way of life, appear unpleasant only after they are *repeated* in the text:

> It was two-thirty in the afternoon, after an enormous dinner at which we had had company—six girls, chattering almost like ready-made bridesmaids—ending with wonderful black, bitter, moist chocolate pie under mountains of meringue, and black, bitter coffee. (648)
> "What do I see? Cake!" (659) –Sister Anne's first words of greeting.
> Uncle Harlan, who could be persuaded, if he did not eat too much, to take down the banjo later. (670)

Welty deepens this critique of the family by holding the portrait of Great-Grandmother Jerrold in tense relation with the photograph of Sister Anne. Their differences are only superficial for Anne's photograph is the comical version of the portrait of the great-grandmother—the same vanity, the same desire to appear to advantage in both instances, above all, the same artificiality in the setting. The photographer uses a backdrop—a "blur of ... yanked-down moonlight"—just as the itinerant painter did, to produce "the same old thing, a scene that never was" (674).

The evocation of the heroic life of the great-grandmother, the founder of the family, is tinted with the same nostalgia and exotic overtones as the views shown in the stereoscope by Uncle Felix: wonderful cities to which the optical machine added the fascination of haziness. In effect, the heroic has become a postcard, rather, a yellowed photograph, something that can be discarded like the old Confederate musket that is kept behind the door like a broom. What the short story "Kin" presents is a series of old-fashioned portraits on the art of living in the South, but it also shows how they were *made up*. Did this legend ever exist? Or was it born out of a series of conventional embellishments? Welty requires that we remove all that is artificial, all that depersonalize, just as we know that the veil behind the photograph or the canvas is not true. Dicey realizes this when she looks at her great-grandmother's eyes, which are her own, strangely authentic in this artificial portrait. As she leaves Mingo, she takes away with her one last "photograph," another faded and yellowed one too, the blurred, indistinct vision of the country neighbors waiting under the porch. Their faces are identical, yet each carries its impenetrable secret, its identity.

The counterpoint upon which the story is built functions like a stereopticon or a stereoscope, both of which juxtapose images that are seen in relief. Whatever the specific mechanism, the principle is one of duality with the result either of increased distinctness or blurring. This provides the key to "Kin." The superimposition of diverse attitudes, nearly identical throughout the ages, gives a unique picture that both permits one to see what is called "the Old South," and at the same time suggests something evanescent. On this apparent contradiction rest the dialectics of "Kin": to seize the myth one must start from the present, not the other way around. "Kin" is a fraud: the fraud of a family picture, the fraud of a loving family. By choosing appearances, artificiality, and the absurdly false, the living perpetuate an *illusion*. Yet, true values are seen, true courage exists. By rejecting false romanticism, Welty says, people can live authentically: the beauty and idealism of the South are all there. In this respect, "Kin" is a plea for the South, this South, which in a purely postmodern reading may amount to *traces* only. Memories are, paradoxically, as evanescent and immortal as smells, the exquisite smells of the pinks and four-o'clocks that Aunt Beck would give to her visitors as she walked them to the gate—as if what is left of people, and life, amounted to no more than mere traces.

In an essay entitled "Literary History and Literary Modernity," Paul de Man arrives at the insight that "one is soon forced to resort to paradoxical formulations, such as defining the modernity of a literary period as the manner in which it discovers the impossibility of being modern" (385). Paradoxical formulations are what would best define Eudora Welty's fiction. The first, as suggested by Paul de Man, is the urge repeatedly to try new techniques to express deeper truths about man and, at the same time, the awareness that this is illusory. There is also the effort to imprison the spirit of the moment and to know that it is past already—which is but one aspect of man's old quarrel with time since he is bound to meet defeat in his very accomplishment. The second paradox is to be very much a Southerner and at the same time to transcend, even disavow, the South, to stand outside in order to see better inside and to know the very desperation and impossibility of the enterprise. And, more important perhaps, it is to be alert and critical and distant and yet to use that very distance to encompass with greater love, with more comprehending love, all that is human. At the heart of Welty's modernity there is a lucidity that is never cold or ruthless even when scalding, a despair that can still love, and is above all a saving comic spirit.

A REREADING OF EUDORA WELTY'S "FLOWERS FOR MARJORIE" (2018)

> Every writer, like everybody else, thinks he's living through the crisis of the ages. To write honestly and with all our powers is the least we can do, and the most.
> —EUDORA WELTY "MUST THE NOVELIST CRUSADE?" (813)

> We all know that Art is not truth. Art is a lie that makes us realize truth.... The artist must know how to convince others of the truthfulness of his lies.
> —PICASSO[1]

> The ability to speak in many voices will be determined by one's cultural, historical, and experiential framework.[2]
> —REBECCA MARK (15)

Eudora Welty's fiction presents an endless challenge for readers and critics. Considered as one of the best literary productions of the twentieth century, her work chiseled to perfection arouses a thoughtful and jubilatory response. Each new reading and new critical exploration further disclose the protean dimension of her text and help understand why this fiction, deceptively simple or adamantly resisting, is so deeply in resonance with the contemporary mind and heart. Welty stressed, contemporarily, the adequation of the work with its times as it reflects the artist's prodigious desire to explore new territories and invent new techniques. We keep in mind her lyrical praise of Twain and Cather:

> Who can move best but the inspired child of his times? Whose story should better be told than that of the youth who has contrived to cut

loose from ties and go flinging himself might and main, in every bit of his daring, in joy of life not to be denied, to vaunt himself in the love of vaunting, in the marvelous curiosity to find out everything, over the preposterous length and breadth of an opening new world, and in so doing to be one with it? ("The House of Willa Cather" 51–52)

The superb formula "the inspired child of his times" addresses the question of the interpenetration of contemporary culture with fiction from a wider perspective than does intertextuality, thus expressing Welty's own attitude towards fiction writing. Here she speaks for herself as well, and she proclaims that her personal interest for all that concerned her times has shaped her narrative strategies and fed her fiction.

Welty was an exceptionally well-read writer, an omnivorous reader, eager since childhood to read and learn about past and present civilizations and their cultures. She was also deeply immersed in the artistic productions of her time, showing equal curiosity and interest towards all forms with utter disregard for any distinction between "lower" and "higher" genres. Her year as a student at Columbia University and then her many trips to New York gave her opportunities to become acquainted with new American art forms such as jazz, musical comedies, and music hall productions and with the new arts of cinema and photography from Europe and the United States. Her early interest for painting made her a frequent visitor of the great exhibitions and art shows, of museums and avant-garde galleries in New York. No field in the arts in the United States as well as in Europe was left unexplored: painting, photography, sculpture, cinema, fiction, poetry, drama, and music, and countless attendance to plays, concerts, and operas. Just as important was the critical, artistic, and creative exchange that went on for years between Welty and "a group of friends who exemplified intellectual daring in many ways and who supported her in fiction" (Marrs, *One Writer's Imagination* 7). With an interest for contemporary history, Eudora Welty was a daily reader of the *New York Times*, and political engagement is ever present in her writings in an oblique way, something she learned from the works of European artists and writers of the late nineteenth and twentieth centuries. Their desire to denounce evil and injustice, and consequently bring about change, implied a new way of looking at people and things, a new perception of the balance of power between individuals and society, and the invention of new techniques in every artistic field. Political and social unrest at the turn to the twentieth century, and more generally the disruption of society brought by the disaster of World War I, caused artists, especially in Germany, to create new forms of representation. They felt they had to shatter the public's certainties and bring people to a new awareness of what the world was really like through the violence of their subjects and their treatments: distortions, dismemberment, a bold displacement of color. The term "expressionism" refers in fact to different groups of painters covering a large scope in time and genre, from Gaugin, Van Gogh, and the early Kandinsky, with mostly the German painters of *The Bridge* and *The Blue Rider* schools, down to such painters as Piet Mondrian, Kazimir Malevich, or Man Ray. The term was first used to characterize the works of the Norwegian painter Edvard Munch in opposition to impressionism and then again in reference to the paintings of the French cubists and fauvists. The American public was better acquainted with the films of those German expressionist filmmakers who had emigrated to the United States in the early 1920s, such as F. W. Murnau.

Another twentieth-century avatar of this political concern can be traced in the surrealists' revolutionary project. Surrealism was not merely an abstract movement focusing on new modes of representation; it was also to "engage" in the chaotic contemporary world and was concerned with bringing about a change in minds and attitudes. This is at the heart of Welty's fiction. A denunciation far more provocative, far-reaching, and inventive than her plain statement, "I was always writing about . . . injustice" suggests, and as the essays collected in *Eudora Welty and Politics* edited by Harriet Pollack and Suzanne Marrs amply demonstrate, constructing a truer and fairer image of Welty from many perspectives ("Fiction" 30). Welty has given her texts this denunciatory dimension, but she fictionalized and disguised it in an indirect way, often as comedy, so that the full shocking import of her message comes belatedly with a careful reading of her texts. What has been misconstrued as utopia turns out to be dystopia. Dystopia surfaces, says Ricoeur, when an excess of the necessary critique of the status quo leads to totalitarianism, presents negative features of the utopian model, and contains the seeds of its potential distortion into the worst of all possible worlds. The term appears in the nineteenth century to become a major and obsessive theme of twentieth-century thinking. Eudora Welty was well acquainted with such texts as Aldous Huxley's *Brave New World* (1932), for instance. The nearly nonexistent critical attention paid to Welty's use of dystopia to denounce social and political evils is due to her subtle control of this bold technique. In Welty's canon is no systematic structure, no complete reconstruction of a totalitarian world as in George Orwell's *1984* (1948) or Margaret Atwood's *The Handmaid's Tale* (1986). Instead, her texts open windows on dystopia; they suggest moods, incidents, turn inside out features that tragic minds could make horrifying. They borrow from cinema and painting, and more often than not, they rely on the full spectrum of laughter to raise the reader's awareness, from slapstick comedy to devastatingly strident or weird laughter, as in *The Ponder Heart*.[3]

"Flowers for Marjorie" belongs to the great innovative stories with which Eudora Welty entered the literary field and, with the title story, is the most intriguing text of *A Curtain of Green and Other Stories*. Close reading brings out the boldness of the young writer's experiment in this exploration of the contemporary world along the aesthetic lines of her times and suggests that the aesthetic statement made in "Flowers" is so strong because it echoes texts written by the founding father(s) of American literature, Hawthorne and Poe, while experimenting with new techniques used by contemporary European artists, writers, and filmmakers. History is at the root of their technical invention. With Hawthorne, it is early American history—Puritanism or British despotism in the colonies as seen in "Young Goodman Brown" and "My Kinsman, Major Molineux." With European expressionist and surrealist artists, it is uprisings, social movements, and World War I. All these artists explored evil, death, and sexuality—the human condition—and favored the form best suited to their subject and purpose. For "Young Goodman Brown," Hawthorne chose the form of a fantastic tale to denounce the evils of Puritanism at the beginning of the colonial period: the obsession with sin and the devil and how a marriage could be forever poisoned by unfounded suspicion. With "Flowers for Marjorie," in order to denounce the evils of the Depression, Welty created a form of resonance with the new sensibilities of her time: combining political dystopia in literature with experiments in representation in the arts, relying on violence, distortion, and dreamlike effects found in expressionistic painting and cinema, hallucinatory effects favored by surrealism. She probed deep into unexpected aspects to reveal hidden evil; this unexpectedness is what brings surprise, and with surprise comes "a shock of recognition" about the truth of her picture.

Placed between "Old Mr Marblehall" and "A Curtain of Green," between a dreamed life and a shamanic experience, "Flowers for Marjorie" is the only text in Welty's first collection that concentrates on a specific historical event—the Depression—which the writer saw firsthand and photographed in New York. Harriet Pollack and Suzanne Marrs subtly decode "The Unemployed in Union Square, New York, 1930s" and "Union Square, New York, 1930s" and adds about the latter, "This photograph and the various images it encompasses establish Welty's very political concern with the Great Depression" ("Seeing" [248]). Welty confirmed this commitment in her 1989 interview with Hunter Cole and Seetha Srinivasan, saying, "These people of the Great Depression kept alive on the determination to get back to work and to make a living again. I photographed them in Union Square and in subways and sleeping in subway stations and huddling together to keep warm, and I felt, then, sort of placed in the editorial position as I took their pictures. Recording the mass of them did constitute a plea on their behalf to the public, their existing plight being so evident in the mass" (qtd. in Pollack and Marrs, "Seeing" [248]).

The writer added a further "plea on their behalf" with "Flowers for Marjorie," a bold narrative experiment to arouse the public's awareness to a major social evil. The story is a textual representation of the Great Depression from the perspective of Southern emigration to the North with a young couple from Mississippi come to New York to find employment as main characters. Doubly faced with estrangement, they react differently to unemployment and starvation away from home. Whereas Marjorie is content with the baby to come in three months and shows spirit and plans for the future, Howard is hopeless, threatened in his manhood, destroyed by despair. The narrative presents Howard's stabbing his wife to death; through the course of his rambling walk in New York City making friends, winning money, hitting the jackpot in Radio City Music Hall with the keys to the city and a splendid bunch of red roses for his wife; and then coming back to his poor room. It belongs to the reader to question the "reality" or the "truth" of these events.

This experiment requires several approaches to seize the writer's intentions and strategies. On a first level, "Flowers for Marjorie" can be read as the written equivalent of an expressionistic painting of the kind produced in Europe some twenty years earlier, with filmic echoes and techniques borrowed from surrealism and German expressionism. On a second level, the contents are manifestly transgressive and as such deserve close attention.

Past the first scene, a transcription in shades of grey of Welty's photographs of unemployed men in Union Square, the reader enters a world of strong forms and colors of violence, distortion, grotesque discrepancies, and a surrealistic use of hallucination. At first, the text may be experienced at one glance like a modern painting that relies on bold colors, great splashes of red and black, and a strong general touch. Soon the reader realizes that Welty invites one to read her character's afternoon as an extended construction—a violent fantasizing in black and red—whose function is to express the traumatic experience of living through the Depression, faced with loneliness and hunger, a sense of abandonment and absolute despair, with bouts of wildest dreams. The text is the projection of what goes on in Howard's mind, first at home in his poor lodgings and then later when he tries to create a more congenial world for himself, as shown by the profusion of happy details borrowed from life in contemporary New York during his long rambling.

The German critic Kasimir Edschmid's formula about expressionistic painting does apply to Welty's writing here: the expressionist painter "does not see, he perceives. He does not depict, he experiences" (qtd. in Travers 167). The hypnotic quality of Howard's gaze on the pansy pinned on Marjorie's coat, then on his wife's body as he examines every detail after "the murder," and later on various places in New York comes from Welty's writing the process itself rather than explaining it—revelation as a visual experience versus understanding as rationalization. A correction in the manuscript about the pansy gives the clue to Welty's method: "It seemed in Herman's wide eyes to lose its identity of flower-size" becomes "it began in Howard's anxious sight to lose its identity of flower-size" (120).[4]

The use of embedded narratives with a blurring of frames to convey the general impression of a horror dream is another device borrowed from contemporary artists, with two levels of utopia turned into dystopia. The narrative starts with the actual world: the realization for unemployed Howard that the utopia of a better life in New York where jobs are available by contrast with Mississippi has turned into dystopia, and the American Dream has dwindled to endless lines of unemployed people in Union Square, demonstrations in the streets, a room that becomes smaller with each moving, and a baby soon to arrive. With no job and no money, just hunger and despair as he sees no end to the present situation, Howard is nothing but a helpless guilty conscience. He has failed his wife in every field: as a lover, a husband providing for his family, a father-to-be. In his subconscious, resentment born of his guilt opens up new ways of apprehending the world. This first enveloping dystopia generates a second one, triggered by the pansy pinned on Marjorie's coat. From that point in the narrative, no event is to be taken literally. They are equivalents to large splashes of red color, dark zones, streaks, and shapes in a painting. "Terrible vision," "mirage," "dream," Welty warns her reader again and again (121, 122, 128). The episode of the bright yellow pansy that Marjorie has found and pinned on her blue coat functions like a *mise en abyme* because it encapsulates all the elements of the story: distortion of real life, Howard's destructive rage against Marjorie's flower, hallucination with the production of a strong sexual element linked to birth, and then the realization that this murderous violence had been a mirage.

> Howard lowered his eyes and once again he saw the pansy. There it shone, a wide-open yellow flower with dark red veins and edges. Against the sky-blue of Marjorie's old coat it began in Howard's anxious sight to lose its identity of flower-size and assume the gradual

and large curves of a mountain on the horizon of a desert, the veins becoming crevasses, the delicate edges the *giant worn lips* of a sleeping crater. His heart jumped to his mouth. . . .

He snatched the pansy from Marjorie's coat and tore its petals off and scattered them on the floor and jumped on them!

Marjorie watched him in silence, and slowly he realized that he had not acted at all, that he had only had a terrible vision. The pansy still blazed on the coat, just as the pigeons had still flown in the park when he was hungry. He sank back onto the couch, trembling with the desire and the pity that had overwhelmed him, and said harshly, "How long before your time comes?" (120–21, italics added)

Deeper probing of the text reveals a transgressive experimentation that only writing could allow. Here, the young writer boldly experiments with the representation of despair. Close reading invites one to read "Flowers for Marjorie" as the dramatization of "self-begetting" when, no longer able to see and face reality, Howard reconstructs the world and creates a personal utopia that will turn into dystopia, in the way surrealist film makers were interested in ultimate transgression in their work. Welty expressed both her awareness and her uneasiness about this bold "leap in the dark" when she told an interviewer, "That's a poor story; I had no business writing that story. That's a kind of an artificial story that's written about a city. I think I wrote it in New York during the Depression. It is too literary" ("Words" 134; "Fiction" 24). As we know, Welty did not disown "Flowers" for subsequent publications. What she expresses here, I think, is the artistic uncertainty she felt as she stepped beyond her familiar field. However, and no doubt about it, the story's technique marks Welty as one of the few major American writers experimenting along the aesthetic lines of their times, plunging into surrealism and expressionism.

What makes the explicit sexual imagery in the pansy episode so terrible that Howard wants to destroy the flower? Not intercourse with his wife, not the birth to come, but his own birth, the one he aspires to with the imagery of a mother's genitals—"the *giant worn lips* of a sleeping crater" (120, italics added). As he hits the very depth of despair, he envisions a second utopia with dystopia at its core; he feels no way out except through terrible transgression—*self-begetting* that entails murder. He subconsciously realizes that the present family order with husband, wife, and baby to come (and love) has been destroyed by the Depression, and in his alienation, he envisions a new order with *himself as the baby to be born*. Howard craves a new start, a new life with no responsibility, no guilt, and people taking care of him.

This implies the need to get rid of his pregnant wife. The filmic narration of Marjorie's murder, seen in slow motion, questions its actuality, as does Howard's noting the perfect balance of the puppet-like body. "How strange! he thought wonderingly" (123). The pool of blood in Marjorie's lap is no proof, just the sign of his guilty hallucination. An addition to the manuscript for the final story further suggests the unreality of the murder: "Yes, of course, he thought; for it had all been impossible" (124).

From then on, with no warning signs as is the case with a fantastic film, Welty pursues her *writing unreality* with a remarkable command of the perilous exercise: to give the illusion of actual events as she writes with accelerated speed and the precision of details found in dreams, and at the same time to question the reality of these events as devices such as *non sequitur*, close up, slow motion, or the use of shadows, extensively present in silent films. Welty's challenge in the description of Howard's rambling through New York, as the young man reconstructs the city and himself positively from the different alienating experiences he has had of the city—the WPA office with Miss Ferguson, Radio City Music Hall, countless people of all sorts, and pretty unusual sights and objects for a small-town Southerner—is to suggest the possibility of its impossibility through excess and a surfeit of details that fulfill Howard's most intimate aspirations.

The subway episode, for instance, expresses the young man's desire for an ontological rebirth under the eye of God—"All along the tile wall was written, 'God sees me, God sees me, God sees me, God sees me'"—just before he experiences birth as he leaves the dark tunnel to enter the world between "two old warm Jewish women" (125).[5] Howard wants acknowledgment and protection; he wants money to share and spend; in a word, he wants *to belong here in New York*, something his final adventure in Radio City Music Hall brings to him as he is given the key to the city with roses for his wife and the public visibility of the press and radio. Like a prince in a fairy tale, he who "was one of the modest, the shy, the sandy haired—one of those who would always have preferred waiting to one side. . . ." has been turned into a public hero (119). At this moment, through the grotesque and threatening perceptions of the world of the powerful, the very excess of this success story generates fear. Howard realizes the enormity of his transgression. From a friendly place, New York becomes a space where fear reigns supreme. Hence the superb description of the young man's panicky return home (with Chekhovian echoes of the short story entitled "Panic Fears"). The dreamlike writing of the end of the story confirms the unreality of the murder, then of the journey through New York City. Like Young Goodman Brown, Howard has dreamed the worst about his wife. And the red stains the policeman sees on his pants (they should be black in a realistic story) are no more proof of the reality of the adventure than is Faith's pink ribbon.

This disquieting effect of the rambling episode comes from the *apparent ordinariness* of sight—places, people, objects, as the young man wanders through New York. In his state of alienation, Howard's mind creates something new; he shapes the world as he wants it to be, yet his visions, those of a badly bruised young man, produce a strangely distorted reality—the poetic form of his ultimate rebellion. Violence is felt as blows and revelation as we see in the paintings of Max Ernst or Max Beckmann in search of modern metaphors to figure the present fight of modern man to survive in big cities as in Beckmann's *The Night* (1918/19).

With this bold innovative story, Welty had the higher ambition to shatter the reader's indifference and smugness towards the evils of the Depression: showing how it affected young people, its first victims, how they were reduced to slow death through starvation, to what extremities despair could lead them. Welty's subtle play on doubt as to the reality of the murder of Marjorie further adds horror as it hits the reader's subconscious with the awareness of its possibility ever present in everyone (as in "A Curtain of Green," the story she placed just after in her first volume of stories), that murderous impulse shown in early surrealist films such as Luis Buñuel and Salvador Dali's *Un Chien Andalou* (1929)—a surreal, violently disjunctive story of desire, gender confusion, and the unconscious, a "call for murder," as Buñuel saw it (34). If, as Octavio Paz puts it, Buñuel's greatest target was the self-assurance of the powerful, his work "develops under the double arch of beauty and rebellion" (157), likewise, with a similar universalizing process, if Welty's target here is the carelessness and indifference of public authorities, "Flowers for Marjorie" takes shape beneath the double arch of assassination and self-creation. Murder and rebirth conjoin as the ultimate form of rebellion when man desperately tries to be "like God."

What are we asked to read in this text? The resisting reader will insist on the reality of the murder, just as he insists on the reality of the journey. He will plead the ambiguity of the end, with Howard's entering his room to look at Marjorie, the stains on his pants, the policeman ready to help, and the little girls picking up the roses. Conversely, the reader who accepts the narrative conventions established by the writer, "a willing suspension of disbelief," continues to read the text as more projections of Howard's mad desire to prove to himself he is the murderer he secretly wishes and regrets (not) to be. What does he see? A corpse? Has he really stopped time, which he had madly accelerated in his crazy flight? Or does he see what his guilty conscience refuses to see—the tired hungry body of a pregnant woman fallen asleep? No mention of the blood pool on Marjorie's lap this time. "He had had a dream" (128). His hurried flight back into the street means a comforting return to the unreal, dreamlike world he has created for himself, with his hands full of roses and no sexual and marital responsibilities, where an unreal father figure offers the balm he needs, and women, the tender irresponsible company of the young girls of his youth.

The strangely elegiac atmosphere of the end as the little girls run stealthily up on the sidewalk and put the roses in their hair functions like a coda to the moment when Howard was looking at Marjorie by the window with "her soft cut hair now and then blowing and streaming like ribbon-ends," and dreaming of "Victory, Mississippi, [where] all girls were like Marjorie—and that Marjorie was in turn like his home" (120). Although everything is left uncertain and blurred, with all the roses gone, we feel the full pathos of the portrait (a self-portrait?) at the end. "The nondescript, dusty figure with the wide gray eyes and the sandy hair," a coda to the portrait of the opening scene, is all the more poignant as we remember the young man's generosity (128). His wildest dreams of the penniless man always meant sharing: "Howard agreed that they should all have drinks around and that his fortune belonged to them all," just as his glorious adventure in Radio City Music Hall meant bringing back to his wife, who found solace in flowers, the most magnificent gift for a country girl, a bunch of red roses (126). This humanity/tenderness in the treatment of the subject characterizes most German expressionist painting, while among American writers who have written about the Depression, few have reached such intensity within such a narrow scope.

Chapter 4

OF HUMAN, ANIMAL, AND CELESTIAL BODIES IN WELTY'S "CIRCE" (2005)

> We are mortal: this is time's deepest meaning in the novel as it is to us alive. [...] Fiction's concern is with the ephemeral—that is the human—effects of time, these alone.
> —EUDORA WELTY "SOME NOTES ON TIME IN FICTION" (168)

"Circe," the shortest story of *The Bride of the Innisfallen* (1955), is also its most secret and intriguing, the resisting burning heart of a collection that explores the antagonistic forces at work in the relations between men and women. With renewed depth and scope over time, space, and theme, *The Bride of the Innisfallen* examines femininity and the many-faceted mystery of its resilience, power, and capability to enforce and endorse transformation and change.

As Eudora Welty states on several occasions, the story was born of her meditation as she was sailing off the Italian and Sicilian coast:

> I had so much fun writing that story. That was on my first trip to Europe. I never thought I was going to write anything. I was looking. I didn't write anything till I got home. We were passing Sicily and all of those other islands where Circe was supposed to be. And I thought, "What would it be like to be condemned to live forever?" To see everybody that you love die and not be able to feel anything about mortality or the preciousness of the moment. That must have been what she felt. ("A Conversation" 19)[1]

To represent this experience outside ordinary human existence Welty firstly reversed the Homeric point of view—Odysseus's telling of the encounter—and made Circe the narrator of her own adventure. Odysseus's visit to her island becomes an event in Circe's immortal life, something that happened to her and changed her perception of self and the world as she recalls that interruption to the endless flow of her time. Second, for Circe's telling, Welty created a poetic idiom that gives depth and mystery to the magician's narrative and fashions a resisting text, one that is often difficult to understand because of gaps and ellipses, devices that demand acute attention to grasp the hidden meaning of the text as it explores the ways this legendary woman can still affect modern readers. At the same time, the writer plays with the familiar and through Circe's humorous comments—voice boasting of her talent as housewife, screeching her scorn for men, or addressing planets and constellations—she throws stitches to bind together the known and the unknown, human grief and everlasting torment, death, and cosmic timelessness.

Welty follows Homer's text with a few changes and several long additions that put special emphasis on the body. Circe is a beautiful woman who seems to promise delight when she brings misery by transforming human bodies into animal bodies: "That moment of transformation—only the gods really like it!" Welty has her say (639). "Men and beasts almost never take in enough of the wonder to justify the trouble" (639). Yet, as she recounts, once a hero resisted her power and firmly rejected her, leaving her forever beneath the fixed and eternal course of heavenly bodies with a strange longing for the perils a mortal body must endure. Yet, the reader feels that something else in Welty's text resists an ordinary revisiting of the well-known myth, something that binds Circe's awareness of her immortal body to fear, a fascination and rejection of the self. I propose to read "Circe" as a story about bodies—human, animal, and celestial bodies—and to explore some of the darker echoes which Welty introduces in her rewriting of the myth. *Simulacrum*, playing with appearances are the well-known key words, yet in a deeper sense Welty's text is an exploration into abjection as Julia Kristeva so superbly analyzes the concept in *Pouvoirs de l'horreur*.

I will examine Circe in her relation to femininity and seduction, to nature when as a magician she denatures nature, then to death when she tries to appropriate death as she plays with the signs and simulacra mortals like Odysseus and his men conceive, and finally in her submission to abjection.

The confrontation on the island opposes a strictly male society—Odysseus and his crew living in a floating moving space (their ship)—to the female society that reigns supreme over the fixed island set on some indeterminate frontier.[2]

It pertains all the more to the *Unheimlich* as it pits a mortal man against an immortal woman, with an endless play on appearance and change. With

Circe, Welty explores together with feminine sexual desire and seduction the limits of femininity, redoubling the very notion of limits by placing her heroine, as Homer did, on an island set at the ambiguous frontier that separates the known world from the unknown world, the civilized from the uncivilized.

As a magician and an immortal, Circe is more than woman. Her first appearance on the threshold of her bright palace is literally a dazzling apparition, as, providentially lit up by the sun (her father), Circe displays the seduction of her fair hair: "I threw open the door. A shaft of light from the zenith struck my brow, and the wind let out my hair. Something else swayed my body outward" (639). This beautiful appearance that promises the joys and comfort of hospitality as the Greeks practiced it is pure deception just as the first word "Welcome" becomes "the most dangerous word in the world" (639). Both prove false as the immortal means treachery and evil power over her visitors. She succeeds with ordinary men—the sailors—but fails with a hero—Odysseus. The sailors are transformed into swine; the captain alone, protected by a plant given by the gods, retains his human shape.

Circe's ambiguous confession, "something else swayed my body outward," takes its meaning once she realizes Odysseus has resisted her magical power: over the only man left unchanged, she will use her sexual power (639). So she plays the temptress, the seductress, determined to enjoy that "magnificent body of his" (640). She lavishes care on him, plentifully giving him the physical attention the sailors had expected but were denied, and offers herself:

> and I, with my own hands, gave him his bath [...] I rubbed oil on his shadowy shoulders, and on the rope of curls in which his jaw was set [...] I took the chain from my waist, it slipped shining to the floor between us, where it lay as if it slept, as I came forth. Under my palms he stood warm and dense as a myrtle grove at noon. His limbs were heavy, braced like a sleep-walker's who has wandered, alas, to cliffs above the sea. (640–41)

Yet, in spite of the deadly threat, Odysseus resists and refuses to see her as if she were not there ("I was invisible"), and he accepts a cup of the potent island wine only to fall asleep on a soft bed (640). Just as her magical power has been defeated by the hero, so is her sexual power. To the frustration of Circe, the immortal, who demands immediate satisfaction of her desire, Odysseus the mortal demands sequential order, since human freedom is the ability given to the individual to correct, even to invent his own relation to time. The hero will not take her before she has given back to his crew their human shapes.

This victorious resistance on the part of Odysseus exposes Circe as a betrayer and a cheat. From seductress she becomes the seduced. Yet for all her apparent defeat, Circe is the winner for a while. She succeeds in keeping her lover and his crew on her island for a whole year, in a relationship that springs from need rather than love, as she and her servants tend male needs: sex, food, and drink. Unlike Calypso, however, Circe is no representation of feminine love and tenderness, only its simulacrum. She is all the more dangerous as her charm eventually operates on Odysseus to make him forget his purpose—to sail back to Ithaca and rejoin his wife and son, Telemachus— Circe's attentions to him have created the illusion that time has stopped and that everyone on the island lives in a no-where and a no-time. So a whole year elapses as one forgetful moment, which Welty's superb craftsmanship represents as ellipse in her narrative.

Circe the magician thus is prime deceiver, an illusion, the pure appearance of appearance. And just as a whole year in her island eludes narration, so does her *persona* since Welty never describes her and only once floodlights her from above, the better to conjure up her seductive ways before her dazzled visitors. Circe is some sublime simulacrum not supported by love—life in death—but supported by evil—death in life—she is pure fascination.

With the very first word of Circe's narration, "Needle in air," Welty departs from the Homeric representation of Circe as a weaver like Calypso, the nymph who fell in love with Odysseus and who offered immortality if he lived with her forever, or like Penelope, the faithful wife in Ithaca, who buys time by weaving and unweaving (639). Instead, Welty provides her character with a weapon that, although a sign of feminine activity, is nevertheless a sign of hostility and power connoting "prick" or "goad." From the first, Circe is depicted as a smirking, heartless woman, taking pleasure in achieving an advantage over men, exercising with scorn what she thinks is her clearsightedness and thwarting the sailors' legitimate expectations of hospitality, booty, and quick departure. What marks her difference and signals her as belonging to another sphere of bodies is her power over the human body. By changing human bodies into animal bodies, the magician denies their humanity, reduces them to a subhuman condition, and commits the unforgivable crime of denaturing human nature. Later, even when she restores the sailors to their original human appearances, Circe exercises one more unnatural control and makes them younger and taller, as in Homer's *Odyssey*. Is this the proof that her power is not subjected to time and nature, or a defiant rejection of the natural process that moves from birth to growth, decay, and death?

With humor and tongue-in-cheek, Welty represents the sinister magician in the guise of a Southern lady keeping control of her vast household and estate, as did plantation mistresses in the past. Her devilish broth has the Caribbean flavor of a New Orleans dish: "I tasted, and it was perfect—swimming with oysters from my reef and flecks of golden pork, redolent with leaves of bay and basil and rosemary, with the glass of island wine tossed in at the last" (640). With distaste, she watches the hungry, tired, and dirty sailors troop into her house after exhausting days of rowing away from danger through a storm, and she immediately transforms them into swine, expelling them from the house with a wry comment on their gender:

> The floor was swaying like a bridge in battle. "Outside!" I commanded. "No dirt is allowed in this house!" In the end, it takes phenomenal neatness of housekeeping to put it through the heads of men that they are swine. With my wand seething in the air like a broom, I drove them all through the door—twice as many hooves as there had been feet before—to join their brothers. (639)

Yet the excess of tidiness rings with more sinister overtones. Despite Circe's lightness of tone and humorous comments on good housekeeping, her drive for dehumanizing bodies, ordering them around like swine and cleaning things up might have brought to the mind of an American traveling through Europe a few years after World War II (Welty's Italian journey took place in 1949) the all-too-recent times and places when human bodies were herded and driven to unspeakable places.

In a less polemical and more philosophical way, the smooth, well-run management of Circe's magic ("there is no mystery in magic," she says), its endless infallible repetition except for that one time, her heartlessness, all bring to mind an automaton—the ambiguous transgressor of limits, the epitome of the denaturing of nature (642). Circe the arch controller of magic and organizer of all activities on the island has denatured herself and become in the very materiality of her physical activities a technical persona—a robot. And perhaps, the text suggests, this very alienation, this draining of one's substance is the essence of immortality.

Confronted with evil and with Circe's endeavor to denature nature, Odysseus's determination to be a man enables him to confound the magician. Welty follows the Homeric tradition and insists in this *humanity* of the Greek hero: he is the character who never forgets he is a man. Threatened by all kinds of natural and unnatural perils, tempted by every sort of spells and creatures, Odysseus has one desire: to get back to his island; one duty: to protect his sailors and ensure safe sailing, and no curiosity about the places and beings he is forced to visit. As Circe deplores: "He cared nothing for beauty that was not of the world, he did not want the first taste of anything new" (642). His urgency and determination are the signs of something that eludes her, "his secret," the sense of mortality: "Only frailty, it seems, can divine it—and I was not endowed with that property. They live by frailty! By the moment! I tell myself that it is only a mystery, and mystery is only uncertainty" (641, 642). When after a whole year Odysseus decides to leave the island and go back to the sea, Circe is brutally confronted with her own immortality.

"What is it like to be immortal?" as Eudora Welty described the problematics of "Circe" in a conversation with me.[3]

Welty had known from the reversed perspective of time transiency and mortality to be central to her fiction. Death alone makes the moment (and life) so precious for mortal men and novelists. The challenge of writing from the perspective of immortality appealed to her all the more as the mythic character of the magician left free range to her imagination. Circe's cosmic lineage (she is the daughter of the Sun and Perseis, herself daughter of Ocean), prompted the first title for the story "Put Me in the Sky!" later discarded for "Circe" that allowed for a deeper questioning of mortality through the negative.

As Welty's story builds up to its climax with Odysseus's departure, one blank in the text puzzles the reader: What happens to Circe during the hero's last night on the island? A lovely description of the place astir with grape-gathering and wine-making under her instructions establishes time as she has always known it and will always know it—the endless seasonal recurrence of farm activities, a routine reasserted later by her nightly inspection of the house. Against this background of repetition and sedentarity, which marks her life as immortal, the event of Odysseus's departure increases Circe's dissatisfaction with her fate to the point of "torment" (645), forces her to invoke celestial bodies that are as fixed in their revolutions as she is, and then leads her to a strange place:

> I looked up at Cassiopeia, who sits there and needs nothing, pale in her chair in the stream of heaven. The old Moon was still at work. "Why keep it up, old woman?" I whispered to her, while the lions roared among the rocks; but I could hear plainly the crying of birds nearby and along the mournful shore.

> I swayed, and was flung backward by my torment. I believed that I lay in disgrace and my blood ran green, like the wand that breaks in two. My sight returned to me when I awoke in the pigsty, in the red and black aurora of flesh, and it was day. (644–45)

What happened in the second paragraph? Circe has just experienced some kind of absence when she wakes up in the pigsty at dawn. She has absented herself from herself and fallen into something that is neither a swoon nor sleep but a state of self-induced temporary absence. She has gone "outside herself." The pragmatic reader will suspect intoxication, especially as the word is present a few lines earlier in connection with Circe's instructing her servants to store all the new wine: "I must consider how my time is endless, how I shall need wine endlessly. They smiled; but magic is the tree, and intoxication is just the little bird that flies in it to sing and flies out again" (644). Yet the text denies intoxication through the sheer poetical force of two words connected with magic: "green" and "wand" in "I believed that I lay in disgrace and my blood ran green, like the wand that breaks in two." What we have here, I think, is a paradoxical "decreation" and recreation of body and self.[4]

Circe has inflicted upon herself some experience in utter degradation, using her own magic against herself, the equivalent of breaking/relinquishing her magic power as represented by the wand, the better to recapture it. "Green" here described as tree sap suggests life, natural rebirth, and in "the red and black aurora of flesh," the body is fully recaptured. This extreme experience in degradation in order to cleanse oneself and revitalize one's potential echoes with shamanic experiences among the Indians, or more closely with the romantic poets experimenting with drugs in England, France, or the United States (Edgar Allan Poe in particular). More in context for a character so obsessed with her inability to experience mortality, Circe has enacted her death and a reverse transfiguration; she has played with the simulacrum of death in an attempt to get closer to that "mortal mystery" that intrigues her so much.

This desire to appropriate death is furthered by Welty's treatment of the death of Elpenor (present in *The Odyssey*) on which she closes the story. The writer opposes human attitude about death to the insensitiveness of Circe. The dead body of the youngest sailor who wanted to prove his manhood with sex and drink and fell to his death the next morning is the object of a ritual that aims at asserting some kind of triumph over death. The corpse becomes "a transformed boy" as death rites are performed in a spirit of love which is the expression of grief:

He [Odysseus] knelt and touched Elpenor, and like a lover lifted him; then each in turn held the transformed boy in his arms. They brushed the leaves from his face, and smoothed his red locks, which were still in their tangle from his brief attempts at love-making and from his too-sound sleep.

I spoke from the door. "When you dig the grave for that one, and bury him in the lonely sand by the shadow of your fleeing ship, write on the stone: 'I died of love.'"

I thought I spoke in epitaph—in the idiom of man. But when they heard me, they left Elpenor where he lay, and ran. (645)

The sailors' horror and flight manifest their rejection of Circe's intrusion into a strictly male human ceremony and their fear of a magic power that could enslave them again when freedom is just at hand. The real cause lies deeper and links death with simulacrum. As we know, through the burial of the dead—a device—man gains his "own nature," his humanity so to speak, as he pits death against itself and endorses it through rites and art, to ensure surviving in men's memory at least. Here, as a corollary to her enacting the simulacrum of her own death in the pigsty, Circe further tries to appropriate death by seizing upon the writing of death—that ultimate game played against death with monuments and carved epitaphs that are nothing but simulacra of man's victory over death.

However, in the dense concluding paragraph of the short story, the text moves the protagonist towards two capital changes. First, Circe does seize upon the writing of death—with her own body. She is pregnant, she says, with Telegonus who will (unknowingly) kill his father in Ithaca. Welty borrows the episode not from Homer's poem but from those epics composed on the Trojan War and its heroes by the cyclic poets who followed Homer: "The little son, I knew, was to follow—follow and slay him. That was the story" (646). This use of a post-Homeric literary tradition confirms Circe as a story-teller. On the morning of Odysseus's departure, it is no longer transformation that matters to her but revelation, the very substance of story-telling. Whereas she reveled in the sight of human bodies transformed into animal bodies before the hero's arrival, she now fully acknowledges her visionary power. No need to watch the Greeks set sail. Instead, as a story-teller and although she has never actually seen it, Circe can tell of the "bright and indelible and menacing world under which they all must go" (646). Because the world has become *a text*, it is indelible; it is a poet's vision and revelation that proclaims that if human lives are too brief and impermanent, stories are lasting and permanent. Yet, Circe's brief comment "but foreknowledge is not the same as the last word" (646) displaces authorship onto Telegonus himself, the young hero who avenges his mother by killing his father, and somehow this gesture provides a metaphor for the maternal origin of language, "this incestuous relation exploding in language," as Julia Kristeva puts it (*Desire* 137). Stories, myths, and legends especially, are retold and reshaped through the centuries and fascinate all the more as they are connected with the outlandish and heroic through the voices of the heroes themselves—Odysseus first, then Telegonus "the little son"—or their heralds—story-tellers who live adventures by proxy like Circe: "For whom is a story enough? For the wanderers who will tell it—it's where they must find their strange felicity" (646). As Circe knows, the episode of Odysseus' visit to her island does not end with his departure, since in her capacity as author, creator, and mother-to-be, the magician has the power to set the story going into new directions, including the hero's death, with no actual experience of the narrated emotions, grief, for instance.

In another way, Welty explores the extreme possibilities of the myth when she probes Circe's awareness of her predicament and superbly ties together the different threads of her narrative. The text opens up new perspectives and becomes one of the great contemporary rewritings of myth. Circe's strange behavior before Odysseus' departure, including what happened in the *pigsty*, is heralded by the word "torment" in "I swayed, and was flung backward by my torment" (645). The word conveys the extreme physical and spiritual violence that tears apart the magician as she is brutally confronted with her immortality/immobility and with her relishing the repulsive power to denature nature: "My cheek against the stony ground, I could hear the swine like summer thunder. These were with me still, pets now, once again—grumbling without meaning" (646).

Welty's use of the word "torment" suggesting the wheel and the rack and derived from "torture" and "twist" is the most appropriate metaphor to express what Circe is going through—abjections as Julia Kristeva describes it. For the philosopher, abjection is experienced when the individual torn between two poles, one desirable, one hateful, is "seized by one of those obscure and violent revolts of the self against what threatens it and seems produced by some outrageous internal or external power, by a gross deviation from the possible, the tolerable, the thinkable" ("Approches" 9).

Quoting freely from Kristeva, I will say that the abject opposes the self, "pulls [Circe] towards the place where meaning collapses," and elicits a shock, a convulsion, a cry. Because of his humanity—his love and respect for other human beings, his mortality, and sense of the ephemeral, Odysseus has altered Circe's vision of her self. What may have been familiar in an opaque forgotten life is now felt like the heavy brutal intrusion of a strangeness that torments her as something radically separate and loathsome. In her evocation of the denatured human bodies that she must live with, the pigs—"pets now," Circe feels torn between attraction and repulsion under the weight of abjection, something on the borderline between inexistence and hallucination, a reality that could annihilate her if acknowledged. This is why in the magnificent last paragraph the magician longs to experience some humanity—grief and death by telling of Hades, the next place Odysseus will visit.

To conclude this reading of bodies in "Circe," I will examine how Welty contrasts "grief" with "torment" in order to dramatically emphasize the opposition between mortals and immortals. Torment is the stronger word, and its etymology suggests "extreme pain or anguish of body or mind." Circe uses it once only to describe what is inflicted on her by her condition as immortal in a statement that flings her so to speak into the simulacrum of death and into abjection. In this context, torment recalls another immortal, a Titan condemned to be forever tied on a rock and tormented by a vulture—Prometheus. The point is to raise sympathy for Circe, who feels confronted with her intolerable fate: endless fixity, with the utter impossibility to leave her island to roam the seas and the world as Welty's wanderers love to do. The point is also to reassert Circe's belonging to that other world—mythology—whose heroes and heroines bitterly fight with one another out of pride or rivalry or an immoderate desire for power and are often transformed into constellations and celestial bodies, like Cassiopeia.[5]

Twice Circe compares her fate with Cassiopeia's. In the last scene as the sailors sail away, with the beautiful evocation of a ship at sea in the light of dawn, Circe once more expresses her predicament as immortal: "The ground fell away before me, blotted with sweet myrtle, with high oak that would have given me a ship too, if I were not tied to my island, as Cassiopeia must be to the sticks and stars of her chair. We were a rim of fire, a ring on the sea. His ship was a moment's gleam on a wave" (646).

Grief, on the other hand, derived from *gravis* (heavy) in Latin, suggests "lasting mental suffering with a tendency to concentrate on one's loss or distress" (Webster). It is a thoroughly human experience, linked with death and loss and mourning, an experience that comes from time, from the measured and limited time of men and the frailty of human bodies. In Circe's distressed mouth, grief is but a word without meaning, and although she repeats it five times in her efforts to fit it with her known experience—celestial bodies waxing and waning, pursuing as definite configurations and visible "shapes" in the sky their endless heavenly course—the feeling eludes her. She cannot conceive the strange relationship that links human bodies and grief. The living human body is the cause of grief when it disappears with death, yet grief is the sign of the absent body, and because it is the sign of something that can neither be seen nor grasped, grief is a ghost:

> I stood on my rock and wished for grief. It would not come. Though I could shriek at the rising Moon, and she, so near, would wax or wane, there was still grief, that couldn't hear me—grief that cannot be round or plain or solid-bright or running on its track, where a curse could get at it. It has no heavenly course, it is like mystery, and knows where to hide itself. At last it does not even breathe. I cannot find the dusty mouth of grief. I am sure now grief is a ghost—only a ghost in Hades, where ungrateful Odysseus is going—waiting on him. (646)

Chapter 5

"THE FICTIONAL EYE"

Eudora Welty's Retranslation of the South (2000)

> The fictional eye sees in, through, and around what is really there.
> —EUDORA WELTY *ONE WRITER'S BEGINNINGS* (929)

> Tout paysage se présente d'abord comme un immense désordre qui lasse libre de choisir le sens qu'on préfère lui donner. (Any landscape first appears like a huge disorder that leaves one free to invest it with a chosen meaning.)
> —CLAUDE LÉVI-STRAUSS *TRISTES TROPIQUES* (60)

> You see, for me the genius of language is that I do not think that language is something that humanity developed just because we somehow physically developed vocal cords. Language begins far before that to imagize, to make one thing stand for another. I think language is an actual way of looking at the world: if we didn't have language, we wouldn't see the world the way we see it now.
> —RUDY WIEBE "UNEARTHING LANGUAGE" (236)

All that pertains to Eudora Welty deserves attention to throw light on her singular vision as a writer. Like her character in "A Memory," she studied painting when a child because she wanted to become a painter. Although she abandoned the idea, visual arts have remained a lifelong interest, and in many ways, they have fed her writing. And like the great innovative artists of this century—Picasso, for instance—she developed early an interest in all forms of popular art and performance, with a sure sense that nothing human was foreign to her. The exploration of New York when she was a student has been of capital importance for the artist because that city introduced her to modernity (including her studies in modern business and advertising at Columbia). Her interest in painting was broadened and deepened as she regularly visited art galleries and discerned avant-garde European painting—a visual and seminal shock that was to sustain her artistic sensibility throughout her life. A comparable shock of recognition came from her appreciation of the new experimental trends in the more popular art of photography, an art whose official and private developments as a recorder of people, landscapes, and events had flowered brilliantly in America since the end of the nineteenth century. Just as visually inspiring for her writing, and as American, were the shows, music hall productions, and various theatricals which she attended almost nightly with Frank Lyell, her childhood friend and fellow student at Columbia University (Cole). Then, almost at the same time, the Depression and its distressing visible effects on the New York population shattered the restricted vision of the young woman and opened her eyes on actual life. Ever since those two years (1930–31) that taught her so much, New York remained a magnetic pole for Eudora Welty, a place frequently visited, always exciting and stimulating because so much was happening in the artistic and intellectual fields.

Welty's frequent trips to New York and across the United States, her extended visit to San Francisco, a city with which she had a love affair, as she says, and her several journeys to Europe, including a one year's stay on a Guggenheim Fellowship beginning in 1949, fed her curiosity about other lands and other people. They also reveal her desire and need "to go away," as did her choice to study at Mississippi State College for Women, many miles northeast of Jackson, instead of at hometown colleges such as Millsaps or Belhaven, across the street from her home (Pitavy-Souques April 1994); her transfer later to the University of Wisconsin; and her graduate study at Columbia. Her desire to be the *traveler*, however, was never a wish to be the expatriate who betrays some dissatisfaction with his homeland or the tourist who travels for the sake of exoticism. Welty's fiction, essays, and autobiographical writing all demonstrate that her travel away from home invariably allowed her to return with an enlarged experience of *otherness*. As traveler, her visionary power always on the alert, she stored forms and patterns perceived in a constantly renewed and enlarged human, literary, and artistic experience. And the place where such epiphanies appear is the white page of her writing. If the aesthetic location is the text, then the geographical location of, say, the typewriter has no importance: "I could write anywhere, in any hotel room," she once said—something she had learned at the university and in the small Mississippi towns through which she traveled for the WPA some years later (Pitavy-Souques November 1993).

No wonder, then, that such unusual training for a young Southern woman of her time and social sphere should have led her to write and work in a way that did change the perception of the South. Unlike Edith Wharton and Willa Cather, her two great predecessors in the twentieth century, Eudora Welty was less interested in pitting the New World against the Old World, the United States against Europe, than in confronting the South she knew so intimately with the South as political and literary tradition. At the time she started writing, the mid-1930s, the Agrarians were in full fledge, creating or recreating a certain image of the South, conservative and agrarian with two distinct races, an image that Eudora Welty has persistently examined in opposition to what was in *her* writer's eye: the South as a place that, although deeply scarred by history, was refusing its nostalgic burden and showing signs of courage and vitality. The Depression-era South she saw in her travels was, in her rendering, a stage on which the immemorial battles against defeat and death were being endlessly reenacted.

Roland Barthes's comment on Julia Kristeva's critical method (after the publication of *Semeiotike* in 1970) illuminates Welty's own attitude to some extent. Like "the Foreigner," as Barthes called Kristeva, Welty "changes the place of things and destroys the *latest* preconceptions . . . what she displaces is the illusion that it has all been said already, that is, she removes the pressure of the signified—in a word, stupidity ("L'Étrangère" 19–20). In subtle ways, and often where least expected, Welty reexamines stereotypes, subverts authority—that is, the traditional discourse about the South—and displays the paradoxical independence of mind of the foreigner (of the stranger, rather, since although she was born in Jackson her parents were not from the Deep South). She writes as if she had had to learn the South as a new language and was thus freer to put things in different places and to avoid preconceptions.

Welty builds her vision of the South as a battlefield where two kinds of Arcadia contend for dominance. The more recent kind is an Arcadia of established order that instituted peace and harmony on a severely controlled hierarchy, an order that tames instincts and life-giving forces. The more ancient kind is darker, "a place of primitive panic," according to Simon Schama's distinction in *Landscape and Memory* (526ff). In this Arcadia, nature is wild and shaggy, filled with disorder and misrule, and clear distinctions such as those between human and animal do not exist, yet its forces are those of life and creativity. Although it seems, Schama argues, that the rough myth was established first, specialists agree on the coexistence of both myths in Western thinking. Welty rewrites this coexistence as a parable of the South she fictionalizes, a South still scarred by slavery and segregation on the one hand, yet redeemed by human life forces at work in spite of extreme poverty and social repression. Welty, whose writer's eye was influenced by her family's position as strangers and by her frequent travels away from Mississippi, was free to combine afresh what she saw as the two aspects of the Arcadian in the South and to give her own translation. This essay will focus on two related developments of her dual vision of Arcadia: first in the short story "Livvie" and then in the collection of photographs *One Time, One Place*.

From the first, Welty has played with a dual vision in her artistic production, quite aware of the dangers inherent in her rather unorthodox use of it (inviting misreading or plain hostility). To understand the extent of her daring—her "leap in the dark"—and the difficulties she set for herself, we must consider that her power to see two things at once as one is at the root of the dual concept of Arcadia that sustains her fiction and photographic work ("Words" 134). To represent the difficult balance necessary to both technique and theme in her unconventional treatment of the world, she has from the first resorted to metaphors borrowed from her childhood experience and her eccentric education in New York, combining physical risk with intellectual daring into two key images—the daring of acrobats and a perilous journey along the edge of a cliff. This is something she has known ever since she composed what we believe to be her first short story, "Acrobats in a Park."[1] In that story, the metaphor for the artist's craft is a pyramid of human bodies erected by itinerant acrobats that suddenly collapses under the realization that the body is but the outside envelope of that most precious thing, the incarnation of passion and spirit. The concept keeps coming up in many disguises in her writing. Metaphorically, the writer Welty is journeying on the edge of a cliff, as she says of artists, real or fictional, a trope that first appears in "Music from Spain," when she uses a cliff near San Francisco to represent the symbolic murder of the father and the acrobatic passage from immature self to creative self, in a story that is for me about *writing*. It is articulated again in a review of Elizabeth Bowen's posthumous *Collected Stories*, to show where this kindred artist's sense of risk springs from: "Firmly at home in the world, Elizabeth Bowen was the better prepared to appreciate that it had an edge. For her, terra firma implies the edge of a cliff, suspense arises from the borderlines of experience and can be traced along that nerve" (Rev. of *Collected Stories* 234).

It is just this borderline of experience, the treacherous path of daring, that characterizes Welty's retranslation of the South, which is far more ambitious and ground-breaking than has been acknowledged so far. This is because Welty examines the very foundations of the South—religion and biracialism—in an entirely new way, iconoclastic, visionary, and ahead of its time. In Barthes's words about Kristeva, "What she subverts is authority—that of monological science, of filiation" ("L'Étrangère" 19). Picking up old myths or stories, Welty substitutes a plurality of voices for monological authority;

she deconstructs characters and narrative, and through her command of words and discourse, her texts fill up all the space they deal with, precisely, to offer, complete and entirely new, iconoclastic vision of the otherness of the South. In the light of this rewriting, we can interpret well-known stories such as "A Still Moment" or "Livvie" as retranslations of the myth of the two Arcadias. Such stories are retranslations and not mere reversals, since the *mise en oeuvre* of the full text, including plot, characters, place, time, and style, restitutes something of the original flavor of the myth she renews, challenging the traditional orthodoxy that superimposed the myth of the happy and pious South to correct the initial mistake of slavery. For example, in "A Still Moment," Welty makes a daring rewriting of the Scriptures so narrowly interpreted in the Bible Belt. The preacher Lorenzo Dow reflects: "He could understand God's giving Separateness first, and then giving Love to follow and heal in its wonder; but God had reversed this, and given Love first and then Separateness, as though it did not matter to Him which came first. Perhaps it was that God never counted the moments of Time" ("A Still Moment" 239).

Likewise, "Livvie" is just as challenging when read as a complex rewriting of slavery. In this text about liberation and feminism in terms of the myth of Persephone, the two arcadias, I argue, contend most fiercely and with bitter irony. Two textual clues should warn the reader. First is the displacement that occurs as the story begins: "Solomon carried Livvie twenty-one miles away from her home when he married her. He carried her away up on the Old Natchez Trace into the deep country to live in his house" ("Livvie" 276). Second is the narrator's repetition of the phrase "it was a nice house" (276, 278), and the revelation that "coming around up the path from the deep cut of the Natchez Trace below was a line of bare crape-myrtle trees with every branch of them ending in a colored bottle, green or blue," that Solomon had spent nine years making with his own hands (277; see *One Time, One Place* 45). Excess of order and control is what destroys life in this carefully arranged and kept place. Through an ironical displacement, it is Solomon, a "colored man that owned his land and had it written down in the courthouse," who here plays the part of a slave owner (276). Because everything that should be good is in excess, the evocation of this apparently benevolent Arcadia turns sour and rings with echoes of the worse discourses that justified slavery in the nineteenth century. And those echoes become deafening, in spite of the deathlike silence that reigns in Solomon's house, when the modern reader projects the sinister echoes of twentieth-century totalitarianism. Solomon's farm, so severely controlled and organized, is run like a fascist organization; it virtually is a form of death camp.[2] In this subtly complex story, Welty suggests that if poor young Livvie is not physically mistreated, she is nevertheless subjected to moral torture: she knows she will never see her family again nor exchange words with anyone except her husband, nor have children to love. She is sentenced to slow death. And just as she is "framed" within the boundaries of Solomon's property, she is framed by language, as textual evidence shows. The very young woman is "forced" to acknowledge that indeed this is a pretty house, that the interior as well as the exterior decoration—in which she has had no part—well meets the aesthetic standards of a simple backwoods black cabin. The repetitive use of "nice" betrays Solomon's excess of power.

The burlesque entrance on stage of the cosmetics saleslady, followed by handsome leaping young Cash, marks the replacement of the peaceful harmonious Arcadia by disorder and misrule and by primitive panic that nevertheless, as Simon Schama has argued, restores sexuality. Dark Arcadia now reigns supreme as a life-giving force. In this interpretation, which, of course, does not exclude a variety of others, Welty as translator of the South celebrates the rejuvenating power of the African American community in the South, its positive role as a life-giving creative force, and its fascination as Other. At the same time she exposes the myth of paternalistic "human" masters running slave plantations, and the fallacy of a "good," because highly hierarchical, society which in fact enslaves people through excess of rules and strict enforcement. Solomon thus appears as the man who emulates the white model once he has acquired property. In spite of his name, he is no wise man. With the names of her characters Welty suggests that Wild Arcadia is the place where traditional agrarian economy is routed by the modern progressive forces of trade. As a herald of the cash economy, Miss Baby Marie, the traveling cosmetics saleswoman from near Natchez, is a farcical avatar of Hermes, the god of communication and commerce. After she is unable to sell Livvie the "golden lipstick which popped open like magic" or any of her cosmetics with "secret ingredients" and suitable for black or white, Miss Baby Marie departs as abruptly as she arrived, taking her sample cases somewhere else (283). Alone again with her old husband, who is sleeping his way into death, Livvie goes outside for a breath of air and immediately sees the dramatically dressed Cash, whose zoot suit attire and magical gyrations do disguise to Livvie the fact that he is "a transformed field hand" who works on Solomon's land (286). "Cash belonged to Solomon," she thinks; "But he had stepped out of his overalls into this" (286). Both dazzled and alarmed when Cash pulls her to him and they kiss, she rushes back inside the house to check on her husband. As she looks at "Old Solomon ... far away in his sleep," "there was a noise like a hoof pawing the floor, and the door gave a creak, and Cash appeared beside her" (287). Solomon rouses long enough to recognize his successor; he gives Livvie his ticking silver watch and dies, and the young couple engage in a dance that Welty's closure fades away from in order to describe "the bottles on the prisoned trees" now filled with sunlight and the peach tree in the yard renewed, radiant "with bursting light of spring" (290).

In this avant-garde story, Welty displaces the issues of the modern South from the traditional white setting onto a black setting, thus integrating the African American community into congruence with the myth of the Wild Arcadia. The highly controlled old world, in which Solomon has sought "respect" by repeating the white planter's acquisition of property and power over people—"Cash belonged to Solomon"—is undermined by the Pan-like figure that the zoot-suited Cash McCord becomes, stepping out of his subservient role and taking Livvie from the moribund household where her youth has been controlled and suppressed.

Wild Arcadia is also discernible in a major trope of her fiction when Welty uses the Mississippi landscape to represent mental and psychological states, especially what I call labyrinths. Obviously, this figure was inspired by the tangled growth and deeply cut paths that captivated her along the Natchez Trace or on the smaller roads leading to the nearly forgotten former harbors and ghost towns along the old Mississippi River such as Rodney and Grand Gulf (Marrs *Welty Collection* 82, 110, 118). And as it keeps recurring, it becomes Welty's major figure to represent what is wildest, most secret, most life giving or death giving in the South. Its textual variations betray a tendency towards abstraction—from realistic or surrealistic treatment to abstract etching. Welty learned this not only as she explored the magnificently vine-shrouded old cemeteries and expired towns, but also as she captured the network of lines, cables, ropes, and tree branches nearly hiding shanty boats on the Pearl River. (One of her three photographs in the 1938 WPA project *Mississippi: A Guide to the Magnolia State* records such a scene [17].) The many snapshots she took on this theme (catalogued in Marrs's *Welty Collection*) show her interest in the visual effect, which is subsequently reflected in the simplifying process at work in *The Optimist's Daughter* or in the broken up spatial structure of *Losing Battles* that transforms that novel into an Odyssey of the New World.

With this modernist technique of the *not-ground* borrowed from the painters she saw in New York, Welty liberates the South from the burden of history (the already said), wipes it clean of the signified, and re-establishes the exact coincidence of myth with reality outside, black with white. The South, she suggests, is *par excellence* the matrix of America, the land of Wild Arcadia. Rosalind Krauss's comment about all modernist artists applies: "The modernist *not-ground* is a field or a background that has risen to the surface of the work to become exactly coincident with its foreground, a field that is thus ingested by the work as figure" (16). Thus, in a way complementary to her fiction, Welty's photographs of Mississippi, especially those taken as she worked for the WPA, present another form of her retranslation of the South. Her aim, it seems now, was to make the invisible visible, to bring front stage those who had been taken for granted as part of the Southern background for a century, and thus to give the African American community its rightful *identity* on the Southern scene. The enterprise was startingly new.[3]

Welty's photographic approach to her subject is comparable to a translator's approach to a text. Because her eye is a writer's eye, she produced the equivalent of a *literary translation* that enables "the work to come up *as a work* because it respects the difference with ordinary language where the text comes into being as something linguistically new" (Berman 201–2). This difference is what makes translation into another language possible, for in a way the translation accomplishes this newness. The native otherness of the work doubles with the enhanced otherness of the translation. The genius of Welty's photographic translation lies in her seeing and capturing the full dimension of the irreducible otherness of the African American community at a time when most Southerners were unaware of it. Then, just as a *retranslator* restores the strange newness of a badly translated text by effacing himself, so Eudora Welty effaced herself the better to bring out something long repressed. What gave her subjects splendid visibility, at last, was her own invisibility: "In taking all these pictures, I was attended, I now know, by an angel—a presence of trust. In particular, the photographs of black persons by a white person may not testify soon again to such intimacy. It is trust that dates the pictures now, more than the vanished years" ("One Time, One Place" 352). Although she uses the fine word "trust," which denotes absolute respect and regard, with the possibility of love in the sense she gives this word in her essays about her writing, Welty intimates an even closer awareness when she writes in the same essay, "One Time, One Place," that she was "moving through the scene openly and yet invisibly because I was part of it, born into it, taken for granted" (351). Here, she is not only claiming her identity as a true Mississippian, but she is also intimating that she was moving about among her own people, *claiming her black heritage*, together with her white heritage, as a Southerner and even more as an American artist in the making. This revolutionary proposition (in the sense of complete reversal) is not quite fully grasped by newsman and author Robert MacNeil, for all his perceptiveness, when he writes in his essay on Welty's photographs, *Eudora Welty: Seeing Black and White*, "Why, back then, did she take so many pictures of blacks?

Why did she? Blacks filled the landscape, of course. Yet for many whites, perhaps for the majority of whites, blacks were invisible. But why go out of her way in the 1930s to take their pictures? It is difficult to say without sounding unctuous; but the answer must be that this photographer recognized blacks as human beings and the circumstances of their lives made her curious" (10).

Another way to understand Welty's eye is to look at the Farm Security Administration photographs of black Southerners. In *The Black Image in the New Deal: The Politics of FSA Photography*, Nicholas Natanson argues that photographs of blacks were rarer than those of poor whites and tended to present types rather than individuals, since both white and black photographers privileged types such as "the noble primitives," "the loyal Georges," the "colorful Negroes," the black-as-extreme-victim (24). Thus, Natanson writes, nearly always in comparison with white subjects, the *identity* of the black subject was denied. Even in the work setting, closeups of individual blacks were much less frequent than closeups of whites: rather than black laborers, black labor—a homogenous background presence—worked the land. And when blacks were given more prominence, their identities were more frequently linked with *the crop* than were white identities (21). Natanson further argues than even in a radically inclined book such as Margaret Bourke-White and Erskine Caldwell's *You Have Seen Their Faces*, "particularly for black subjects, an angry camera becomes a demeaning camera, with the effect intensified by Caldwell's fictionalized quotations used in the captions" (26). On the other hand, Natanson's fine comment on a photograph by Robert McNeil, "'New Car,' South Richmond, Va. 1938," throws light on Welty's own attempts: her insistence on individuals rather than on stereotypes: "Rather than paragons of black success, rather than symbols of Race Pride, these are young men enjoying the conversation, the feel of a new car, and the attention of two young women on a porch in the background. To the extent that McNeil's subjects are responding to the camera (no hidden-camera tricks here), they seem to be responding as individuals, not race- or class-role players" (45).

From a broader perspective, what differentiates Welty's photographs from those of anthropologists or commercial photographers? She was intensely aware of people's ineradicable individuality, and even more, of transiency in the revelatory gesture. Paradoxically, the permanence of Welty's photographs comes from their being rooted in the transient. Whereas the function of an anthropologist's photograph is to represent a *generality* about a people in the diversity of its occupations, attitudes, clothes, and ornaments and of the multiple reproductions of old postcards flooding the market at present all aim at *instructing* about the aspect of a city, a street, or a village at a certain time and a certain hour of the day—by virtue of which all those pictures are pure documents, Welty's photographs were not taken with a view to generality or representativeness. Their only purpose—and present meaning for us today—was to show human beings. To the general impersonal attitude of the commercial photographer for his subject, Welty opposes specificity and timelessness because she selects a moment of high emotional intensity. On her photographs, all gestures are true, and therefore charged with a high *iterative* value, because they are signifying; they never are indifferent or commonplace, as on postcards. The commonplace for Welty does not come from low social status or occupations but from low feelings. Through empathy, the passions and emotions she captures are renewed with each new viewing and thus become timeless. Because she was so intensely aware of the theatricality of the events she captured, she herself became audience and actress, as the camera recorded the Southern social comedy in its uniqueness.

The beauty of her pictures is born of a balance between the specific moment when a gesture, pause, or smile betrays a person and the truth of that gesture, which is the eternal, and not the anecdotal. Looked at from this perspective, the photographs compose a panorama of life: the exotic fades behind the universality of the situation or gesture, surprise is natural. "The pictures now seem to me to fall most naturally into the simple and self-evident categories about which I couldn't even at this distance make a mistake—the days of the week: workday; Saturday, for staying home and for excursions too; and Sunday" (Welty, "One Time, One Place" 351).

Thus, timelessness is what charms the viewer of those photographs. The writer's eye selected her approach, and many decades later its life-giving power is just as effective. Welty's restriction that the photographs she selected for *One Time, One Place* are pure documents and refer to a specific time must not blind us to the exceptional quality of what we see ("One Time, One Place" 351–52). Her pictures are brimming with life and meaning. A reflection by Claude Lévi-Strauss shows the difference between the anthropologist's eye and the fictional eye. In his introduction to *Saudades do Brasil*, published in 1995, a reprinting of the photographs he took of the Nambikwara between 1935 and 1939, he writes,

> Viewed again those photographs leave me with a feeling of emptiness, of the absence of what the objective is fundamentally unable to capture. I can see the paradox of publishing them, more numerous, better printed and centered than when they first appeared in *Tristes Tropiques*: as if in opposition to me, readers could find some substance because they have not been there and must be satisfied with this mute illustration, and above all because all this, seen again in its

setting, would appear unrecognizable, and because in many ways, it no longer exists. (3)

Interestingly, Lévi-Strauss and Welty both came from privileged backgrounds in this quest of the Other; they both felt the same deep kinship with fellow human beings. But Welty's quest was of the spirit, whereas Lévi-Strauss's was of the mind. The anthropologist was studying manners and ways of life in order to understand their functioning (and subsequently to come upon his theory about the laws regulating marriage and alliances); the writer was probing hearts and souls as she was photographing bodies in their poses and gestures in the hope of unveiling the mystery of the human heart. In both instances, vision was required, yet Lévi-Strauss was looking for general rules, and Welty, for individual revelation.

In a way, the photographs were her sketches or studies, the necessary apprenticeship of an artist; at a deeper level, because the revelation they brought required some wording, they "precipitated" those uncommon ingredients that go into Welty's fiction to make it a unique production. Her true subject is neither love, nor family, nor the South, but the universal yet most modern quest of the *Other* and *otherness*, while her mode, to use a musician's language, or tone and coloring, to use a painter's language, is the South. Eudora Welty does not write *about* the South but *with* the South, a unique combination whose emblematic figure, or mathematical "form," is the artist as Perseus slaying the Medusa with the help of a mirror-shield. As with the shield, the flat image and apparently realistic representation of the real as seen on photographs always reveal an abstract content that implements both technique and meaning. She learned substance and technique in an inseparable way: what to see, how to see, how to write with what Rudy Wiebe suggests is the eye that is language in a way comparable to a painter's experience, "painting and writing, always the closest two of the sister arts (and in ancient Chinese days only the blink of an eye seems to have separated them)" ("Place in Fiction" 783).

As she was exploring the geographical surface of Mississippi, her native state but not that of her parents, Welty learned about individuals as they came in the variety of their social, economic, and racial backgrounds. At the surface level, taking pictures in the whole state of Mississippi was equivalent to learning to draw in the streets for young Matisse. In a 1925 interview with Jacques Guenne, Matisse tells how when as an art student he used to visit the Louvre, his professor Gustave Moreau told his class: "Don't be content with going to the museum, go into the streets." Matisse comments: "In effect it's there that I learned to draw. . . . We were forcing ourselves to discover quickly what was characteristic in a gesture, in an attitude" (qtd. in Flam 54). Welty implies just the same when she writes:

> I learned quickly enough when to click the shutter, but what I was becoming aware of more slowly was a story-writer's truth: the thing to wait on, to reach there in time for, is the moment in which people reveal themselves. You have to be ready, in yourself; you have to know the moment when you see it. The human face and the human body are eloquent in themselves, and a snapshot is a moment's glimpse (as a story may be a long look, a growing contemplation) into what never stops moving, never ceases to express for itself something of our common feeling. Every feeling waits upon its gesture. Then when it does come, how unpredictable it turns out to be, after all. ("One Time, One Place" 354)

Welty's pictures reveal another link with a writer's sense of dramatic development in time of emotion—the photographer's and later the viewer's—caused by that disquieting element, that *punctum*, which Roland Barthes perceives on the photographs he likes: "this unexpected chance detail which, in it, points at me (and also hurts me and grapples me)" (*La Chambre* 49). With Welty, it is most often a detail seen afterwards only, which betrays not the distress or the great poverty of these people in the sense of an insufferable weight crushing them down, but the reality of a difficult life, and an instinct for happiness. "Making a date/Grenada" in *One Time, One Place*, an exquisitely tender and respectful picture, shows a young woman taken at the moment when, perhaps half aware of Welty's presence, she raises a finger to her left nostril in a gesture full of modesty and embarrassment, while the young man she is facing is seen in profile with a smile on his lips. The *punctum* comes from the torn trousers of the man, then from his worn shoes that direct our gaze towards the downtrodden shoes of the young woman (*OTOP* 67). As with the close-up on Jack Renfro's worn-out shoes in *Losing Battles*,[4] so unexpected when it comes, and so free of any comment, we see on this picture Welty's homage to people's fortitude, and her belief that to show (or write) about human beings encompasses universal feelings and the weight of their plight. As Welty scanned her photographs afterwards, she learned that a close-up, that is, a brief description, is more powerful to present directly to the reader's mind a sociological and moral comment while arousing his emotion, than any wide-angle shot or authorial comment through the narrator's voice. Technically, such close-ups are the shading or the splash of unexpected color on the canvas.

The secret relationship Welty's photographs entertain with death is not the least source of their enduring fascination. Take for instance their disquieting connivance with that secret of femininity they try to capture in the abandoned bodies lying in a porch swing (*OTOP* 32), or leaning against a banister (*OTOP* 31), in a variety of postures and gestures with the general carriage of the whole person (*OTOP* 15, 18, 26, 28, 33, 34, 85, 91, etc.), in the bodies half revealed beneath the supple material of the straight clinging dresses falling down to the ankle after the fashion of the time, which gives them timeless grace while adorning them (*OTOP* 60). Those are pictures of the living flesh cognate with the funerary statues that haunted Welty's eye for a time.

In "An Abundance of Angels," her fine introduction to the photography collection *Country Churchyards*, novelist Elizabeth Spencer insists on a thread of laughter in Welty's choice of funeral monuments: "Unlike skipping about on graves, this thread of laughter is no part of irreverence. Anything Eudora Welty puts her hand to, had laughter lurking somewhere, ready to break in. And that too, she viewed as part of life" (20). While conferring upon women the quality of Greek statuary, the fashion of the thirties transformed them into the ideal representation of triumphant Woman and, for the perceiving eye of the novelist, also into those stone mourners celebrating death and grief she had photographed in old cemeteries. No wonder that nearly all of Welty's feminine characters carry courting with death in their bodies. Often, at the same time, they are the vessels of triumphant motherhood or the vulnerable battlefield where all deadly forces contend, from Ruby Fisher of "A Piece of News," Easter of "Moon Lake," and the unnamed American heroine of "The Bride of the Innisfallen" to Gloria Renfro in *Losing Battles*.

In the much debated scene where other women force watermelon down Gloria Renfro's throat in a splash of red juice in order to make her admit that she is a Renfro, the act is less a form of rape performed by women on another woman, as some critics would have it, than the mock enactment of a mutilating feminine ritual of integration, a symbolic form of human sacrifice—a fitting scene in a novel more violent than it seems, which dramatizes the violent undertones of sacrifice: the collective sacrifice of food-offering to mimic death and thus assuage it, the private self-sacrifice of Nathan's cutting off his hand in expiation, or the ruthless sacrifices performed by society with every unjust prison or death sentence. A mock version of this dramatizing of the coalition of the social body against the private body is presented in "Lily Daw and the Three Ladies," a fitting overture to Welty's fiction as the first story in her first collection. Here, in this subversive little text, Welty shows the ultimate triumph of the "irrational" body (Bourdieu 165ff). Lily Daw, said to be half-witted, has a knowledge of the world through her body ("une connaissance par corps"), which, at the moment of the lives of the three ladies and in the present state of the little town of Victory, proves superior to theirs; rational bodies are defeated (there are ample signs of distress in the sweaty bulging forms of Mrs. Watts, Mrs. Carson, and Aimée Slocum). This story is the fictionalized version of the formidable *presence* of Welty's photographs, something that must have come directly from the scanning of her snapshots.

This insistence on the individual rather than on roles is the secret of the enduring charm of Welty's photographs of African Americans. A radical reconsideration of race relationships touches upon the artist's imagination and its identity. The loving gaze that Welty sends on all those around her is especially pregnant when it concerns black subjects. Although it has been objected that there are too few African Americans in her fiction, from the moment they become characters, African Americans are drawn with such intensity that their *presence* fills more than the short story where they appear. In some ways, they are the best known of her characters; often they give their names to the story ("Powerhouse" and "Livvie") or they haunt the reader's imagination long after he/she has closed the book, like Phoenix Jackson of "A Worn Path" at the close of the collection *A Curtain of Green*. Although white prejudice is always fictionalized in the stories where they appear, Welty represents her black characters not as dark doubles, the disquieting possibility of the obverse self, as Faulkner does, nor as victims (Keela has overcome the episode of his exploitation as the outcast Indian maiden with better success than the guilty barker who used him). Welty paints African Americans as life forces, filled with creative power and very old lore, but that of course is a role she assigns to many of her women characters, too. In a way, the African Americans are the mythical counterparts of her commonplace ordinary characters. Because they straddle two worlds, they are messengers, or even angels, with the power to establish communication with the invisible world, although their weight in suffering and daily experience is always asserted. Despite their apparent earthiness, they give a spiritual dimension to the world. In our period, which is so intrigued by the coming back of angels, whether in scholarly interest in the function of pictorial angels or in the filmic use of angels as in Wim Wenders' *On the Wings of Desire*, it seems to me that Eudora Welty, once more ahead of her time, felt the need for such characters. They beckon mysteriously to the reader from their disguises—Old Plez in *The Golden Apples* and Phoenix Jackson in "A Worn Path"—or function like doubles of the artist herself—Livvie and Powerhouse, for instance. Their mythological names are discreet clues, inward jokes, yet Minerva, "the old beggar woman, the old black thief" who is alone with Virgie Rainey at the end of *The Golden Apples*, "listening to the magical percussion, the world beating in their ears," is present to impart to Virgie the beauty and wonder of the world, her wisdom, and, we would hope, the creativity of the Roman goddess ("The Wanderers" 555, 556). Old black Minerva is also one of those beggars or hoboes we see every day around us and whose function is to tell us of the underworld of poverty, exploitation, humiliation for it has always been the role of angels to help people communicate, to open their eyes and see the humble as well as the luminous. What Virgie Rainey perceives, thanks to Minerva, is the cosmic dimension of her life. No wonder then that Welty chose the photograph of a young black angel, the "Baby Bluebird, Bird Pageant" (*OTOP* 94), for the cover of the paperback edition of *Collected Stories*,[5] for who could better invite her readers to enter fiction's surprising territory?

As a conclusion to this reading of Welty's fiction and photographs as a retranslation of the South, I would like to insist also on identifying the images she took of others as a series of self-portraits of the artist. In a way—and Welty knew it instinctively—those photographs into which she put so much of herself were the fragments of a deconstructed self-portrait. In those faces and attitudes she saw the reflection of her own "high spirit and joy of being alive," the very words she will use to characterize the final leap into freedom of the characters that truly make it, male and female, characters who are all avatars of Perseus, her emblematic figure of the artist: "If I took picture after picture out of simple high spirits and the joy of being alive, the way I began, I can add that in my subjects I met often with the same high spirits, the same joy. Trouble, even to the point of disaster, has its pale, and these defiant things of the spirit repeatedly go beyond it, joy the same as courage" ("One Time, One Place" 352).

Seen from this perspective, *One Time, One Place: Mississippi in the Depression: A Snapshot Album* opens on a self-portrait with the photograph of the heroic woman [ii][6] as a portrait of the artist, in the way Philippe Sollers calls self-portraits those portraits where Cézanne expresses mental attitudes or depths of reflection on life akin to his, be they nephews, sons of friends, or Vallier, his old gardener (141–44). Looking at the face of this woman, marked by suffering yet undefeated, a "heroic face," Welty had the revelation of what an artist's soul encompasses ("One Time, One Place" 353). At that moment, I believe, Welty became the artist for times of distress that she is: a writer of inner depths of infinite depth, and as Sollers writes of Cézanne, "in every part of [her text] an adventurer of what is most interior in the heart, there where Thinking and Memory, Thinking and Awareness, Thinking and Sensation meditate together" (91). In Welty's praise afterwards, we read those qualities that belong to Welty's own vision of the artist:

It was after I got home, had made my prints in the kitchen and dried them overnight and looked at them in the morning by myself, that I began to see objectively what I had there.

When a heroic face like that of the woman in the buttoned sweater—who I think must come first in this book—look backs at me from her picture, what I respond to now, just as I did the first time, is not the Depression, not the Black, not the South, not even the perennially sorry state of the whole world, but the story of her life in her face. And though I did not take these pictures to prove anything, I think they most assuredly do show something—which is to make a far better claim for them. Her face to me is full of meaning more truthful and more terrible and, I think, more noble than any generalization about people could have prepared me for or could describe for me now. I learned from my own pictures, one by one, and had to; for I think we are the breakers of our own hearts. ("One Time, One Place" 353–54)

We can interpret the photograph of the woman in the buttoned sweater as a pictorial self-portrait—the portrait of that defiant artist heroically coming to terms with her knowledge of human suffering, defeat, and death—just as we can read "Powerhouse" as a companion piece, a fictionalized self-portrait, to place side by side with those two other major figures of artists: Miss Eckhart and the guitar player in "Music from Spain." (The presence of an artist of mythic dimension in "Music from Spain" justifies the inclusion of the story in *The Golden Apples*.)

Retrospectively, it seems appropriate that Welty should have published her photographs at the time she was writing "The Optimist's Daughter"[7] into a book—her first fiction to include much autobiographical material. Just as her novel constitutes a displaced autobiography, the collection of photographs constitutes a series of displaced self-portraits. In both instances, the shock of her mother's death led her to a reappraisal of her heritage *as an artist*, and she found out that her heritage exceeded by far the South within which critics had confined her until then.

Photographs (1989) presents other pictorial self-portraits whose significance deserves attention as they suggest Welty's early awareness of the possibility of representing the darker and disquieting side of the artist in three roles: Perseus slaying the Medusa with the help of a mirror-shield. If Welty's photographs of Mississippians, black and white, figure Perseus and his defiant heroic gesture, or his exuberant spirit, then the comic photographs of young Eudora Welty and her friends collected in *Photographs* reveal the artist's somber complement with the face of the Medusa and the mirror-shield when we probe their significance. They were taken as jokes by the small, dedicated group to which she belonged at the time, and the elaboration they required with the full participation of Eudora Welty herself allows us to call those photographs self-portraits indeed.[8]

In a less obvious way, photography taught Welty how to do away with traditional depth and perspective and how to experiment with the background in the way avant-garde painters were doing it. Welty saw Henri Matisse's first large one-man show exhibition in New York in November 1931, just as she saw the work of young American painters in the early thirties who had adopted a similar technique. That technique represents a capital invention because it helped Welty solve the technical difficulty of dealing with the South while giving her fiction a universal dimension. She learned it, I think, partly from photography, especially with the general scenes she took of New York during the Depression (in Union Square for instance), and later on with views of back streets and social events in Jackson and New Orleans. Those photographs exemplify political attitudes that will feed her fiction later, and they taught her too about narrative technique. The camera eye takes in everything, yet a certain amount of control can be achieved through framing, distance, and selection of the right moment, as Welty wrote repeatedly. More important for the present discussion is what she learned from her photographic work through improving composition by cutting off parts of the photographs afterwards, thus *re-placing* her characters into the (proper) background. What she refused to do was to *pre-organize* and manipulate her subject, as the official WPA photographers did, in order to convey a required political message. Welty's purpose had a wider, more universal scope, especially as her technique followed that of the modern painters she had seen in New York. Her photographs of large cities are crowded with details: publicity, posters, people. They give no sense of depth; rather, they *flatten* their subjects, and this is true even of the photographs with reflections in shop windows. This flattening creates an effect similar to that achieved by such modern painters as Piet Mondrian or Matisse. And this rejection of perspective emphasizes the value of the ground. The proliferation of signs reflecting the social and political background of the thirties nearly hid her subject but had the subtle effect of integrating subject and social background completely.

This practice, I think, lies at the source of Welty's use of the South in her fiction. At any rate, understanding this integrative flattening of figure or subject and ground helps us understand the South's unique position in Welty's work. The South is prominent ground whose features and spirit fill the picture, so that her characters and themes become nearly indistinguishable from it. Welty writes *less about the South than with the South*, and her narrative techniques re-evaluate or retranslate the respective parts played by the black and white communities, and by depicting these things as interrelated and often undistinguishable as figure or ground, Welty repeatedly composes a story of the South as a dramatic, inclusive, and as yet unfinished human battleground where the struggles of ordinary people matter greatly.

Chapter 6

PRIVATE AND POLITICAL THOUGHTS IN *ONE WRITER'S BEGINNINGS* (2001)

> She communicates vastly more than she writes.
> —WILLA CATHER ABOUT KATHERINE MANSFIELD *STORIES* (878)

> I glimpse our whole family life as if it were freed of that clock time which spaces us apart so inhibitingly, divides young and old, keeps our living through the same experiences at separate distances.
> —EUDORA WELTY *ONE WRITER'S BEGINNINGS* (946)

Though seldom overtly assertive or militant, Southern women writers have been committed to the political since the end of the nineteenth century. They have long known that writing fiction is never a neutral activity, that all great texts are revolutionary because they change attitudes—mental, social, and political. Though Southern women writers have generally had their parts cut out for them, they have redefined those parts in the course of their work. Moreover, they have played their redefined roles with the utmost commitment, all the more since they knew they were composing from a region where the violence of History doubled their responsibilities as writers and artists.

Because their art touches their deepest convictions so intimately and because it gives rise to sharp criticism for either excess or deficiency of engagement in political causes, many Southern women writers have felt the need to publish autobiographies, usually for the purpose of justifying themselves and their fiction, which they feel has been misread. Thus, any evaluation of the political in these women's work must necessarily include an evaluation of their autobiographies, a task that requires insight as well as discrimination on the part of the critic. Despite the recent reappraisal of feminine fiction and the considerable achievement of feminist criticism in this field, there still lingers the suspicion that feminine writing is not on a par with masculine writing. Harold Bloom's book on the Western canon, with its blatantly unfair omissions, is proof of this ongoing battle that women writers must continue to fight in order to see their works fully acknowledged.[1] Critically at least, and politically as well when they belong to ethnic groups outside the dominant white majority, they are treated as members of a minority, and more or less consciously, they adopt the strategies of minority people of both sexes when writing their autobiographies: paradoxically, they portray themselves as both victimized and guilty. Yet some are strong enough to write in defiance of such commonly accepted strategies and produce proud affirmative texts.

Eudora Welty's autobiography must be read in such a light, especially since the event that led her to pen *One Writer's Beginnings*—the inaugural William E. Massey Sr. Lectures in the History of American Civilization at Harvard in April 1983—attests to how politically oriented her talks were, a preoccupation further corroborated by Welty's first declining the invitation and then accepting it at Daniel Aaron's suggestion that she speak about what made her into a writer. The aging writer was glad to pick up the challenge and trace those informing patterns that had fashioned her imagination, technique, and political attitudes. Moreover, implicit in her tracing of these patterns is a rejection of the mutilating label of regionalist writer—a Southerner writing in the wake of William Faulkner. The lectures turned out to be immensely successful, and *One Writer's Beginnings* (their published form) was on the bestseller list for over ten weeks. Some deep chord in the American heart and imagination must have been struck. The book proved truly meaningful to Welty's newly gained audience, which read it as a reflection of the nation's destiny.

One Writer's Beginnings' implicit call for a reorientation of critical approaches was not so successful. While perceptive readers were confirmed in their critical guesses, the narrow-minded and politically biased continued to be prejudiced against a work to which they applied ill-fitted critical tools. Misunderstanding is not over yet.[2] Along with the popularity of cultural studies and multiculturalism on the current American critical scene, the old academic activity of comparing authors and their works is still going full speed, making for all sorts of pairings. The validity of such activity rests on respect for authors in the form of an honest attempt to understand their intentions, to compare what is comparable, and to locate new cross-cultural insights when seemingly divergent texts are read together. That this technique is not always appropriate, respectful, or fair is evidenced by two recent essays (among others) that compare Welty's autobiography with, respectively, that of a black male writer, putting the emphasis on racial issues only, and that of a white woman writer of the preceding generation, concentrating on the paintings of the self alone.

Richard Brodhead's "Two Writers' Beginnings: Eudora Welty in the Neighborhood of Richard Wright" is an indictment of Welty's blindness to segregation in Jackson at the time she grew up, an indictment that would be appropriate if Welty's purpose had been to draw a picture of Jackson in her childhood and youth. But it wasn't. Similarly, in a sensitive collection of essays titled *Feminine Sense in Southern Memoir,* Will Brantley compares Ellen Glasgow's *The Woman Within* with Welty's *One Writer's Beginnings.* In his insistence on emphasizing the sheltered life, Brantley reduces the scope of Welty's project and achievement. As is evidenced by the origin of Welty's text and by the very title she chose for the publication of her three lectures delivered to an audience that included Harvard historians, she clearly meant to depart from Richard Wright's racial pleas or from Glasgow's plea for a true self. Indeed, before they have opened her book, Welty's readers are warned that this is not an ordinary autobiography, but what Michel Beaujour defines as a self-portrait, which he differentiates from the autobiography: "Self-portrait," he explains, "differs from autobiography by the absence of a continuous narrative, and by the subordination of the narration to a logical development, made up of elements brought or joined together, that provisionally we shall call thematic elements" (Beaujour 8).

In this disruptive light that negates continuity and supposes a reorganization of the facts, a more judicious comparison would bring together Zora Neale Hurston's *Dust Tracks on a Road* and *One Writer's Beginnings.* Both books share comparable techniques and intents: a desire to control rather than privilege the writing of the self and to transcend the burden of history. Above all, as each rewrites a history of the development of the American imagination, with all its cultural components, each takes her turn addressing the issue of the political at its highest level, emphasizing a positive assertion of multiculturalism rather than concentrating on victimization. In her superb study of *Dust Tracks on a Road,* Françoise Lionnet calls Hurston's book an autoethnography: "that is, the defining of one's subjective ethnicity as mediated through language, history, and ethnographical analysis; in short, the book amounts to a kind of 'figural anthropology' of the self" (99). While I will not compare Hurston's and Welty's autobiographies here, I will make occasional use of *Dust Tracks on a Road* to clarify various points I make about Welty. Hurston's highly criticized stand on racial issues stems from a political attitude not unlike Welty's, and she also is a victim of hasty judgments. Great women writers of the South have shown more daring and broader views than their male counterparts, although this has been little acknowledged as yet.

This essay will focus on the quintessential relationship Eudora Welty entertains with the political in *One Writer's Beginnings*, a book that, paradoxically, defines American mythologies rather than Welty's private ones. Briefly defined, the political indicates a concern with the general, with public and social ethics, including the issues of race, class, gender, and history. Though adamantly refusing to write fiction polemically, Welty has always been a progressive *engagé*, an active supporter of Adlai Stevenson, and a courageous lecturer at the worst time of the civil rights movement, as Suzanne Marrs argues in "'The Huge Fateful Stage of the Outside World': Eudora Welty's Life in Politics." Moreover, Welty produced two of the finest stories on the sixties' conflicts, the first written out of her personal anger at the racist mentality that had resulted in the murder of Medgar Evers. More generally, she has shared the democratic values of the Founding Fathers of the American Republic from the first, taking pride as she recently told me, in being born on the same day as Thomas Jefferson, the thirteenth of April: "Jefferson is my hero and as my mother would say 'at least that was something I could do for you'" (Personal Conversation 1997). Educated in a family from which racism was absent, Welty's stand on racial issues led her to write stories about African Americans, which have won her the respect of the black community.

With regard to *One Writer's Beginnings*, the question is not really Welty's particular brand of liberalism, using Brantley's definition of liberalism as "a belief in human rationality and accountability, and if not a belief in human perfectibility (as O'Connor would have it), at least a desire to make life better for the entire diversity of the nation's citizens" (7). Instead, Welty shows a genuine concern for the general and the abstract, and above all for the representativity of her own biography. Therefore, I propose to examine *One Writer's Beginnings* from an American point of view rather than from a strictly Southern point of view in order to show how Welty's Americanness inscribes her production solidly within the canon of American literature.

The technique of the self-portrait—as exemplified by Augustine or Michel de Montaigne, for example—gives writers great freedom to play with light and shade, to privilege that side of themselves they want to reveal to the public eye. And Welty had a double purpose in composing her self-portrait: to meet the requirements of the Massey lectures on the history of American civilization, she chose to emphasize the Americanness of her family background and education, and to place her canon in a true perspective, she chose to dismiss the image of the Southern regionalist by emphasizing what had been there all along—the general and the universal.[3] These gestures of the writer will be restored with each new reading, as Welty's slim volume feeds the meditation of future generations in the tradition of great self-portraits.

Eudora Welty achieves her ultimate triumph of style and composition in this text, written with as much passion as courage. The style she chose explains the misreadings as well as the praise. The superbly crafted language is designed to achieve a delicate balance between the specificity of the self with its private world and the representative portrait of a continent fostering dreams and illusions. Throughout her career, Welty has polished and perfected her style, adapting it to the genre of the work: the fiction is written in an elaborate, elliptical, resisting manner, verging at times on the overwrought. In the essays, the language is simpler, yet still dense and terse, with a fine sense of formula. Finally, the ongoing simplifying process reaches its climax in the autobiography. Here Welty refines her style to its utmost simplicity, yet without compromising its elegance and precision; more importantly, she plays with the multilayered possibilities of language, which itself then becomes motif and theme. Language functions as motif when its naked spontaneity echoes the pragmatic language of the pioneers Welty celebrates, especially that of Benjamin Franklin—a language meant to arouse the reader's reflection rather than his emotion as fiction does. Language becomes theme when it serves Welty's purpose to present a general picture of America rather than the private picture of her life, when she scrapes off the surface of her narrative the too salient telling of intense anecdotes and minimizes personal emotion. This meticulous work on the texture of her style creates the very tension of the autobiography, which achieves a balance between the specificity of the self and the representative depiction of a life. The work's dramatic strength, like its originality, rests on this paradox, which feeds it, polishes it, and fashions the strategies Welty adopts. Yet, for all the book's guardedness, Welty's violence is there all the same—lucid, angry, and militant.[4]

The technique she uses to paint her panorama of an American childhood stems partly, I suggest, from her experience as a photographer, especially from the pictures she took of Union Square in New York during the Depression and later from views of backstreets and social events in Jackson, New Orleans, and France. Those photographs exemplify political attitudes that would feed her fiction later; they also taught her about narrative technique, as Harriet Pollack has shown in two essays on the relationship between Welty's photographs and the techniques of her story composition.[5] The camera eye takes in everything, so that the photographs of large cities are crowded with details: publicity, posters, people. They give no sense of depth, instead flattening their subjects, and this is true also of the photographs with reflections in shop windows. I will argue that this flattening creates an effect similar to that achieved by modern painters when they discard perspective and emphasize the value of the ground (what Pollack calls the details "of life around the figure ... circumstances" ["Photographic" 26]). For this pictorial technique, Rosalind Krauss describes how Piet Mondrian covered his canvas with a grid to eliminate successiveness and figured forth simultaneity "in this brilliant obsessional hatching. It would be his first truly systematic reinvention of the ground as fiction" (16).[6] The disconcerting effect Welty achieves in *One Writer's Beginnings*, which critics like Brantley find difficult to sum up, comes from a similar technique. Since Welty builds her narrative upon an accumulation of small details, she multiplies information about her home life and family background, schools and libraries in Jackson, summer travels through the country, and life in the early days of the pioneers, always insisting on mirror effects through endless echoes and multiple repetitions that work like so many small touches of paint on a canvas, or like Mondrian's grid, to convey the intellectual perception of what life was like in America at a certain time.[7] At the end of our reading, we feel the simultaneity of hundreds of perceptions and thoughts, rather than the sequentially organized sensory experience of impressionism. The background has become exactly coincident with the foreground.

The possibilities offered by this technique of the ground as figure help Welty define her attitude toward the South and make her point on such controversial issues as racism or history. She treats racist bigotry in an exemplary way, showing its absence rather than its presence, and, more subtly, she implies that black voices and black talents for story-telling were part of her education as a fiction writer. Race relations is the oblique reference when throughout *One Writer's Beginnings*, and specifically in the first section, "Listening," Welty shows how Jackson taught her the sounds of life and the voices of Southern story-tellers, and how early she became aware of the creative power of those voices. Not least among them is Fannie, the African American seamstress, whom Welty places side by side with her mother's white friends in the acknowledgment of her debt as a writer. She writes eloquently and lovingly and wryly of Fannie's teaching regarding the dramatic possibilities of a good telling of family gossip.[8] Welty's point is that her early education gave her no sense of racial difference or inferiority. Quite the opposite, for Fannie is given the title of author: "The gist of her tale would be lost on me, but Fannie didn't bother about the ear she was telling it to; she just liked telling. She was like an author. In fact, for a good deal of what she said, I daresay she *was* the author" (*OWB* 854). In this example, Welty shows the background exactly coinciding with the foreground: in the South black culture and white culture work together to yield the unique Southern culture.

The same attitude of open acceptance and admiration colors Welty's treatment of African Americans in her fiction. She shares Hurston's political project to place the emphasis on celebration rather than on victimization. And just as Hurston fully integrates black culture into the American experience and celebrates her ethnic heritage, Welty claims her own American heritage in the story "Powerhouse." With it, she boldly asserts that jazz music represents the most outstanding American artistic contribution to the arts in this century. Thus, by placing "Powerhouse" directly before "A Worn Path" at the end of her first collection of short stories, with both texts celebrating the greatness of the black community and its deep interaction with the white community that sees it as Other, Welty builds up an aesthetic and emotional climax that is also strongly political: she proudly claims her black heritage as an American citizen, at the same time undermining the white Southern prejudice present in both stories. What Françoise Lionnet writes of Hurston applies at least to some extent to Welty's political attitude: "I would thus argue that [Hurston's] unstated aim is identical to Fanon's later formulation: to destroy the white stereotype of black in culture not by privileging 'blackness' as an oppositional category to 'whiteness' in culture but by unequivocally showing the vitality and diversity of nonwhite cultures around the Caribbean and the coastal areas of the South, thereby dispensing completely with 'white' as a concept and a point of reference" (105).

This ground-as-figure technique inspires Welty's treatment of her family's political background in reference to historical events. She may have borne in mind Willa Cather's own research and the technique that author used in *Death Comes for the Archbishop*, about which Cather explains: "The essence of such writing is not to hold the note, not to use an incident for all there is in it—but to touch and pass on" (*Later Novels* 973).[9] Similarly, Welty uses short genealogical sketches to draw a political map of the United States, establishing, for instance, West Virginia as a place where slavery was refused and the lofty ideals of the Republic fulfilled, without dwelling too long on the point. With the same lightness of touch, she asserts the origins of her family's devotion to independence and its rejection of racism:

> The Cardens had been in West Virginia for a while—I believe were there before West Virginia was a state. Eudora Carden's own mother had been Eudora Ayers, of an Orange County, Virginia, family, the daughter of a Huguenot mother and an English father. He was a planter, fairly well-to-do. Eudora Ayers married another young Virginian, William Carden, who was poor and called a "dreamer"; and when these two innocents went to start life in the wild mountainous country, in

the unknown part that had separated itself from Virginia, among his possessions he brought his leather-covered Latin dictionary and grammar, and she brought her father's wedding present of five slaves. The dictionary was forever kept in the tiny farmhouse and the slaves were let go. One of the stark facts of their lives in Enon is that during the Civil War Great-Grandfather Carden was taken prisoner and incarcerated in Ohio on suspicion of being, as a Virginian, a Confederate sympathizer, and lost his eyesight in confinement. (900, 903)

Beyond facts and history, this incident picks up again the debate about private and public guilt, alluded to earlier in the autobiography, and as it completes the picture, it clearly states Welty's project, for in *One Writer's Beginnings*, Welty shows how her sense of guilt was displaced from the traditional Southern guilt over slavery, racism, and the Civil War to a more generally American sense of guilt of an ontological nature: the Puritans' or Hawthorne's. This deeply political gesture has liberated not only Welty herself but younger Southern writers after her.

The guilt in *One Writer's Beginnings* touches on the origin of writing. "Listening" literally "stages" language, with this first chapter generating dislocation and estrangement through a journey *into* language, a strictly lexical adventure. The intimation of mortality present on the very first page is a poetical strategy, an exploration by language of that hinterland prowled by death, the supreme form of otherness, which will be at the heart of Welty's fiction as both metaphor and theme from "Death of a Traveling Salesman" to "The Demonstrators." The method reflects Welty's political options, in the displacement resulting from the strategy of metonymy, that is, contiguity, which Welty uses to link together incidents ranging from the particular to the general. As a supreme manifestation of the carnivalesque, verbal games assert that any act of language is linked with death through its transgressive nature of exceeding boundaries. The first incident, based on the revelation of the secret of life and death, is the mother's admission of the birth and dramatic death of an eldest brother, which starts for young Eudora a network of guilty feelings associated with the principle of pleasure.[10] The metonymic construction of the page invites the reader to speculate upon that universal link that relates the functioning of the mind by associations of ideas to the pleasure/guilt polarity, right to the ontological guilt of survival. In the telling, Welty insists on dramatization, which once more leads to serious thinking on guilt and expiatory modes; in addition to the guilt of the survivor, there is the guilt connected with sexuality, with the parent-child relationship, with excess of tenderness or with a wish for happiness, and above all with a desire to transgress the laws of piety, filial or religious—a supreme transgression that will become the source and the theme of all Welty's writing. Thus, the political intrudes where a reflection on writing is a reflection on life or vice versa and where the lexical and mental structures are altered as is shown by the next two increasingly complex incidents, which are built upon the principle of theatricality and the reader/audience response.

The first plays upon a lexical alteration (for the rhyme) and upon the passage from biological necessity to poetical necessity to assuage the fear of death:

> In the Spanish influenza epidemic, when Edward had high fever in one room and I high fever in another, I shot him off a jingle about the little boy down our street who was in bed with the same thing: "There was a little boy and his name was Lindsey. He went to Heaven with the influenzy." My mother, horrified, told me to be ashamed of myself and refused to deliver it. (*OWB* 880)

The second piece of writing plays upon literalness. Welty takes to the letter a phrase commonly used in the South ("by an act of God") and, by a turn the young student had not anticipated, her public, in the person of H. L. Mencken, read the joke literally in his turn:

> After the great floods struck the state and Columbus had been overflowed by the Tombigbee River, I contributed an editorial to *The Spectator* for its April Fool issue. This lamented that five of our freshman class got drowned when the waters rose, but by this Act of God, it went on, there was that much more room now for the rest of us. Years later, a Columbus newspaperman, on whose press our paper was printed, told me H. L. Mencken had picked up this chirp out of me for *The American Mercury* as sample thinking from the Bible Belt. (*OWB* 923)

Welty thus makes her point wittily: all misreadings come from political prejudice and an excess of literality. By doing so she gives her audience something to consider when passing judgment upon her as a woman writer from the South, or more generally when the North and South appraise each other (a sly echo of the past with the fate of her great-grandfather, and of that present with the North's self-satisfaction during the civil rights movement).

The echoing effects of these sketches link together transgression, guilt, and writing—or, to put it differently, Welty invites her reader to read them as political statement: all serious writing aims at disrupting known forms of authority, as it does in the description of Welty's mother's attachment to the Bible: "Then from time to time her lips would twitch in the stern books of the Bible, such as Romans, providing her as they did with memories of her Grandfather Carden who had been a Baptist preacher in the days when she grew up in West Virginia. She liked to try in retrospect to correct Grandpa too" (*OWB* 877). Furthermore, all serious writing, in Welty's case at least, aims at fully accepting the guilt, the better to transcend it; this is the meaning of her central metaphor for the artist—Perseus slaying the Medusa. Pure exhilaration comes from this liberating gesture of the artist and her characters.

Moreover, what makes *One Writer's Beginnings* such an exemplary American piece is recasting of the American myths of the frontier. The project to write about the American imagination itself is emphatically and modestly stated on the first page. The theme is deceptively simple: time and space. The manner is emphatic: Welty's favorite narrative strategy of dramatization/theatricality, which means displacement or transgression when applied to a genre other than drama. To dramatize a scene or moment is an eminently political gesture because it shifts the respective positions of reader and writer from intimate exchange to public performance: it transforms the world (of the work) into a stage, on which everyone ceases to be an individual and becomes character *and* audience in a formal dialectical relationship. Thus, like drama originally, the autobiographical text does not aim at transmitting information about the self, but at reiterating that word that founds all societies. The intimate confidence becomes the public reiteration of the origin. By a mirror effect, the writer establishes herself as stage director, and in the distance she has just introduced, she places a reflection on fear and death, while at the same time celebrating her art. *One Writer's Beginnings* opens onto a cosmogony, a staging of the origins of the world in which the writer was born, thus establishing her within a community. Conversely, Richard Wright in *Black Boy* chose to stress his personal family configuration (the opening scene is the pitiable image of a four-year-old child scolded by his mother on the day his grandmother died) and then proceeded to present bleaker and bleaker variations on this theme, as Richard Brodhead's study of the revisions of the manuscript shows (113–16, 121). If we go back to the beginning of Hurston's *Dust Tracks*, however, we find another cosmogony, splendid, militant, and highly political:

> Like the dead-seeming, cold rocks, I have memories within that came out of the material that went to make me. Time and place have had their say....

I was born in a Negro town. I do not mean that the black back-side of an average town. Eatonville, Florida, is, and was at the time of my birth, a pure Negro town—charter, mayor, council, town marshal and all. It was not the first Negro community in America, but it was the first to be incorporated, the first attempt at organized self-government on the part of Negroes in America. (1)

Welty's cosmogony is just as present on the page as Hurston's, but it is deconstructed, represented by elements that seem disparate yet function together as in a Paul Klee painting. By choosing to stage sound effects, Welty puts time, the emblem of the living world, at the origins of her text. The striking and chiming of clocks in the Weltys' house places her within the genealogy of her family (Swiss ancestors), as well as within the American tradition of mixed ancestry. When Welty goes on to discuss the scientific use of the instruments her father loved, she opens the family house and the child's imagination onto the cosmos and its temporality, and she also asserts the full cosmic dimension of the American frontier (*OWB* 839–40). Under the appearance of the familiar and the anecdotal, Welty reveals what characterizes the universal writer for her: an obsession with the flight of time toward inexorable death. In the essay "Some Notes on Time in Fiction," she observes, "We are mortal: this is time's deepest meaning in the novel as it to us alive" (168).

"My father loved all instruments that would instruct and fascinate" (*OWB* 839). The word "fascinate" asserts that science is the daughter of imagination and feeds it. Beyond the narcissistic quest of the self, Welty stresses the general and indicates an opening. Hurston places her infancy on the historical and political American scene. Likewise, on the first page of her autobiography, Welty draws the great axis of the American (and feminine) imagination—the vertical axis of the cosmic vision. That she should relate in similar terms her epiphany at the top of the mountain in West Virginia, where she has the revelation of both her independence and her vocation as a writer, shows her will to acclaim herself fully an American writer (*OWB* 899). As we know from similar experiences by other women writers, this insistence on the vertical axis and its reversibility (Welty sees stars in the well [899]), the depth of the earth and the clouds in the sky all contribute to suggest some gigantic volcanic eruption emblematic of the creative experience of a feminine "venue à l'écriture," in Hélène Cixous's phrase. No doubt Miss Eckhart should undergo such transfiguration when she becomes at last the great artist she is before two ignorant little girls.[11] Welty's experience is in no way to comparable to Ellen Glasgow's, although Will Brantley writes that she "describes a naturistic experience on a West Virginia mountain top that helped to crystallize her love of independence (a moment that bears comparison to Glasgow's experience in the Alps)" (112). Glasgow clearly writes of a pantheistic moment, which followed the death of the man she loved. After despair over the haunting persistence of death in her life, she experiences "union," "peace" that comes from integration into the great natural cycle of decay and renewal. Welty experiences an opposite pull, not into but out of, something she will fictionalize in "A Memory," with its images of volcanic eruption at the moment the girl has an intimation of creativity and of the forces of death—the artist's great theme.

As the narrative of *One Writer's Beginnings* unfolds, Welty establishes through the figures of her mother and father the paradoxical quality of the American myths. In so doing, she is not defining her own self as would be expected in an autobiography: rather, she is defining the American identity as simultaneously a reaffirmation of the Puritan past and a reshaping of it in the name of the future. With her mother's ancestors—preachers and lawyers, schoolteachers and scholars—she establishes the link with the drafters of the American Constitution and beyond that with the Puritans and their intense preoccupation with New Beginnings.

It is worth noting that Welty reorganizes the mythical geography of America. As she recaptures her heritage in order to see how much of it went into her writing, she identifies West Virginia, her mother's country, as both Eden and the Promised Land—an Eden for her mother, but the wild promised land where she will have to fight ceaselessly to ensure her independence. Recoiling from the encroachment of the pigeons is the negative counterpart of her epiphany at the well (*OWB* 899). Both events lead to freedom and independence, which is what her whole production as an artist has aimed at. Ohio, on the other hand, her father's country, becomes the place where, for her, the myths of American pragmatism and simplicity and efficiency begin. Welty soon discards the negative aspect related to a sad private past in order to recreate the pristine simplicity of the frontier through sensations and sparse telling: a simpler frontier, closer to most of her readers' experience, yet full of promises since it produced that typical American—her father, a man who loved scientific instruments and was always ready to experiment with new technologies as his final achievement, the Lamar Life Insurance Building, Jackson's first skyscraper, amply proves. She further presents him as filled with the pioneer's lover of change and movement, ready to seize new opportunities in places far away from home (such as his prospective trip to Niagara Falls [*OWB* 942]) and eager to reenact with the same spirit of adventure the exploration of the width and depth of the North American continent. Welty's insistence on the role played upon her creative imagination by railroad journeys with her father defines, it seems, wandering as the quintessential American dream and shows how deeply ingrained the wanderer is in the heart of a writer some have called a Southern "recluse," as it is deeply ingrained in the nation's imagination (Welty, "Eudora Welty: 'I Worry'" 142). Indeed, traveling for Welty has always meant a journey toward freedom, exploration, and creativity under the auspicious ministering of angels such as the African American woman who provided coffee to night travelers in Welty's student days and who figures in "The Key," one of her best stories about writing fiction (*OWB* 937).

When she chooses to quote her maternal grandfather Ned Andrews's "dedicatory address for the opening of a new courthouse," the eighteenth-century rhetoric (one can even hear the accents of Chateaubriand's celebration of the New World in *Attala* or *Les Natchez*) exemplifies the nature of the American West (this is West Virginia, for a Virginian) as both invitation and end, origin and destiny (*OWB* 888). Here the landscape is haunted by the ruins of former democracies and former empires, and the assertion of America's Manifest Destiny. We find some of the rhetoric of the Puritans celebrating the founding of the New Jerusalem and the unwavering belief in Progress. As a true revolutionary "son," if we follow George Bancroft's theories, Ned Andrew is obeying his Puritan fathers. He is also a true man of the New West in the nineteenth century and sees the West not as wilderness but as empire-building country:

> The student turns with a sigh of relief from the crumbling pillars and columns of Athens and Alexandria to the symmetrical and colossal temples of the New World. As time eats from the tombstones of the past the epitaphs of primeval greatness, and covers the pyramids with the moss of forgetfulness, [the architecture of the building] directs the eye to the new temples of art and progress that make America the monumental beacon-light of the world. (888)

Thus, as Welty finally perceives the pattern that organized her heritage, the gap between her parents' families does not seem as wide as she had first imagined. One line of ancestors, the mother's side, represents the side of the myth that is the fulfillment of a promise. In her important essay "'Pockets of Life': Rediscovering America in Paul Auster's *Moon Palace*," Kathie Birat uses Sacvan Bercovitch's analysis of American cultural history to show how "the projection of a scriptural consecration into an uncertain future prepared the way for other fruitful paradoxes of openness and enclosure" (135) and how Auster "consolidated the myth of a new set of fathers," thereby setting in motion the process by which America would "prove its promise from one frontier to another" through "rhetorical invention" (Bercovitch qtd. in Birat 135). On the other hand, Welty's father in *One Writer's Beginnings* embodies a man turned to the future, always seeing America as the Promised Land, a land of technological invention, progress, and unlimited hope. So, the strategy established in the book rests on the dialectics of the literal, achieved by the mother's many speeches and comments, and the metaphorical, the silent text, represented by the father's optimistic belief in the future of America.

By introducing distance between the personal and the general, the private and the public, Welty liberated the self from the danger of exposure. This gesture corresponds to that deep strain visible in every form of her production as an artist—photography included—which is a continual movement toward abstraction. In this respect, Welty thinks along the lines of Willa Cather. She simplifies, erases, and leaves only a rarified substance that her readers or viewers must interpret. Such a technique is responsible for the intemporal beauty of her work, which will make it endure time and repeatedly fascinate readers and viewers. I further argue, in the light of *One Writer's Beginnings*, that Welty writes not so much *about* the South than as *with* the South.

Just as Rembrandt's magnificent last self-portrait (October 1669) teaches much about an artist's enterprise and risk through the veins, scars, and marks of life on a face, the very texture of *One Writer's Beginnings*, presenting as it does the eroded yet forever alive and animated face of Welty's world, teaches us much about America and the risks of writing about her. This book is Eudora Welty's most secret piece of work, filled with holes in its texture, blanks in the writing, and silences in the voice. In its secret,[12] there lies an excess of meaning and brooding guilt—the guilt of a writer's venture. For there is forever the lucidity inherent in the secret that doubts and battles against the unsayable and yet tries to the last to say it. It is no wonder then that the self-portrait should end like *The Golden Apples*, the work "closest to [her] heart," with a magnificent rewriting of the American Dream ("'The Interior'" 42). Virgie's portrait is Welty's feminine counterpart of Fitzgerald's vision of the Dutch sailors (156). By a daring *effet de superposition*, Welty represents Virgie as both America and the Quintessential American since the two parts of a long sentence about Virgie in *One Writer's Beginnings* apply equally to the woman and to the land (946). America seen as battered (not waste) land and Promised Land, while, sitting on the stile in silent companionship with Minerva, the old African American woman who functions as her double in a mysterious and mythical way, Virgie is shown as the buffeted yet undefeated

American adamantly sustained by his/her sharing of the Promise—which has always been Welty's subject: "Passionate, recalcitrant, stubbornly undefeated by failure or hurt or disgrace or bereavement, all the while heedlessly wasting of her gifts, she knows to the last that there is a world that remains out there, a world living and mysterious, and that she is of it" (*OWB* 946).

With this forceful reiteration of her acceptance of the full American heritage, Welty also celebrates the undaunted spirit that creates this mysterious world. America as the Pilgrim/Pioneer's dream and challenge, America as the writer's secret territory: the political gesture of the writer will be restored again and again with each new reading, as Welty's slim volume feeds the meditation of future generations in the tradition of great self-portraits.

Chapter 7

EUDORA WELTY AND THE MERLIN PRINCIPLE

Aspects of Story-Telling in *The Golden Apples*— "The Whole World Knows" and "Sir Rabbit" (2009)

> Specific in the work, in the mind, but not describable anywhere else— or not by me; shape is something felt. It is the form of the work that you feel to be under way as you write and as you read. At the end, instead of farewell, it tells over the whole, as a whole, to the reader's memory.
> —EUDORA WELTY "WORDS INTO FICTION" (143)

> We all know that Art is not truth. Art is a lie that makes us realize truth.... The artist must know the manner whereby to convince others of the truthfulness of his lies.
> —PICASSO[1]

Writing in praise of two American writers with whom she felt some spiritual kinship—Willa Cather and Mark Twain—Welty stressed contemporaneity, the adequation of the work with its time as it reflects the artist's prodigious desire to explore new territories and invent new techniques, and thus expresses her own attitude towards fiction writing:

> Who can move best but the inspired child of his times? Whose story should better be told than that of the youth who has contrived to cut loose from ties and go flinging himself might and main, in every bit of his daring, in joy of life not to be denied, to vaunt himself in the love of vaunting, in the marvelous curiosity to find out everything, over the preposterous length and breadth of an opening new world, and in so doing to be one with it? ("The House of Willa Cather" 51–52)

Written in 1974 to commemorate the hundredth anniversary of Willa Cather's birth, at a time when feminist critics were beginning to raise gender issues, "The House of Willa Cather" places Twain and Cather side by side and compares Cather's treatment of history to Faulkner's. Here as in her essays and later interviews and like the truly great women writers in the twentieth century, Welty emphasizes the important feminine issues in her work precisely by ignoring the gender distinction and choosing to discuss the achievement of women writers and men writers on a par, considering that great artists transcend the sexual difference, a conclusion which does not preclude something similar to what Bakhtin described as "*translinguistic procedure*" (Kristeva, *Desire* 66).

Welty's superb formula, "the inspired child of his times," addresses the question of the interpretation of contemporary culture with fiction from a wider perspective than intertextuality does. Welty's acute mind, her commitment to the writing of fiction with its exhilarating challenges and constant questioning, and her keen interest in all that concerned her times have shaped her narrative strategies and fed her fiction. Reflecting on fiction, Kristeva says that the ability to speak in many voices will be determined by one's cultural, historical, and experiential framework (*Desire* 200–208). There is little doubt that Welty's knowledge and awareness of her "ruptured, inverted, and refashioned time" (Kristeva 207). This essay proposes to track some voices less often examined in Welty's fiction that mark this writer as one of the most original creators of the twentieth century for Welty explores the contemporary world by experimenting along the aesthetic lines of her times.[2]

In *Pour un tombeau de Merlin, Du barde celte à la poésie moderne* [*In Homage of Merlin: From Celtic Bard to Modern Poetry*], the French critic and scholar Yves Vadé traces the specific creative principles related to the figure of Merlin in the avant-garde production of twentieth-century writers and poets and adds that Merlin's influence is pervasive, as his aura reaches everybody's imagination in today's popular culture. He concludes that the Merlin principle characterizes most aesthetic experiments in the twentieth century and can even be considered as the distinctive mark of creativity in the century. The conceptual cluster associated with Merlin seems an appropriate key to analyzing Welty's fiction under a new light, especially as this mythic Celtic figure looms large in the background of Yeats's poetic and dramatic work, which was to be a seminal revelation for Welty at the University of Wisconsin.

The limited scope of an essay necessarily restricts analysis, allows only for indications and new paths to explore. After a short presentation of "the Merlin principle," I propose a rereading of two stories in the artistic context of the first half of the twentieth century that illustrate two aspects of the

Merlin principle. One is the first story Welty wrote for *The Golden Apples*; the other is the last one. Both are about desire and feminine sexuality: "The Whole World Knows" experiments along the lines of what modern painters were doing and "Sir Rabbit" along what sculptors were doing. The first is a dark modern composition brooding on older texts, the second, a playful liberating text that dramatizes Virgie's meditation on the near identity of opposites. Welty's rewriting the myth of Leda and the Swan in deep resonance with the representations made by the sculptors Maillol and Brancusi. These two texts open up perspectives that illuminate Welty's whole production. The point is to show that there are affinities, confluence, and no strict decoding.

As Vadé argues, the figure of Merlin represents creative imagination in its wildest, most exuberant manifestations, with all possible forms of invention, disruption, and transgression. In many respects Merlin embodies the spirit of our times, with his appearances and disappearances, disguises, primitive violence and association with the forest, nature, and animals (more especially with birds): above all, perhaps, with his subversive, even revolutionary attitude. A protean figure coming down from the most archaic myths, Merlin is a seer who was present at the creation of the world and who knows the past as well as the future. This figure of change and movement, whose name associates him with the sea, possesses immortality and omniscience, like older gods in Greek mythology in relation with the sea (Proteus, Nereus, Glaucus). Another strong character of the Merlin principle is the identification with poetic writing: in Arthurian legends, Merlin does not write himself but tells his exploits to the monk Blaise, who writes them down. Merlin thus becomes the creator of his own legend, of his own heroic character, so that the formula "the writing of his adventures in the adventure of writing" seems fitting here (Vadé 24). Howard Bloch sees in Merlin the patron saint for writing in the Arthurian world, the strongest image of the writer produced in medieval times, the very embodiment of the writing principles since his status as seer warrants the contents. Somehow, Merlin functions like a modern author, using innovative artistic techniques such as those inherited from surrealism, expressionism, dystopia in politics, and the insistence on illusion.

The classical age preferred Greco-Roman art, considered the figure of Orpheus as a civilizing principle, and favored the vision of a harmonious world where the poet-musician tamed wild animals in opposition to Merlin, who is associated with disorder, chaos, wild poetry, war, and wilderness. Orpheus represents realism, control, a logical organization, elucidation that privileges the intelligible over the sensuous. Merlin corresponds to the Celtic principle of illumination, privileging universal rhythm, the polysemy of symbols. The opposition can be compared with Simon Schama's statement:

"There have always been two kinds of Arcadia; shaggy and smooth; dark and light; a place of bucolic leisure and a place of primitive panic"; panic Arcadia is the place of creativity (517, 526–31). It took the revival of Medieval Celtic studies in France and the British Isles during the nineteenth century to revive the Merlin tradition, and the publication of the influential "L'enchanteur pourrissant" (the rotting enchanter) by the French surrealist poet Guillaume Apollinaire at the turn of the twentieth century to reestablish Merlin as a key figure. Vadé stresses the role of this text that celebrates the essential closeness of the poet-seer with death and argues that the subversive cluster of artistic, poetical, and political concepts that had emerged with the new century and transformed art in Europe can be said to participate in all that the figure of Merlin stands for. This creative trend he calls "the Merlin Principle," a principle that became a dominant influence not only in avant-garde artistic movements in Europe and later in the United States in the early twentieth century, but also down to the present time. In some respect the cluster of aesthetic and political ideas at the core of the Merlin principle partakes of what Bakhtin identified as the carnivalesque.

Welty's fiction reflects that spirit: an intense preoccupation with narrative technique and its exigencies, together with a very modern interest in what I will call modern technology that links science to painting and music, similar to what contemporary artists were doing, as we shall see. This comment [in a review of] Virginia Woolf's *A Haunted House and Other Stories* in 1944 illuminates the background of Welty's own creativity: "Instead of science, I should have named painting and music as being most closely allied to the writing of Virginia Woolf, which seem far more obvious counterparts. Yet it is in the science of these arts that the counterpart lies, and in that she is also meticulous as an astronomer and bold as an engineer" (27).

To appreciate Welty's special brand of creativity, we must remember that she was an exceptionally well-read writer, eager since childhood to read and learn about past and present civilizations and their cultures. She was also deeply immersed in the artistic productions of her time, showing equal curiosity and interest towards all forms with utter disregard for any distinction between "lower" or "higher" genres, what Axel Nissen calls "camp Welty," which is, I think, one aspect of the Merlin principle. Her years as a student at Columbia University and her frequent trips to New York gave her many opportunities to become acquainted with new American art forms such as jazz, musical comedies, music hall productions and with the new arts of cinema and photography from Europe and the United States. Her early interest in painting made her a frequent visitor of the great exhibitions and art shows, of museums as well as avant-garde galleries in New York. No field in the arts in the United States and Europe was left unexplored: painting, photography, sculpture, cinema, fiction, poetry, drama, music, countless plays, concerts, and operas. Just as important was the critical, artistic, and creative exchange that went on for years between Welty and her friends. Stressing the importance of one or more supportive individuals in the inner life of creators, Suzanne Marrs writes, in her sensitive *One Writer's Imagination*: "Eudora Welty was extremely fortunate, as are we her readers, that she found [. . .] a group of friends who exemplified intellectual daring in many ways and who supported her in fiction" (7). We know the role played by John Robinson. And Michael Kreyling, in *Author and Agent*, has provided us with an invaluable tool to understand the throes of creation, through his comments and the exchange of letters between Welty and her agent Diarmuid Russell. With an interest in contemporary history, Welty was a daily reader of the *New York Times* and more actively involved in American politics than has generally been acknowledged, as Peggy Prenshaw, Barbara Ladd, Sharon Deykin Baris, Suzanne Marrs, Noel Polk, and others, in the essays edited by Harriet Pollack and Suzanne Marrs have shown. The boldness and violence of Welty's denunciation of political and social evils, often unperceived, is present from her first collection, *A Curtain of Green*, especially in "Flowers for Marjorie" and "The Whistle," in *The Robber Bridegroom*, *The Ponder Heart*, and the last two stories about the civil rights movement, "Where Is the Voice Coming From?" and "The Demonstrators." Besides politics, some aspects of the Merlin principle are especially strong in Welty's production: the emphasis on the art and craft of the story-teller, stories illustrating their own functioning, the emphasis on illusion and uncertainties, on fragmentation, endless reflections, and, most important, the belief that death as it informs the notion of fascination and creation is at the core of the writer's experience.

For me, *The Golden Apples* (1949) is the quintessential Merlin work in Welty's fiction. That there is no mention of Merlin in the text, just as she never names Zeus and other mythic figures, is part of her strategy.[3] Yet she provides one textual clue that must have been obvious to her 1949 readers: the use of the word "hideous"[4] in relation to two figures/avatars of Merlin: the foreign musician in "Music from Spain" and the elusive living legend in Morgana, King MacLain. Both times "hideous" is explicitly linked to fascination. In the first occurrence Eugene and the Spaniard are watching a cat holding her prey in the power of her gaze: "The Spaniard, when Eugene looked to him, was making a hideous face over the lighting of another cigarette. The muscles of his face grouped themselves in hideous luxuriousness" ("Music" 501–2). The second occurrence, in "The Wanderers," shows the defiant smile of Welty's Merlin-like character before Katie Rainey's coffin: "Mr. King pushed out his stained lip. Then he made a hideous face at Virgie, like a silent yell. It was a yell at everything—including death, not leaving it out" (538). This "hideous smile" becomes part of Virgie's vision at the very end of *The Golden Apples*: "She smiled once, seeing before her, screenlike, the hideous and delectable face Mr. King MacLain had made at the funeral, and when they all knew he was next—even he" (555). This is fascination for one's own death, as we shall see. Among the good pieces of criticism written about *The Golden Apples*, Thomas McHaney's major essay states that the book resists known categories, investigates whether Welty "has discovered or elaborated a tradition of her own," and provides many insights into this great work ("Falling" 175). I wish to pursue this line and suggest how *The Golden Apples* gains some new coherence when seen in the light of the Merlin heritage, differing in my approach from Rebecca Mark's in *The Dragon's Blood* (1994), an extensive study of the background that places Welty's feminist issues in their relation with Celtic myths, Joyce, and Faulkner.

One primary reason for Welty's attachment to *The Golden Apples*—her masterpiece—comes from her having successfully met the self-imposed challenge of exploring fiction in the making. From different angles each of the seven related stories tackles narration, stages representation, and more generally deals with the problematics of literary creation to convey Welty's vision of life. What makes *The Golden Apples* so central to Welty's fiction and places her work in the very midst of twentieth-century philosophy is her magnificent wording of the myth of Perseus's slaying of the Medusa that brings, on the last page of "The Wanderers," a unity and perspective not only to the cycle but to her whole work. I will briefly recall the three elements of the myth since it is at the very core of the two texts I have chosen.[5] The center of this trinity is fascination—Medusa's deadly gaze, or rather fascination defeated, overcome by another gaze—Perseus's in the mirror. At the level of human relations, it refers to that spell, that *abus de pouvoir*/abuse of power by which we tend to objectify the Other, to make him lose his identity and become a thing, an object. In his phenomenological study of the gaze in *L'Etre et le Néant* (1943), Sartre was perhaps the first to show that fascination is central to the problem of the gaze and to the relation of one being to another. Beyond the inconciliable duality of our relation to the Other, Sartre says, there is the body, apprehended as the purely contingent presence of the Other. This apprehension is a particular type of nausea. We can see how seduction and the wish to possess the body of the Other are, eventually, another form of fascination with one's own death. The third constituent of the myth, the mirror, points to the fascination of Perseus—his awareness of horror and its fascination for him. The place of desire, the mirror becomes the door to death. A reflection, it is the sign of the near identity of opposites, as Virgie reflects when coming back home at seventeen for a "new" life. The endless doubling upon oneself is fascination—again. And this is true not only of "moments" but of the short stories themselves as structures. They are built on this endless reflection, which doubles and doubles again. There are two parts or two movements in each story that are based on the ambiguity between a real experience and a dreamed one, between asserted reality and hypothetical reality.

I propose to read from this perspective two of the three shorter stories in *The Golden Apples* whose function is to dramatize the art of writing through freer shapes that comment on the contents and technique of the volume obliquely and "at the end, instead of farewell, tell over the whole, as a whole, to the reader's memory," as Welty says of "shape" ("Words" 143). She had felt the need to add shorter stories ("Sir Rabbit" and "Shower of Gold") that would reveal the hidden coherence of the collection (Kreyling 137). Though "The Whole World Knows" was written before the six other stories, it functions as a third shorter text because of its experimental dramatizing of nausea.

Technically the most complex and experimental of the three if not of the whole collection, "The Whole World Knows" explores that psychic territory where beyond the inconciliable duality of our relation to the Other, the individual faces the body, apprehended as the purely contingent presence of the Other (Sartre), and is overwhelmed by a desire to kill, even himself. The text is built on Ran MacLain's narrative, which moves into murderous hallucinations that blur borders between his raving mind, close to madness, and the actual surrounding of the events he is telling. Like great artists, Welty felt the aesthetic necessity of her bold technique here. In response to Diarmuid Russell's questioning of the "meshing of two types or 'reality'" and his feeling unsure that the "shifts from one to the other always occurred smoothly," Welty wrote: "I don't think I know the answer to the transition question—I think I had better leave it ambiguous, because I felt it like that—I think part in the mind and part real" (Kreyling 118).

With a technique that partakes of the vampirism of creators, Kristeva says that "any text is constructed as a mosaic of quotations; any text is the absorption and transformation of another" (*Desire* 66). Welty draws from older, well-known texts, extracting the spirit rather than the text, in order to word her own new vision of human desire that is closely related to the fascination with death, which is present in love, hatred, and sex. Close analysis reveals the working of Welty's creative imagination. Valid for herself is her comment about Woolf's "An Unwritten Novel": "Here, like a technique of a technique, is the writer writing before her own eyes" (Rev. of *A Haunted*

House 28). Her text achieves a "form" comparable to what modern painters were doing at the time. Welty's choice of older texts covers a wide range in time, space, and genre, from the medieval English ballad "Lord Randall," as critics have said, to a complex nineteenth-century book loved by children, Lewis Carroll's *Alice's Adventures in Wonderland*, a successful contemporary novel, Fitzgerald's *The Great Gatsby*, and Welty's "A Memory." With the four texts Welty condenses all the features of the negative tradition of women as bullies or victims: the wife as betrayer and murderer, the evil Queen with her constant orders for beheading ("I pictured to myself the Queen of Hearts," Carroll wrote, "as a sort of embodiment of ungovernable passion—a blind and aimless Fury" [109]), the generously seductive flapper, the flirtatious young woman courting danger, the pitying mother siding with her son, the domineering mother-in-law, and a chorus of three old gossips and meddlers. Facing these women, the men equally belong to tradition: the cocksure young lover, the lecherous roving absent father, the betrayed husband mad with self-pity and murderous desire. In other words, those characters belong to the bourgeois drama or children's literature or a musical comedy on Broadway, ready to move in and out of the melodrama of ordinary life. Welty transforms them into her own textual characters through rhetorical figures such as inversion when the Queen of Hearts becomes Ran, redoubling when Alice becomes Jinny and Maideen, metaphor when the Cheshire Cat becomes King MacLain or the Spaniard in "Music from Spain," a text written at about the same time. Translated into the world of painting, the overall effect of this gallery of grotesque characters is comparable to expressionist James Ensor's paintings. Welty's self-imposed challenge in "The Whole World Knows" is bolder as regards narration itself: to invent a new narrative syntax that will transform characters and events into verbal equivalents of pictural elements. This was her preoccupation as an avant-garde artist at the time, as her self-revelatory review of Woolf's *A Haunted House and Other Short Stories* (1944) reveals. It expresses such deep understanding of what Virginia Woolf was doing that one feels firsthand research and practice on the part of Welty, as through her comment on Woolf's technique, she provides clues to decipher her own fiction: "In the broader organization and development of her themes she makes one always think of musical composition, indeed she gives musical terms as titles to some pieces. And in the delineation of character and in detail she makes one think of painting. We are likely to see profile and full face and reflection and dream-image simultaneously" (Rev. of *A Haunted House* 27).

Sent two years later to her agent, "The Whole World Knows" represents Welty's experimental research at its sharpest and most narratively determined at the time. Several painters come to mind. First and obviously, Picasso, inventing the revolutionary technique of superposing faces seen from different angles (profile, full face, reflection, dream image) as he struggles with the artist's representing (and the viewer's grasping) the complexity of the human personality. As one narrative equivalent, Welty uses voices to represent the enormous pressure put on Ran by the community with its multivoiced advising or disparaging comments about him as the furious husband and his unfaithful wife. The text becomes a fabric woven with the multiplicity of voices echoing (or not) Ran and Jinny's story, voices endlessly telling and retelling firsthand, repeating like Maideen, abstaining like Miss Lizzie, blaming like Tellie the black servant.

Second, Welty transcribes how surrealist painters such as Max Ernst represent the unconscious through weird and frightening figures by revealing Ran's visions of wounded or murdered bodies, as in sudden hallucinations he sees his murderous desire come true. As in dreams, the hallucination is presented realistically and rationally. Three instances are rather developed. Ran first sees himself breaking every bone of his rival's body with his croquet mallet ("The Whole World Knows" 459) and then suddenly shooting unfaithful Jinny as she is sewing a button at his demand:

> I fired point-blank at Jinny—more than once. It was close range—there was barely room between us suddenly for the pistol to come up. And she only stood frowning at the needle I had forgotten the reason for. [...] I was watching Jinny and I saw her pouting childish breasts, excuses for breasts, sprung full of bright holes where my bullets had gone. But Jinny didn't feel it. She threaded her needle. (463)

Ran's third victim is Maideen, a girl of eighteen, who "looked like Jinny. She was a child's copy of Jinny," whom he takes to a motel in Vicksburg after making her drunk (456). "Maideen came into the space before my eyes, plain in the lighted night. She held her bare arms. She was disarrayed. There was blood on her, blood and disgrace. Or perhaps there wasn't. For a minute I saw her double. But I pointed the gun at her the best I could" (471).

Third, a painter like Piet Mondrian, for instance, helps us appreciate the overall composition of the story. Rosalind Krauss describes how Mondrian covered his canvas with a grid to eliminate successiveness and to figure forth simultaneity, discarding perspective in order to emphasize the ground (16). Welty does something comparable to the grid when she provides a strong musical and visible structure (through italics) with the imaginary ballad/dialogue between mother and son, shadowed by Ran's invocation to his absent father, and puts the emphasis on a wealth of fragmented, superimposed, at times blurred and nearly erased elements of the narration in order to represent the increasingly murderous and nearly mad anxiety of Ran. The brevity of the ending "I had her so quick," followed by Ran's whining reproach to Maideen for killing herself later ends the story on a jarring note, of both color and sound (471, 472). Interestingly, when criticized about Cornella's message at the end of "The Winds" (267), Welty justified her technique through reference to painting in a way that applies here: "You know how in a painting a required note of intensity or a certain unmixed color will be placed maybe on otherwise irrelevant material, as far as subject matter goes, for the sake of the whole composition—the final compensating thing" (qtd. in Kreyling 70).

Two other echoes corroborate and open widely the serious matter discussed in "The Whole World Knows." First is Welty's dramatic musical accompaniment to prolong the traumatic perception of the Other. Rather than Faulkner's *The Sound and the Fury*, as Rebecca Mark insists, especially with the figure of the black boy sounding the palings with his stick (150–51; Welty, "Whole World Knows" 471), Welty's "A Memory" is brought to the reader's mind. That major early story already dealt with the discovery of fascination by the young narrator, as Sartre defined it, especially the nausea linked to the flesh and the self, the body apprehended as the purely contingent presence of the Other. The continuous repetitive noise in the background of the scene in the motel which so terribly dramatizes nausea in "The Whole World Knows" is a distant echo of the continuous laugh the young narrator of "A Memory" finally identifies as, watching a group of vulgar bathers on the beach, the revelation of the closeness of sex, death, and the Other: "from the man's hand, the sand piled higher like the teasing threat of oblivion. A slow, repetitive sound I had been hearing for a long time unconsciously, I identified as a continuous laugh which came through the motionless open pouched mouth of the woman" (95).

Second, a very fine thread started inside the first two stories written simultaneously, "The Whole World Knows" with heartless, unfaithful Jinny Love, and "June Recital" in which defiant Virgie played a prominent part, leads the collection to its superb conclusion in "The Wanderers." This thread ties *The Great Gatsby* to *The Golden Apples*. In "The Whole World Knows," what is new, very much inspired by the times rather startling at this point in Welty's production, is the specific role of Jinny Love as a Southern avatar of the flapper Daisy Buchanan. Jinny, flat-chested, wearing expensive sandals and boy's shorts, first seen cutting off locks of her hair and playing high-handedly with everybody ("The Whole World Knows" 463, 454), her role in the text is to cross borders, to *deterritorialize* not only this story, but the whole cycle as it prepares the reader for the feminist code with which Welty chose to end *The Golden Apples* in the last story she wrote for the collection in order to tie together all the volume's various threads. The very end of "The Wanderers" discreetly echoes *The Great Gatsby*—that great American novel that encapsulates the historical movement of the 1920s while opening the perspective across time and space—when Welty magnificently rewrites the American Dream. Virgie's portrait is Welty's feminine counterpart of Fitzgerald's vision of the Dutch sailors.[6] The terrible beauty of the "shape" of "The Whole World Knows," a text which Welty refused to alter, is that it held already a vision that the writer may not have fully conceived then but that she fully acknowledged when she put the collection into perspective and certainly wished to argue strongly since she made an explicit comment about it in *One Writer's Beginnings* (943–46).

Trapped on this side of the mirror, Maideen/Alice dies because she refuses to see the murderous game being played by Jinny and Ran: Mattie Will, on the other hand, talks herself through the looking-glass and frees herself in "Sir Rabbit."

As a narrative variation of the two-part structure, based on the ambiguity between a real experience and a dreamed one, "Sir Rabbit" follows the simple pattern of two sequential parts told in chronological order. The first, the narrative of young Mattie Sojourner's romping with the MacLain twins at fifteen, belongs to fact; the second, the narration of her encounter with King MacLain, suggests daydreaming and presents remarkable invention on the part of Mattie Will. More than "The Whole World Knows," "Sir Rabbit" has given rise to much good criticism, especially over the reality of Mattie Will's encounter with King MacLain. Patricia Yaeger never doubts its unreality: "If Mattie Will is a figure of the artist as a young woman, she is also a symbolic site where the dialogic interactions of text and intertext become visible (151). Using frame analysis as a tool, Daun Kendig provides a well-informed discussion of different views and concludes quoting Welty: "A fiction writer's responsibility covers not only what he presents as the facts of a given story but what he chooses to stir up as their implications; in the end, these implications, too, become facts, in the larger, fictional sense" ("Is Phoenix" 816). In *The Golden Apples*, "Sir Rabbit" functions as a brilliant demonstration of the story-teller's mastery of her art, Mattie Will's and Welty's. Mattie Will is presented from the first as a story-teller in the main two activities of *invention* and *reiteration*:

> Tumbling on the wet spring ground with the goody-goody MacLain twins was something Junior Holifield would have given her a licking

for, just for making such a story up, supposing, after she married Junior, she had put anything in words. Or he would have said he'd lick her for it if she told it *again*.

   Poor Junior! ("Sir Rabbit" 402)

Placed at the end of part one of the story, the information is a warning to the reader as well as an invitation to pleasure and complicity—the joy of active participation in the creation of an encounter that gives visibility and substance to King MacLain so far talked of and never seen, an invitation to appreciate the representation of an erotic myth. Just as Mattie Will had expected to see King in the woods when fifteen, now a young married woman, she is again expecting to see the mythic seducer as she accompanies her husband on a Saturday morning hunting trip. The place is typically King/Merlin's territory—wild woods—and a witty subtext of jokes with double meaning, including Mrs. Stark's forbidding the presence of "Pigs With or Without Rings," betrays Mattie Will's obsession with sex and with King (407). Welty's mastery of a double vision doubling upon itself plays here with the representation of seduction, and consequently with the reader's willingness to decipher a comic rustic rewriting of the seduction of Leda by Zeus. Humor, exaggeration, ludicrous theatricals with marked stage directions, and a refusal of plausibility: such are the narrative ingredients in the line of the Merlin principle. At times, Mattie Will sounds like Rosamond in the highly derisive and seminal *The Robber Bridegroom*.[7] From the first word, Mattie Will literally conjures up King MacLain's presence—he takes gradual shape as she keeps reflecting and inventing under the very nose of her clumsy husband. The whole construction of Junior's coarse humor when she mentions King, of his missing his target, then conveniently falling into a faint, even of her speculating that King must be an old man, down to her causally dismissing a witness ("'Turn *your* self around and start picking plums!' she called, joining her hands, and Blackstone turned around, just in time" [408]) is the proof of Mattie's *acceptance*—in her daydreaming.

   This episode is no rape, nothing like the rape so powerfully described in Yeats's "Leda and the Swan," whose textual presence is discreetly attested and reiterated. Instead, the writing of the scene *en décalé* marks Mattie Will's disappointment, her seeing through the legend: a great seducer is nothing but a mirage and functions like an idol that gives nothing, not even pleasure. The fascination embodied by King MacLain refers to that *abus de pouvoir* by which we tend to objectify the Other, to make him/her lose his/her identity and become a thing, an object. Yet, from the moment Mattie Will *words* this abjection, turns herself into a legend instead of a dishonored woman, she is freed and saved: "She was Mr. MacLain's Doom, or Mr. MacLain's Weakness, like the rest, and neither Mrs. Junior Holifield nor Mattie Will Sojourner; now she was something she had always heard of. She did not stir" (409). We note the reversal in the dramatization of gender positions, symbolized by the reversal in the use of shame. Whereas "The Whole World Knows" denounces tradition with Maideen's shame that led her to kill herself after a real rape she had not imagined possible (turning his murderous impulse against the girl when Ran brutally deflowers her), "Sir Rabbit" is about imagining a "rape" severely controlled by the woman that leads her afterwards to put King to shame as she holds him in the murderous power of discourse. Her leisurely crawling around King equates sleep with death: she sees the legend of a sexually powerful man as just an old body of no "more use than a heap of cane thrown up by the mill and left in the pit to dry"; the fascinator has become an empty slough (410).[8] In her extended analysis of this text, Rebecca Mark insists on King as "a potential fertility consort. This heap of cane is dead but Mattie knows he will not stay that way" (107). Within the narrative contract of this story, I think that Welty is at this moment doing away with King MacLain, as Aristide Maillol absented the swan, suggesting instead through Leda's bent head some pitiful bird. Welty's text is in resonance with contemporary views of Leda, that great favorite with sculptors, painters, and writers since Ancient Greece. Giving substance to a myth with words is strangely similar to the work of a sculptor, as Virginia Woolf felt and Welty too, since she quotes in wonder and approval a note in Woolf's diary about a work in progress: "I am not very far along, but I think I may have my statues against the sky" (qtd. in "The Art of Fiction" p. 75).

With her defiant retelling of the myth of "Leda and the Swan," Welty raises her statue against the sky, breaking away from traditional representations, introducing distance, control, even full creativity with respect to Mattie Will/Leda. What makes this text so compelling is that as a text about fascination it functions like fascination: the character's and the writer's with their own texts. Mattie Will/Leda is fascinated as the young woman discovers the power to control the event while satisfying her curiosity; Welty the writer becomes fascinated with her displacing the significance of the myth onto the woman and her body in a spirit that reflects the Merlin principle as it inspired two sculptors.

Welty's innovative gesture displaces the significance of the myth onto the woman herself who, as "inventor" controls the occurrence, as the French sculptor Maillol had done before.[9] At the same time, Welty's use of uncertainty, blurred effects, and reflections brings to mind Brancusi's *Leda*, which she may have seen exhibited in New York in 1936 or at least have heard of.[10]

All three works deconstruct the traditional representation of a beautiful naked woman close to a beautiful swan and introduce instead something new. As an artist/inventor of modern sculpture and spiritual father of such avant-garde sculptors as Jean Arp and Brancusi, Maillol was interested in form, in discovering a way to express the intemporal idea behind voluptuous form. Rejecting details and Rodin's tragic representation with an overworked surface, Maillol was after simplified forms tending towards abstraction with highly polished smooth surfaces that alone could express the figure transcending reality. He started from the torso and then worked from the inside to produce totally new sculptures: his only theme was the feminine body, which he endlessly represented in many different positions, each expressing by its form the abstract idea of femininity. Conceiving of existence as flux and perceiving happening in a fashion similar to Henri Bergson's *durée*, Maillol, like his friend Henri Matisse, wanted to evolve forms that would express the elusive "present" even as it was eroded by the mutual interpenetrations of past and future. This is what happens in the invented encounter between Mattie Will and King, something that Nina Carmichael will discover about the pears in "Moon Lake" (428). What Jack D. Flam writes of Matisse does apply to Maillol and also to Brancusi's *Leda*, as we shall see: "The goal of the process is to arrive at an absolute which, paradoxically, has only relative validity: that is, for a given situation" (33).

The novelty about Maillol's *Leda* is the oblique suggestion of *acceptance* and his doing away with the swan. This small bronze statue, four inches high, carved in 1902 at the beginning of Maillol's career, represents a buxom, naked young woman sitting and looking down at some unseen creature to her right. The intemporal obliqueness of Leda's reaction comes from her hands: the raised left hand, palm facing the viewer says no, while the right hand hidden by her thigh says yes. The swan is not represented: "I did not know what to do with the swan," Maillol said (qtd. in Lorquin 19). What is suggested instead is the disparaging smallness of the seducer. The spirit behind Maillol's statue is very similar to Welty's representation of her character's desire to seize the day and make the most of the present: "Of course she was not denying a thing in this world, but now had time to look at anything she pleased and study it" ("Sir Rabbit" 410). I further suggest that Welty must have visualized other small statues by Maillol, especially *Femme accroupie* (1930), when she represented Mattie Will's bravado a little later, defiantly sure of her femininity: "Then she approached softly, and down on hands and knees contemplated him," and even more so a few lines later: "Mattie Wills subsided forward onto her arms. Her rear stayed up in the sky, which seemed to brush it with little feathers. She lay there and listened to the world go round" (410).

In a more visionary way, Brancusi altered Maillol's proposition and carved an abstract figure representing Leda as the arch feminine swan. "Art is different from life, art is its transfiguration," he used to say (qtd. in Lemny 38). Here he condensed the myth into a single form, originally carved from one piece of white marble in 1920, shaped like an egg with a slanting shaft like a pyramid upside down at one end that suggests penetration or the neck of a bird. Later, he made a single copy in highly polished bronze, which he set off in a dramatic way. Brancusi had already used mirrors when he exhibited his work: for *Leda* he contrived a pedestal made of three pieces of different shape and material and used modern technology to make it revolve.[11] Placed on top and slowly revolving, the highly polished bronze reflected Brancusi's studio or the room around when exhibited in New York and made a strong impression on the American visitors in 1933 and then again in 1936 at the Museum of Modern Art in the *Cubism and Abstract Art* exhibition. Brancusi kept the sculpture in his studio as long as he lived, a proof that *Leda* had a special significance for him, somewhat similar to Welty's attachment to *The Golden Apples*. As the Bulgarian art critic V. G. Paleolog understood early, Brancusi solved the technical problem of light with *Leda* by trying to reverse roles. Whereas sculptures usually absorb light, his use of modern technology—the revolving pedestal and elaborate lighting that gave the illusion of movement and life—illuminated the sculpture, which in return sent back light (Paleolog 31).

In full resonance with the spirit of her time, Welty created a beautiful textual object with *The Golden Apples* comparable in its intent, technique, and effect to Brancusi's *Leda*. The sculptor's obsessions with the multiplication of reflections, contingent and redoubling upon one another, is voiced in Virgie Rainey's meditation on life in "The Wanderers": "Virgie never saw it differently, never doubted that all the opposites on earth were close together, love close to hate, living to dying; but of them all, hope and despair were the closest blood—unrecognizable one from the other sometimes, making moments double upon themselves, and in the doubling double again, amending but never taking back" (546).

I will add an intriguing further kinship, a shadow echo to Brancusi's love of modern technology and his invention of a revolving pedestal to express the most of his statue. It finds its equivalent in Welty's love of cinema, another modern technology/art that inspired writers. The writing of a screenplay of *The Robber Bridegroom* with John Robinson coincided with Welty's completing and revising the stories for *The Golden Apples*. Although the film was never made, I have a feeling it must have haunted Welty's mind as a wealth of visual possibilities: images, disguises, multiple identities and likenesses, trick and light effects, confusing, disturbing, enchanting, especially if they had in mind Cocteau as a possible film director.[12]

Brancusi's *Leda* obliquely illuminates *The Golden Apples*, even her whole fiction. Like Welty, Brancusi knew he had given a visible form to his artistic conception. As the lit-up statue slowly revolves on its pedestal, it sends back to the viewer reflections from the world around, distorted and constantly changing through circumstances yet carefully controlled by the artist through form, speed, and light. In a word, *Leda* represents Brancusi's *idea* of art. *Leda* is art made visible. The artist's play with reflection, fragments, uncertainty, and contingency corresponds to Welty's narrative technique in *The Golden Apples*; at the same time, it represents Welty's idea of the artist as Perseus slaying the Medusa, with emphasis on fascination as Sartre defined it. *Leda* thus becomes the visible representation of fascination at the heart of Welty's research. I will add a further point: as the sculpture becomes illumination through an excess of reflections, it disappears, so to speak, to proclaim the abstract and temporal idea of creation. This is exactly what Welty writes when she chooses to word her idea of the artist's struggle with the representation of the world as she conceived of it on the last page of her masterpiece when her beloved character Virgie Rainey has an illumination which allows her to condense her vision of the world through the myth of Perseus slaying the Medusa.

The spirit of the Merlin principle links and informs the three shorter stories in *The Golden Apples*—"Shower of Gold," "The Whole World Knows," "Sir Rabbit"—through their commitment to the art of story-telling. Welty plays with the deadly Looking-Glass in "The Whole World Knows" and "Sir Rabbit," wherein the two texts function like two mirrors placed *en vis à vis* endlessly reflecting one another. Using distortions and transformations, dubious gender identity, blurred distinctions between the feminine and the masculine, women and birds, male and female, sufferer and murderer, the body and the mind, her text crosses centuries from the Middle Ages, through the nineteenth century, and down to the present time, all the while infusing with a new impulse and eroticism the age-long battle between men and women, or the ancient myth of Leda and the Swan that endlessly radiates its fascination. We see then how this re-vision of realities led her to the writing of a screenplay from *The Robber Bridegroom* with the hope that the aesthetic and political kinship between the novella and the recent stories would find an adequate representation through fantastic and political cinema. The reality of King's encounter with Mattie Will in the woods is the reader's and the critic's problem; the reality of King's visit to his family on Halloween in "Shower of Gold" is the story's problem. Welty has displaced the narrative problematics from interpretation to narration; the reader realizes that the "proof" of King's visit lies in the highly hypothetical first part.[13] As incipit to *The Golden Apples*, "Shower of Gold" warns the reader: the seven stories, like a series in modern painting or sculpture, read as a series of experiments in narration. Furthermore, the moment that gives its full significance to "Moon Lake," itself placed at the center of the volume, and thus functions as a shaping principle of *The Golden Apples*, is the scene about writing with the mutual discovery made by Nina and Easter—two faces of the story-teller—through writing their names. From the moment Nina the observer is able to put herself in the place of Easter, to renounce her own system of differentiation and to acknowledge true "separateness," she becomes a writer, just as Easter asserts herself through and by writing, and opens up the whole field of literature through the body of legends and sacred texts handed down to be rewritten in different contexts and places by each age ("Moon Lake" 430). Easter's falling into Moon Lake and her coming back to life from near death completes this metaphorical representation of fiction writing. Literally, as well, she brings to the minds of the watchers/readers death's territory/the unconscious, which is fiction's territory. What the French surrealist playwright and poet Roger Vitrac said of Brancusi in 1933 for an exhibition at the Brummer Gallery in New York is strangely in resonance with Eudora Welty's work as a twentieth-century writer: "In the image of his own sculpture, which is slender, glossy as though destined to traverse space in all its elements, Brancusi, unconcerned with epochs, has traversed them all with the same tranquil faith, the same serenity. And this double parallel phenomenon enables us to ascertain, even now, that his work will last, since it affirms both an immediate and permanent expropriation of time and space" (1).

"THE INSPIRED CHILD OF [HER] TIMES"

Eudora Welty as a Twentieth-Century Artist (2010)

> It is of course the *way* of writing that gives a story, however humble, its whole distinction and glory—something learned, and learned each writer for himself, by dint of each story's unique challenge and his work that rises to meet it—work scrupulous, questioning, unprecedented, ungeneralized, unchartered, and his own.
> —EUDORA WELTY "HOW I WRITE" (242)

When asked to define what made her into a writer for the lectures that would inaugurate the William E. Massey Sr. Lectures in the History of American Civilization at Harvard in April 1983, Eudora Welty chose to open the series with a remarkable cosmogony. On the first page of what became *One Writer's Beginnings*, she writes the creation of the world of her childhood as very American, very progressive, with a passion for discovery, new technology, and a sense of wonder. Though deconstructed, this cosmogony is represented by three elements that function together as in a painting by Kandinsky: time, space, and modern technology to see beyond appearances. First are sound effects associated with clock time, chronology, and genealogy—her Swiss ancestors. Then is an awareness of space, within the house, abroad in Europe, and beyond with the immensity of the cosmos apprehended through her father's telescope. That telescope, which Loch Morrison, a young figure of the artist, uses to spy on his neighbors in "June Recital," symbolizes in this emblematic cosmogony the scientific discoveries that so radically changed the perception of the universe, of time and space, with Einstein's theory of relativity, which Welty fictionalized in her magnificent representation of the artist. "My father loved all instruments that would instruct and fascinate" (*OWB* 839), such as those held in the drawer of the library table: a folding Kodak, a magnifying glass, a kaleidoscope, and a gyroscope. All three children received the same questioning, future-oriented education that culminated for Eudora with two years at the University of Wisconsin plus one year in New York at Columbia. Welty had been fully trained at home and at school to explore, understand, and make the most of what the twentieth century would offer her. I propose to show how in her fiction and essays she was both the child and the thinker of twentieth-century creativity.

Invited to give a speech for Willa Cather's centenary in 1974, in her praise of two American writers with whom she felt some spiritual kinship—Willa Cather and Mark Twain—Welty stressed the adequation of the work with its times as it reflects the artist's prodigious desire to explore new territories and invent new techniques, thus expressing her own attitude towards fiction writing:

> Who can move best but the inspired child of his times? Whose story should better be told than that of the youth who has contrived to cut loose from ties and go flinging himself might and main, in every bit of his daring, in *joy of life not to be denied,* to vaunt himself in the love of vaunting, in the marvelous curiosity to find out everything, over the preposterous length and breadth of an opening new world, and in so doing to be one with it? ("The House of Willa Cather" 51–52, italics added)

If for a moment we may be tempted to take the "opening new world" literally since Cather's and Twain's times were those of the last frontier, of the opening of the whole American continent, we soon realize the power of Welty's metaphor, heralding modernity itself and the twentieth century on its way: "The works of these two are totally unalike," she writes, "except in their very greatest respects, except in being about something big, in the apprehension of the new, and in movement, tireless movement in its direction" (51). Her superb formula, "the inspired child of his times," addresses the question of the interpenetration of contemporary culture with fiction.

Welty's critical awareness, her commitment to the writing of fiction with its exhilarating challenges and constant questioning, and her passion for all that concerned her times have shaped her narrative strategies and fed her fiction. As she takes a bold "leap in the dark," Welty explores the contemporary world by experimenting along the aesthetic lines of her times ("Words" 134).

Welty's fiction belongs to the artistic revolution that marked the advent of the twentieth century, a period characterized by great changes in sciences and in the arts, that brought, with new technologies, fresh perceptions of man and the world. She grew up in the age of the remarkable development of visual arts: a revolution in the old arts of painting and ballet, the flourishing of photography, and, above all, the invention of the cinema soon acknowledged as the seventh art, an age marked by new artistic and philosophical modes of translating reality in order to represent for larger audiences emotions, the impact of historical events, and a new understanding of the great political, social, and psychological currents. This historical background influenced the political engagement that was a marked feature of the aesthetic revolution that started in Europe, especially in expressionism, surrealism, and futurism with the emphasis on movements in Italy. Social unrest at the turn of the century and, more generally, the disruption of society brought by the disaster of World War I caused artists in Germany to invent new forms of representation known as expressionism. They felt they had to shatter the public's certainties and bring people to a new awareness of what the world was really like through the violence of their subjects and their treatments: distortions, dismemberment, a bold displacement of color in order, hopefully, to cause a change of attitudes. The term "expressionism," a technique marked by overemphasis, refers, in fact, to different groups of painters covering a large scope in time and genre, but it soon became adopted by writers. At the same time, poets and writers in France started another artistic movement, creating a revolution in language and, later, in painting. Surrealism was not merely an abstract aesthetic movement, focusing on new modes of representation with emphasis on Freud's discovery of the unconscious; it was also politically *engagé* in the contemporary world.

Those were inspiring times for artists and their public when there were no frontiers between the continents and no barriers between the different forms of art, times when artists knew each other, worked together, and shared, as the twentieth century developed new horrors, a similar desire to reveal the truth about a terribly chaotic world torn and destroyed by wars, fascism, unimaginable massacres, and revolting poverty. Against such a background and with equal commitment, though not immediately perceived by her critics, Eudora Welty wrote a powerful and original fiction that continues to challenge her readers.

After a brief sketch of Welty's personal background, I will present some characteristics of twentieth-century art, and then I will select some aspects of her fiction that I find in resonance with her time, as they reflect the fertile turmoil of the artistic production of the century. Finally, I will trace the development of the figure of the artist as it exemplifies Welty's avant-garde conception of representation and places her among the very great writers and artistic leaders of the twentieth century. I will often rely on the visual arts, painting, and sculpture, to show what Welty was doing as her creative imagination worked along those lines. "I have a visual mind, and I *see* everything I write," she would say ("Art of Fiction" 85). This is not a matter of influence, rather of confluence.

Welty was an exceptionally well-read writer, eager since childhood to read and learn about past and present civilizations and their cultures. She knew every form of the artistic production of her time, which, like other artists of the period, she welcomed with equal curiosity and interest and with utter disregard for distinctions between *lower* or *higher* genres. Her year as a student at Columbia University and her frequent trips to New York gave her many opportunities to become acquainted with indigenous American art forms such as jazz and music hall and musical comedy and with the new arts of cinema and photography from Europe and the United States. Her early interest in painting made her a frequent and fervent visitor of museums, avant-garde galleries, and great exhibitions in Chicago, New York, New Orleans, San Francisco, and Europe, wide open to contemporary creativity.

No field in the arts, sciences, and technologies in the United States and Europe was left unexplored. Just as important was the critical, artistic, and creative exchange that went on for years between Welty and her friends, including the Irish writer Elizabeth Bowen. Such visual knowledge fed her art and also gave her a poet's attitude towards language: an extraordinary craftsmanship and inventiveness in her use of words and syntax never freed her from a painful awareness of both the power and the limits of language.

She was especially alert to new approaches to the visual, telling by pictures borrowed from painting, sculpture, cinema, dramatic or musical performance, and photography—she was herself a good photographer. Echoes can be traced in her fiction as comparable experiments. They create vision and style, open depths to reveal the unconscious as with Georgia O'Keefe (see Claxton) and German expressionists in "Flowers for Marjorie." They create images, metaphors, and rhythm as when Eugene MacLain's rambling through San Francisco in "Music from Spain" reads like a written journey through twentieth-century painting. Or they suggest a whole social, cultural, and political background through the technique of the ground as figure as in Mondrian in *One Writer's Beginnings*, for example. One should note her indebtedness to Picasso's revolutionary technique of superimposing faces seen from different angles (profile, full face, reflection, dream image), the recurrent theme of the Minotaur, which gives mythic depth to "Music from Spain," and Picasso's play with ludicrous juxtapositions. Welty is indebted also to the cinema for the way she structures her texts: the sequential organization of the narrative in scenes, the absence of transitions, an abundance of ellipses, and the use of shadows and dark zones that leave much unsaid.

I have selected four narrative aspects that Welty has brilliantly developed in her fiction that are particularly akin to twentieth-century art: two belong to technique—displacement and transformation; two belong to the philosophy of art—emotion and vision, but they all work and combine together. These are the characteristics stressed by Welty when reviewing contemporary art (*Occasions* 89–123).

The new emphasis on technique reflects a displacement of priorities in the twentieth century when artists begin to feel the necessity to question representation as practiced until then, and they favor a double movement—reflecting on their own practice while inventing it. They subvert prevalent techniques, borrow from older ones, and create new concepts in order to be true to a vision that springs from emotion and aims at causing the vibration of spiritual cords, at moving the soul. "The real dramatic force of a story depends on the strength of the emotion that has set it going," Welty writes ("Is Phoenix" 817). For writers, painters, sculptors, and musicians, the twentieth century means a new approach to *form*. "Whatever our theme in writing, it is old and tried.... It is only the vision that can be new," and that vision means a new use of their medium: words for writers, colors for painters, musical instruments for jazzmen ("Place" 796). Likewise, displacement is at the root of *indirection*, that great device that characterizes twentieth-century art. The artist does not say or show things directly. He hides his real intention or meaning behind masks, screens, or a partial vision so that the full import of his work is not immediately accessible. The surface functions as a lure; behind the apparent picture or story, there lies another one, much more instructive or disturbing. Deconstruction, so very present in Welty's texts, can be considered as one aspect of indirection.

In "Powerhouse," an early story about a jazz musician (Fats Waller), displacement is all the more brilliant, as it is *the telling itself* that becomes jazz music. A nineteenth-century realist would have dramatized the social background, emphasized the white audience's response only, and stayed at the periphery. Instead, with the joyful daring of a young twentieth-century writer, Welty transposes the writing of a story into *the writing of a piece of jazz music*. She starts with the condescending attitude of the white audience towards a great black American artist, and then she moves on to the composition of a jazz piece when the musicians meet in a small café during intermission—a pure jazz improvisation around a theme launched at random by Powerhouse himself, the recent tragic death of his wife. With real titles and words from jazz songs, and a superb mastery of dialogues mimicking music, Welty captures the essence of this great American contribution to twentieth-century art—the wonderful play on bouncing echoes between the musicians themselves as each in turn improvises his piece in competing solo and between the responsive black audience and the musicians. If the theme is death, then it is because art knows no other theme.

The second characteristic, that of the emphasis on movement and transformation, reveals the change from the nineteenth century's favoring of the gothic to the twentieth century's favoring of the grotesque. As motif, the grotesque originated in Rome, was rediscovered in the late Middle Ages/ early Renaissance, and flourished again at the turn of the twentieth century. It is a form of art based on the continuous transformation of the subject into different natural realms or orders. For instance, a pillar becomes a tree, then a woman, and then a bird or a flower. With painting or writing, the process implies a blurring of borders or categories, as what the Austrian painter Gustav Klimt does in his portraits of women: the dress and the face blur into the background in works like "The Waiting" (1905–1909). In fiction, we find a similar fluidity, a blurring of distinctions in the narrative, indecision between reality and reflection. This appears in such stories as "Old Mr Marblehall," "Asphodel," "Ladies in Spring," or "Kin."

Another aspect of movement is the dramatic form, more precisely a tendency to dramatize, so characteristic of twentieth-century art, a technique that Welty practiced and admired in the creations of her contemporaries. Welty points this out by quoting LeRoy Leatherman about the modern choreographies invented by Martha Graham, an artist she much admired: "Martha aimed for . . . ways of moving that would communicate varieties of human experience which the art of dance had never before attempted . . . and ultimately for dramas that would be acted through movement alone" (qtd. in Welty, Rev. of *Martha Graham* 141). In a similar spirit, Welty wrote her novels in such a manner that they might be read as dramas or plays.

If we now turn to the creative process itself, what I call a new philosophy of art, we find two creative principles hitherto little exploited: emotion and vision. Twentieth-century artists started from within instead of starting from the outside world. They started from emotion, something Welty had learned from photography, a form that captures "the moment in which people reveal themselves. [. . .] The human face and the human body are eloquent in themselves, and a snapshot is a moment's glimpse" ("One Time, One Place" 354). This moment's glimpse concerns the soul. What artists discovered with primitivism—Picasso, Brancusi, and Cocteau, for instance, worked in their *ateliers* with the African masks and statues they had bought—is *the spiritual force* behind simplification and abstraction. They felt the urge to discard realism and concentrate, instead, on the emotional value of form, color, material, or pattern, to make visible the invisible. Startling the viewer into a deeper perceptiveness through the vibration of spiritual cords, as Kandinsky developed in his influential *Du Spirituel dans l'art* [*Concerning the Spiritual in Art*]:

> When we look at colors on the painter's palette, a double effect happens: a purely physical effect on the eye, charmed by the beauty of colors firstly, which provokes a joyful impression as when we eat a delicacy. [. . .] But this effect can be much deeper and causes an emotion and a vibration of the soul, or an inner resonance, which is a purely spiritual effect, by which the color touches the soul itself. (105, 107)

Art is inspired technique, as the Canadian painter Emily Carr experienced when looking at a Haida totem pole in the forest of British Columbia: "The power that I felt was not in the thing itself, but in some tremendous force behind it, that the carver had believed in" (36). Welty had the same revelation on discovering the windows in the cathedral of Chartres, the capitals in the cathedral of Autun, and the mosaics of Torcello.

> I painlessly came to realize that the reverence I felt for the holiness of life is not ever likely to be entirely at home in organized religion. It was later, when I was able to travel farther, that the presence of holiness and mystery seemed, as far as my vision was able to see, to descend into the windows of Chartres, the stone peasant figures in the capitals of Autun, the tall sheets of gold on the walls of Torcello that reflected the light of the sea. (*OWB* 877)

With words that bring up the vision of an abstract sculpture, Welty defines her own aesthetic principles of shape or form as a concept analogous to Kandinsky's *inner necessity*: "Specific in the work, in the mind, but not describable anywhere else—or not by me; shape is something felt. It is the form of the work that you feel to be under way as you write and as you read. At the end, instead of farewell, it tells over the whole, as a whole, to the reader's memory" ("Words" 143).

Form then results from what Welty calls "a personal act of vision," which is both the starting point for the story and the unique use of words to tell that particular vision ("Words" 137). She describes this impetus to get at the "idea" as a spark: "the imagination has to be involved, and more—ignited" (139). And she puts the emphasis on language: "If this makes fiction sound full of mystery, I think it's fuller than I know how to say. Plot, characters, setting, and so forth, are not what I'm referring to now; we all deal with those as best we can. The mystery lies in the use of language to express human life"

(137). Welty's view of words is in resonance with Kandinsky's use of colors. In a book published in 1967, Robert Scholes defined avant-garde writers by the role of words in writing, and the power of abstraction in contents—in a way that fits Welty's technique very well, though he was thinking of Iris Murdoch's *The Unicorn*, among others: "Fabulation, then, means a return to a more verbal kind of fiction. It also means a return to a more fictional kind. By this I mean a less realistic and more artistic kind of narrative: more shapely, more evocative; more concerned with ideas and ideals, less concerned with things" (12).

In modern fiction, the writing of a story from the vision of the writer leads to a second aesthetic principle: the building of the narrative towards some ultimate revelation or illumination brought to the character or the reader, what Joyce called "epiphany," and Virginia Woolf and Welty called "vision." Remember the last sentence of Woolf's *To the Lighthouse*, when the painter Lily Briscoe is at last able to complete her picture: "I have had my vision" (310). This is something Welty had known from her first published story, "Death of a Traveling Salesman." For Welty, if the material (the theme) of the story is not new, what matters is the writer's inner belief—imagination—that creates a new dramatization to give her reader a shock of recognition.

Another aspect of twentieth-century art is the reader's/watcher's active participation. Because twentieth-century art plays with indirection and is not immediately accessible, critical attention is expected from the audience to interpret or decipher the work. Modern painting, especially abstract painting, requires critical distance and the capacity to adapt one's evaluation criteria to new modes of representation, and so does fiction. Consequently, the active participation of the reader, as audience, is in itself a form of creativity: "Before there is meaning, there has to occur some personal act of vision. And it is this that is continuously projected as the novelist writes, and again as we, each to ourselves, read" ("Words" 137). Misreading is the danger. Quite often, the deceptively charming or familiar social surface functions as a lure that stops the reader before he starts probing deeper into the text and grasping the whole as a whole:

> The novel or story ended, shape must have made its own impression on the reader, so that he feels that some design in life (by which I mean esthetic pattern, not purpose) has just been discovered there. And this pattern, shape, form that emerges for you then, a reader at the end of the book, may do the greatest thing that fiction does: it may move you. And however you have been moved by the parts, this still has to

happen from the whole before you know what indeed you have met with in that book. [...]

It is through the shaping of the work in the hands of the artist that you most nearly come to know what can be known, on the page, of his mind and heart, and his as apart from the others. [...]

This ordering, or shape, a felt thing that emerges whole for us at the very last, as we close the novel to think back, was to the writer, I think, known first thing of all. It was surmised. And this is above all what nobody else knew or could have taught or told him. ("Words" 144)

If we now turn to composition itself, we find the major aesthetic principle of reflexive writing: the story itself dramatizes or represents the writing of a text or one aspect of writing. Twentieth-century writers favored that technique because it presented, indirectly, a reflection on their art and its provocative issues. In her use of reflexive writing, Welty's insistence on the visual as a narrative detour is her distinctive mark. I will briefly examine two stories that use the South as background and pretext: the aristocratic myth in "Old Mr Marblehall" and family tradition in "Kin."[1]

Published in Welty's first volume of stories, *A Curtain of Green and Other Stories*, "Old Mr Marblehall" is a story about the imposture of writing; it dramatizes the creation, the "fabrication," of a character and its limitations. Once again, the surface is deceptive; the apparent subject of the narration is a picture of the decadent society of the Old South, the South seen as myth, and consequently reduced to *staging* with sets and costumes.

In reality, the story stages the specificity of the literary act, the questioning of the nature of poetical invention and what happens at the moment invention becomes a narrative. The clue is given in the revised version by the addition of the verb "Watch," an injunction to the reader to become the active spectator of the pantomime, for indeed this is Welty's visual detour here. To create her character, Welty raises two basic questions at the same time: How do we define a character? How do we give him a fictional existence? Character, as it appears in traditional novels, can be said to be defined by family, house, and social life. Welty plays with doubles (Mr Marblehall is a bigamist) that are not quite identical and uses brilliant pastiches to paint the two families. The whole story is based on the deconstruction of the characters; by stressing the unimportance and artificiality, she presents them as literary constructions. If we look at the last scene, when old Mr Marblehall imagines he is discovered by his second son, we are warned that *it cannot happen* for the whole passage is based on the sum of all the different signs attached to his different lives. This scene is purely fictitious. Writing is a matter for illusion: it begets it while it feeds upon it. "Old Mr Marblehall" is the imposture of narration.

At the other end of Welty's production, and emblematic of the narrative complexity of *The Bride of the Innisfallen*, "Kin" also deals with imposture—what a fraud a family portrait is—and functions like an optical device, the stereopticon used by the narrator's Great-Uncle Felix, which provides the clue to the narrative complexity of this text, itself a reflection on Welty's late research. Structured upon the principle of the play within a play (*structure en abyme*), the text rests on a counterpoint between past and present.[2] Welty uses the device of a mirror that does not reflect directly the scene presented to the spectator or reader, but the fragment of another scene, of which it constitutes the only material proof, thus putting the first picture into perspective. One must look at the portrait of the great grandmother in order to understand the meaning of a story about people coming to have their pictures taken. "Kin" treats the myth of the Old South after the manner of Monet or Vuillard: only fragments on the shimmering surface. The counterpoint upon which the story is built functions like a stereoscope that juxtaposes images that are then seen in relief. The principle is one of duality with the result either of increased distinctness or blurring. The superimposition of diverse attitudes, nearly identical throughout the ages, gives a unique picture that both permits one to see what is called "the Old South" and, at the same time, suggests something evanescent. On this apparent contradiction rests the dialectics of "Kin": to seize the myth one must start from the present, not the other way around. "Kin" is a fraud, the fraud of a family picture, the fraud of a loving family.

We see why the short story was Welty's privileged mode: it allowed her a complexity that could be best expressed in the short form. The *telling* is what matters because only through narrative technique, "the *working* insight, which is what counts," "words used in certain ways" can the writer show something new, yet timeless ("Words" 135, 134). The reader's mind and heart are equally solicited: "Both reading and writing are experiences—lifelong—in the course of which we who encounter words used in certain ways are persuaded by them to be brought mind and heart within the presence, the power, of the imagination. This we find to be above all the power to reveal, with nothing barred" (134).

Indeed, Welty used mirror effects quite early, that modernist feature favored by Virginia Woolf in her short stories and by surrealist filmmakers like Jean Cocteau in *The Blood of the Poet* and *Beauty and the Beast*. This visual technique, which played with distortions, blurred or half-seen reflections, appealed to Welty for its political possibilities, as we see in two novels, *The Robber Bridegroom* and *Delta Wedding*. A brief comment on the latter text, which so far has escaped critical attention from that perspective: I read *Delta Wedding* as an anti-plantation novel, which, through indirection, stages Welty's reflections on contemporary issues such as World War II, race, the place and role of women, the tyranny of family ties, and a changing society. We can see her technique as an equivalent of Brancusi's invention with his statue of *Leda* (Giedon-Welcker); even more, I will say, as a re-appropriation of the seventeenth-century baroque technique of a catoptric theater, very apt if we consider that the novel, with its explicit reference to Shakespeare's *A Midsummer Night's Dream*, is a comedy. From the Greek *catoptron* (mirror), "catoptric" relates to the reflection of light by a mirror and to means produced by or based on reflection. The stage was set with a series of candles and mirrors endlessly reflecting, multiplying, and distorting characters and action to suggest that the world is a stage where illusion reigns supreme. From the first, in spite of its apparent hugeness, the Delta and the plantation appear to Laura as a closed world limited by reflection: the sky mirrors the fields, the name Fairchild refers to the place as well as to its inhabitants, and characters come and go between two identically furnished plantation houses. The black waters of the bayou reflect a house that was never lived in. Above all, the golden light of evening or the clouds of dust raised over the fields create a magic, blinding atmosphere. The family thrives on countless repetitive actions, traditions, and family narratives that are as many traps, and this setting culminates with the theatrical symbol of the bird cage where the young cousins seem imprisoned. This closed narcissistic world symbolizes the Fairchild family and its enormous pressure on individuals through expectation, repetition, and endless violence. The Delta becomes a stage where illusion and narcissism reign supreme, and far from being a new development of the plantation novel as the first critics said, *Delta Wedding* is an anti-plantation novel. It tells of seduction and fascination and cruelty and plays subtly with the clichés and conventions of the genre to lure the reader into the pleasant illusion of recognition and complicity until she realizes, as does Laura who refuses to live at Shellmound, that the Delta is an evil place for all its enchantment. Hawthorne's garden with the beautiful lethal flowers in "Rappaccini's Daughter" is not very far.

I now come to that important aspect of twentieth-century writing, political commitment. Although never absent from a work that invites one to read oblique comments on world affairs and the world's history, it is foremost when Welty feels personally concerned and writes bold innovative texts in resonance with the political and aesthetic movements of her times such as surrealism, expressionism as in "Flowers for Marjorie," or when she uses fairy tales, mythology, tall-tale, and musical comedy to denounce greed and the frontier in *The Robber Bridegroom*, or creates dystopia to indict McCarthyism in *The Ponder Heart*, or dramatic soliloquy and displaced violence for the two stories about the civil rights movement, "Where Is the Voice Coming From?" and "The Demonstrators."

In "Must the Novelist Crusade?" Welty argues that the great difference between a crusader, say a politically engaged journalist, and a writer is that by reverting to art, which is the condensation of a vision, the writer reaches an intensity and a form that will more surely reach the heart of the reader because a work of art is the expression not of anger or outrage or the wish to reform, but the expression of the writer's vision of something much more complex and wide-ranging—humanity: "There is absolutely everything in great fiction but a clear answer. Humanity itself seems to matter more to the novelist than what humanity thinks it can prove. [. . .] The novelist's real task and real responsibility lie in the way he uses [life around him]" (806).

"Flowers for Marjorie" is the only text in Welty's first collection that concentrates on a specific historical event, the Depression, that the writer saw firsthand and photographed in New York, betraying a very political concern. The Depression is seen from the perspective of Southern emigration to the North with a young couple from Mississippi come to New York to find employment as main characters. Doubly faced with estrangement, they react differently to unemployment and starvation away from home. Whereas Marjorie is content with the baby to come in three months and shows spirit and plans for the future, Howard is hopeless, threatened in his manhood, destroyed by despair. For me, the text is the written equivalent of an expressionistic painting of the kind produced in Europe some twenty years earlier, with filmic echoes and techniques borrowed from surrealism. Violence felt as blows and revelation, as we see in the paintings of Max Ernst or Max Beckmann in search of modern metaphors, figures as the present fight of modern man to survive in big cities. In her text, Welty faces a writer's challenge: to give the illusion of actual events as she writes with the precision of details found in dreams or nightmares, and at the same time to question the reality of these events with devices such as non sequitur, close-up, slow motion, or the use of shadows, all extensively present in silent films. Welty has the ambition to shatter the reader's smugness. Her subtle play on doubt as to the reality of the murder of the pregnant wife by her husband further adds horror as it hits the reader's subconscious with the awareness of its possibility ever present in everyone—that murderous impulse shown in early surrealist films such as Buñuel's *Un Chien Andalou*. "Flowers for Marjorie" takes shape beneath the double arches of (self)-destruction and (self)-begetting. Murder and rebirth conjoin as the ultimate form of rebellion, when man desperately tries to be "like God." Close reading invites one to read "Flowers for Marjorie" as the bold dramatization of self-begetting, with the hallucinatory episode of the pansy as a transgressive sexual key when Howard no longer gazes at a lovely young flower but at his mother's genitals ("the giant worn lips of a sleeping crater" [120]). Because he is no longer able to see and face reality, Howard reconstructs the world and creates a personal utopia (his rambling through New York when everything turns out so well and fulfills his deepest wishes) that will turn into dystopia, in the way surrealist filmmakers were interested in ultimate transgression in their work.[3]

Likewise, for all its entertaining comedy, with the exorbitant power of language at its center, *The Ponder Heart* is a brilliant dystopia. Sharon Deykin Baris was first to denounce Uncle Daniel as a projection of President Eisenhower's attitude towards Julius and Ethel Rosenberg. For me, the short novel is a devastating indictment of McCarthyism in the United States and of the terror brought by a general suspicion of language and minds. It is also about women being denied language and speech and about dirty money made during the Civil War.

Welty also denounces twentieth-century horror in Europe. I think we ought to read "Livvie" as Welty's first writing about concentration camps. In the depth of the Natchez Trace, old Solomon's farm and "nice" house has the enforced organization of a slave plantation or of a death camp as it dramatizes the imprisonment of a young wife torn from family and country, sentenced to a slow death (276). The very symbol is the "line of bare crape-myrtle trees with every branch of them ending in a colored bottle, green or blue" made by Solomon over the nine years of his marriage "in labor amounting to about a tree a year, and without any sign that he had any uneasiness in his heart" (277, 278). The deathlike silence that reigns inside and outside thunders with deafening echoes when the reader realizes what the text is about. The ironical ending precipitates the evil invasion of modern capitalism, heralded by Miss Baby Marie peddling cosmetics—a modern avatar of Hermes the God of communication and trade—followed by Cash, the brash young man, whose name symbolizes the free circulation of sex and money. A more ruthless though oblique version of concentration camps looms in "Circe," her 1949 story, the first set in Europe. Circe has the terrible power to denature nature, to enthral men and reduce them to the abject condition of animals. I think that despite Circe's lightness of tone and humorous comments on good housekeeping, her drive for dehumanizing bodies, ordering them around like swine, and cleaning things up, might have brought to the mind of an American traveling through Europe a few years after World

War II, the all-too-recent times and places when human bodies were herded and driven to unspeakable places.[4]

In this last part, I would like to stress Welty's inventiveness as she establishes links and correlations between the anthropological, scientific, and philosophical discoveries that were changing mentalities and the problematics of representation in the arts—especially in the reflexive texts where the artist is present.

The figure of the artist appears in an early story, "A Curtain of Green," published in 1937 in *The Southern Review*, which Diarmuid Russell, Welty's newly self-appointed agent, had liked (Kreyling 27–30). Unlike "Powerhouse," which centers on the figure of the black jazz musician, "A Curtain of Green" has, so far, attracted less critical attention than it deserves, mostly, I think, because it is one of those resistant texts that require special tools to open them. I suggest reading it as Welty's brilliant experimentation with *shamanism as motif* because this animistic form of religion from northern Asia and Europe, long known in Europe, had attracted much attention by anthropologists in the first years of the twentieth century when it was evidenced in its northern American forms. It is characterized by its use of Nature and the mediumistic trance. Surrealist poets were already well acquainted with its links with the discoveries of Sigmund Freud and Carl Jung. British, American, and Mexican painters also became interested in its artistic possibilities.

For the great American painter Jackson Pollock, shamanism was precious, as it provided him with an artistic medium with which to convey his interest for Jung's theory of the collective unconscious and his desire to bring some form of cure to a world sick with World War I, the Depression, and totalitarianism. The American art critic Stephen Polcari, who co-organized an exhibition in Paris ("Jackson Pollock et le Chamanisme," Pinacothèque de Paris, 15 October 2008–15 February 2009) was the first to point out shamanism in Pollock's work ("L'idée").

Why speak of shamanism in regards to Welty's story? Because "A Curtain of Green" stages an exorcism, therapy through violence, with the intervention of superior forces that come from Nature: the finger that parts the hedge (215). Deconstruction gives a clue because it is the written equivalent of what avant-garde painters were doing at the time. Pollock's canvas *Bald Woman with a Skeleton*, painted circa 1938–1940, thus after Welty's story, helps readers understand Welty's technique here, especially the puzzling "finger that parted the hedge" ("Curtain" 133). On the symbolic level, the text stages a ritual sacrifice and the promise of rebirth. The elements of a shamanic cure are present: chaos, trance, sacrifice, and healing. To identify them, the reader must not stop at the realistic level, always present in Welty. Instead, as is the case between a modern abstract painting and its viewer, the text requires from the reader a crossing of appearances, a desire to enter the psychic space where the artist creates a spiritual vibration that will enable him to explore a world hitherto unexplored, to read, to see differently in order to (re)capture the buried relationship between the unconscious and the world, that is to say, creativity.

Chaos in "A Curtain of Green" is the accident, the unforeseen, the unaccountable that kills the husband and sinks the young widow into the depths of her garden, whose uncontrolled vegetation becomes the visible sign of the chaos of death and of the wreck of the heart. Through deconstruction, the trance is presented in three moments. First as it affects the garden, it opens a scene for a shamanic ceremony: "the sun seemed *clamped* to the side of the sky. [...] the stillness had *mesmerized* the stems of the plants. [...] The shadow of the pear tree in the center of the garden lay *callous* on the ground" (133, italics added). The transgressive arrest of the course of the sun suggests fire, always present to heal and purify. Then Mrs. Larkin falls into a form of trance in the original meaning of the word, "extreme fear, terror" when she feels as if addressed by superior forces: "She felt all at once terrified, as though her loneliness had been pointed out by some outside force whose finger parted the hedge" (133).

The sacrifice is present, too. Shortly, there occurs the third moment, a disturbing incident when Mrs. Larkin raises her arm in a murderous impulse to revenge her husband's death by killing the innocent Jamey, her black gardener. Nature—whose healing cure had begun when it had shattered Mrs. Larkin out of her hardness and brought her to see Jamey in his difference—by sending the rain now, transforms the intended murder into the simulacrum of a sacrifice. Yet there remains an echo. Welty's vision is disquieting because she intimates, at this early stage of her production, that the artist is a potential slayer. In the Medusa-like instant that mesmerizes every plant and creature just before the rain, Mrs. Larkin is about to kill Jamey. (In her second collection, *The Wide Net*, the artist does become the slayer, in "A Still Moment," for instance.) For all its benevolence, Nature is also endowed with the power to kill with the fall of the tree on Mr. Larkin's car. As in a shamanic cure, the apparition of death is here associated with a new psychic state that divests Mrs. Larkin of all resentment and hatred. She falls to the ground in a swoon-like trance as the falling rain completes the cure: "Then as if it had swelled and broken over a daily levee, tenderness tore and spun through her sagging body" (135).

The next question raised by this reflexive text, which defines good practice in reverse, is who is the artist? The artist here is represented by three figures:

Mrs. Larkin, Jamey, and the garden, and this is the scandalous character of the text. Mrs. Larkin is the figure of the failed artist, what one must not be, the artist that lets herself be carried away by her personal passions instead of rising above herself to reach the universal. The young widow represents the danger that threatens the artist when she fails to control her abundant material, whether it be overcoming personal grief and loss, as Welty did successfully after her father's death, or judiciously selecting and discarding among the excessive riches of life. In the metaphor of the garden, the excess of material, personal or not, becomes the excess of vegetation Mrs. Larkin no longer controls. An aesthetic necessity Welty later emphasizes in "Words into Fiction"—"It grows clear how [the writer] imposes order and structure on his fictional world" (142). Here, the narrator suggests what the writer/gardener must do and must not do and defines at the same time the writing practice Welty displays in the entire volume: a superb control of plot and narration, a dense precise style, strong, yet filled with nuances, so inventive in its condensation that it often reads like poetry:

> Only by cutting, separating, thinning and tying back in the clumps of flowers and bushes and vines could she have kept from overreaching their boundaries and multiplying out of all reason. The daily summer rains could only increase her vigilance and her already excessive energy. And yet, Mrs Larkin rarely cut, separated, tied back.... To a certain extent, she seemed not to seek for order, but to allow an overflowering, as if she consciously ventured forever a little farther, a little deeper, into her life in the garden. ("A Curtain" 131)

Jamey is the Other of the writer, the person he understands and becomes in the act of creation at the moment he writes the world without exclusion: "to imagine yourself inside another person [...] is what a story writer does in every piece of work; it is his first step, and his last too, I suppose" (*OWB* 883). Here, as often in her first stories that are variations of sorts on the very fine photographs she took as she was discovering what would become her territory as an artist, Mississippi during the Depression, the Other is black. And the dream that fills him with "a teasing, innocent, flickering and beautiful vision" is the secret of each individual, as elusive and fascinating as a mirage ("A Curtain" 134).

More challenging is Welty's treatment of the garden as a figure of the artist. The garden falls into a trance like a person, as we have seen. It is also the finger that points out Mrs. Larkin's loneliness and makes her realize where her predicament lies: in her indifference to the presence of the Other, in her refusal to see the Other's wonder. Immediately after, she looks at Jamey and sees him at last: "She forced herself to look at him, and noticed him closely for the first time" ("A Curtain" 133). This is precisely the meaning of the shamanic cure: to restore Mrs. Larkin's ability to feel and love, her full awareness of human life, so essential to the artist. The garden represents that side of the artist that through intuition reaches the truth of the heart. The artist is Nature with the Emersonian emphasis on intuition. We remember Jackson Pollock saying, "I am Nature," in his desire to create like Nature, not to represent it (qtd. in Polcari, "L'aboutissement" 92). When, years later, Welty uses again the metaphor of the finger that parts the curtain of green, in "One Time, One Place," to describe her *venue à l'écriture*, she says nothing else:

> In my own case, a fuller awareness of what I needed to find out about people and their lives had to be sought for through another way, through writing stories. But away off one day up in Tishomingo County, I knew this, anyway: that my wish, indeed my continuing passion, would be not to point the finger in judgment but to part a curtain, that invisible shadow that falls between people, the veil of indifference to each other's presence, each other's wonder, each other's human plight. ("One Time, One Place" 354–55)

With this beautiful metaphor, Welty acknowledges her spiritual kinship with the transcendentalism that defined American philosophy at the beginning of the young Republic. Yet, the intriguing introduction of "some outside force" in "A Curtain of Green" definitively marks her as a twentieth-century writer. This is not mysticism, as Michael Kreyling suggests in *Author and Agent* (28–30), but rather, perhaps something in relation with the diffuse pantheism of A. E. Russell, Diarmuid Russell's father, who wrote, "I prefer the spiritual with its admission of incalculable mystery and romance in nature" (qtd. in Kreyling 28). Certainly, something in relation with what Welty knew of shamanism and its beliefs was rooted in the very depths of archaic animism, and even more certainly in relation with modern thinking as Welty knew through her reading of Sir Arthur Eddington's *The Nature of the Physical World*, "a treatise on the philosophic import of modern science" (Marrs, *Eudora* 49). This popular book, which Welty read as early as 1934, and that is still on the shelves of her house in Jackson, brought to the general reader Einstein's theory of relativity. It comforted Welty in her questioning intellectual attitudes, her distrust of the relationship between perception and reality, her suspecting the existence of powerful and invisible forces that give substance to what we know to be largely empty space. More important for her fiction, as Saye Atkinson suggests, were two new concepts: firstly, "no frame of reference offers us a better, clearer, or truer insight into the nature of the world around us than any other," and secondly, the ambiguous nature of time and space, and the challenge it presents to the notion of linear time (10).

Because it illuminates Welty's vision as a writer/photographer and a connoisseur of modern art, *Camellia House*, a photograph of entangled lines and squares, very much an abstract modern painting, which Welty took and used to promote a story from her collection *A Curtain of Green*, will function as a transition between Mrs. Larkin's garden and the Natchez Trace.[5] I remember coming upon this extraordinary photograph in the Welty collection in the archives with the instant awareness that this was Mrs. Larkin's garden and wondering which came first, the photograph or the text. The geometrical pattern with embedded squares, blurred and redoubled by a profusion of lines and shadows, creates a mysterious atmosphere that suggests the idea of a dark entangled garden or of the wilderness in the Trace. It also evokes the overabundant surface of Pollock's paintings in the thirties haunted by shamanism and prefigures the all-over drip paintings of the forties or fifties.

More boldly representative of the impact of scientific discoveries is the treatment of representation in "A Still Moment," first published in 1942. Here, Welty sharpens her reflection on the Other and the visible when it is affected by the presence of an absence, and on the necessary deconstruction in representation. She presents a remarkable construction of the artist and the creative act with three characters that have existed, and stages the action somewhere along the Natchez Trace, the highly emblematic place for American creativity in her fiction. In the center, a triple figure of the artist: Audubon, the official artist, a painter, and a naturalist, and two other figures that represent the darker sides of the artist, his devils. Murrell, the bandit who craves to dominate and tear off the secret of life from his dying victims, announces the figure of the Medusa, and Lorenzo Dow the preacher is convinced in his teleological vision of the world that his mission is to save souls. All three men are consumed by a passion to possess their objects to the point of removing lives or souls. This is what Audubon does when he kills the beautiful white heron the three men are looking at in order to paint it. The painter's meditation on representation asserts deconstruction as an aesthetic necessity, a device Welty had used herself in "A Curtain of Green" to represent shamanism: "He knew that the best he could make would be, after it was apart from his hand, a dead thing and not a live thing, never the essence, only a sum of parts" ("A Still" 239). Faced with this "murder" inextricably bound to creation, Dow, the philosopher—the thinking side of the artist, puts into words the very questions that postmodernists will raise later:

"He could understand God's giving Separateness first and then giving Love to follow and heal in its wonder; but God had reversed this, and given Love first and then Separateness, as though it did not matter to Him which came first. Perhaps it was that God never counted the moments of Time; Lorenzo did that, among his tasks of love. Time did not occur to God" ("A Still" 239). If time no longer prevails, the logical organization of the narrative sequence no longer matters. And indeed, the text is about "a still moment." Moreover, in as much as the necessary similitudes or dissimilitudes disappear, representation can move farther away from the original. Representation becomes, in effect, a reflection on the distorting power of absence over presence; absence is then a kind of echo, not the thing itself.

"A Still Moment" places the reflection on a philosophical level and presents, aesthetically, an avant-garde solution. The artist faced with the impossibility to represent pure essence has become a cliché, as Welty, the fervent reader of Virginia Woolf, knew too well. Here, Welty innovates in comparison with her modernist predecessors when she shows that representation implies a fracture, a construction that is a deconstruction. Moreover, she acknowledges the presence of an absence with the symbol of the dead bird used to represent a bird alive. "Separateness" in this context (Dow's despair) signifies the attempt to reject the principle of causality, the effort to run away from the terrorist world of narrative causality. Audubon's gesture is a liberating gesture. This text dramatizes a darker face of the artist in Welty's fiction and thinking. As suggested in "A Curtain of Green," the artist is a slayer and a healer. The artist with the ruthless gaze who denounces all fallacies, injustices, and horrors is a healer when he brings understanding and solace to bruised hearts and opens up the beauties of the world. But before that, he must have envisioned, and in the act of creation, embodied evil. This is what Virgie Rainey discovers in "The Wanderers": the artist is the Medusa as well as Perseus.

In the last story of *The Golden Apples*, that great book about writing, Welty words a superb representation of the artist through a great classical myth, strong, ambiguous, and rich with infinite developments: Perseus slaying the Medusa. As Reynolds Price insisted in an essay meaningfully entitled "Dodging Apples," "The central myth of the artist is surely not Narcissus but Perseus—with the artist in all roles, Perseus and Medusa and the mirror-shield" (8). Because a myth is outside sequential time and rests on repetition, it is the very image of that escape from the principle of causality. Welty writes, "In Virgie's reach of memory a melody softly lifted, lifted of itself. Every time Perseus struck off the Medusa's head, there was the beat of time, and the melody. Endless the Medusa, and Perseus endless" ("The Wanderers" 555).

Considered as a whole in its richness and diversity, Eudora Welty's production dramatizes, with its themes and techniques, the general philosophical movement of her times as Michel Foucault defined it in *Les mots et les choses*. She was no longer to think in terms of radical difference and "alterity" as was the case in past ages for the demented, for instance, considered as the Other both inside and alien and as such to be kept apart, but to think in terms of likeness, similitudes. Our modern thinking, Foucault argues, becomes a history of likeness, a history of the Same, of what in a culture is both spread apart and kindred and as such to be distinguished through marks and collected into identities. We see here the influence of Claude Lévi-Strauss, the great French anthropologist who invented structuralism to study other cultures and a modern way of apprehending the universal functioning of the human mind. One must study differences first, in order to identify the universal invariants in man's thinking and organizing life in society.

Welty's insistence on the closeness of opposite feelings, on doubling and redoubling, on similarities and persistence in myths and aesthetic productions, in social manners despite apparent differences and in private, political, and historical thinking, attests not only the modernity of her vision, but her theorizing ahead of her times in *The Golden Apples*. She writes, "Virgie never saw it differently, never doubted that all the opposites on earth were close together, love close to hate, living to dying; but of them all, hope and despair were the closest blood—unrecognizable one from the other sometimes, making moments double upon themselves, and in the doubling double again, amending but never taking back" ("Wanderers" 546).

Moreover, the movement towards abstraction visible in the structures of Welty's narratives, in the simplifying of her style reflects a commitment to innovation that, like Matisse in painting, places her among the most influential twentieth-century writers throughout the world. Especially illuminating for Welty is this comment painted on a wall at the entrance of the Matisse permanent collection in the Musée de l'Annonciade in Saint-Tropez: "Matisse is so vast, his work encompasses everything, including the large and colorful early stirrings of abstract art. He remains a powerhouse."

Chapter 9

"MOMENTS OF TRUTH"

Eudora Welty's Humanism (2014)

> He taught her to draw, to work toward and into her pattern,
> not to sketch peripheries.
> —EUDORA WELTY, *THE OPTIMIST'S DAUGHTER* (980)

The title of the conference for which this essay was originally written—"Everybody to their own visioning: Eudora Welty in the Twenty-First Century"—raises two questions that address the critical problem of the role and future of literature.[1] Mrs. Katie Rainey's comment, "Everybody to their own visioning," on the freedom and subjectivity of narrative imagination in a story that plays with visions, invention, distortions, anamorphosis, as well as with bits of facts, the better to mislead the reader to the truth or reality of incidents that may have been fabricated, and all on Halloween, raises the question of the visible and the invisible, of the traces of an absence ("Shower of Gold" 326). Second, the subtitle "Eudora Welty in the Twenty-First Century" asks implicitly: Will Welty's fiction still be read in our new century? And if so, where and by whom? Why and how will her fiction bring pleasure, enchant new generations of readers in a changed world, and still instruct (not teach) through her awareness of what life is about? Will she rank as one of the major writers of world literature? In fact, the critical question is, what can literature do? What future for literature? (Compagnon, Mathé).

    I will attempt to give some elements of response, drawing on the concept of "moments of truth" as Roland Barthes defined it in his 1978 lecture at the College de France, whose title is the first sentence of Marcel Proust's *Remembrance of Things Past*, "Longtemps je me suis couché de bonne heure" ("For a long time I used to go to bed early"). He takes as example two death scenes from *War and Peace* and *Remembrance of Things Past*. Interestingly, Barthes's critical reflection on Proust is valid for Eudora Welty herself. Barthes argues that Proust was led to write *Á la Recherche du Temps Perdu*—a fictionalization of his desire to write—by the death of his mother and, with a departure from his previous texts, to reach the splendid invention of a new form that solved his aesthetic indecision between the essay and the novel. This is not unlike what Welty experienced herself emotionally and intellectually with a comparable creation of new modes of writing.

The gap between *The Bride of the Innisfallen* (published in 1955) and *Losing Battles* (published in 1970) reveals a major crisis in Welty's life and views on writing. Those were years of private grief and loss, as well as years of great political turmoil in the South and the nation at large. The experience of the closeness and ineluctability of death on the one hand and the increasing awareness of the writer's responsibility on the other hand built a new urgency for Welty over those fifteen years that led her to write new forms of fiction. Welty's last texts should be examined together as a new "period" (as we say of painters) in Welty's production, which may be this writer's best claim to the general public's love and deep appreciation in the future. At any rate, they won the aging writer success and a fame she had never known before with the general public. In 1970, *Losing Battles* became Welty's biggest seller and precipitated re-issues of her earlier work. In April of 1972 *The Optimist's Daughter* won the Pulitzer Prize, and in May, Welty received the Gold Medal for Fiction of the National Institute of Arts and Letters. In 1984 *One Writer's Beginnings* won the American Book and National Book Critics Circle awards. All these texts, including the two stories on the civil rights movement and foreword she wrote for *One Time, One Place*, her photographs of Mississippi during the Depression,[2] evidence a departure from previous modes of writing, a renewal of aesthetic achievement, increased ethical concern, and the invention of a form that partakes of pathos for it "expresses and transcends suffering" (as Barthes says of Proust, "Longtemps" 335). Despite technical differences, *Losing Battles*, *The Optimist's Daughter*, and *One Writer's Beginnings* share the use of the long form and great affinities in theme and spirit; they were written, or imagined, at about the same time. They read as variations on the form of the novel, hitherto seldom practiced by Welty, with creativity and the writer's art as dominant themes. Why this new direction for an artist celebrated for the excellence of her short stories? It springs from a desire to reach a wider audience and to address new readers that until then may have been put off by the complexity of her modernist technique. Now the time had come, Welty felt, to write at length about burning issues long known or recently felt, public or private, in a way that would assuage her private grief and awareness of her responsibility to the public. This required inventing new modes of communication: the longer form versus the shorter form.

Whereas the short story as Welty practiced it rests in the power of words and elaborate structures that rush the text through mirror effects, reversals, and condensation—a demanding form that requires insight from the reader—the novel as she saw it rests on the power of emotion, its slower pace allowing for the growth of feelings and relationships, the interplay of memories, digressions, echoes, and uncertainty. As such, the novel appeals to many readers caught up in the emotional atmosphere of a representation of life as they know it, personally and collectively, firsthand or from hearsay. Because it takes time to read a novel, readers slip into a friendly companionable experience that teaches them much about life and themselves. This applies equally to *Losing Battles*, written out of a sense of moral debt to those whose poverty and defiant courage to face life ignited her eye, heart, and imagination when she was working for the WPA; to *The Optimist's Daughter*, written out of grief and mourning and the realization of the end of a world after the death of her mother and two brothers; and to *One Writer's Beginnings*, written out of her probing the roots and sources of her "coming to writing" ("venue à l'écriture"), as Hélène Cixous says.

More importantly, the spirit of that last period is born of Welty's double stance towards writing: a new preoccupation with the origins of her writing, the people, places, private events, and culture that have shaped her mind and heart and now inspire new forms; and her stance as a twentieth-century writer with simplified structures, a shift towards the universal, with myth and drama as "form," and an increased appeal to the reader's intellectual and emotional participation through a move towards scenes—"moments of truth." Barthes coined the phrase and explains, "All at once, literature (for this is what I am talking about) absolutely coincides with an emotional wrench, a scream; deep in his body, as through memory or anticipation the reader experiences separation from the loved one, there rises that transcendental question: what Lucifer created is love and death at the same time" (Barthes, "Longtemps" 343).

In this same lecture, Barthes assigns, among others, two missions to the novel that throw light on what Welty does in her last period. First, the novel, should *represent* activity without *saying* it is a feeling that is on the side of love, pity, compassion. Obliquely, the character's role is to speak his or her emotions, to give free range to pathos, for pathos is "sayable,"—"le pathétique y est énonçable" (344–45). Then, Barthes concludes: "Out of this subjectivity, this intimacy that I have developed for you, the novel should express both the brilliance and suffering of the world, what fascinates me and makes me indignant" (346). In Mathé's words: "To express, from the heart of intimacy and subjectivity, 'the brilliance and suffering of the world'" (19). The result is three strong texts with a renewed emphasis on humanism—"the essential interwovenness of our being in the world," in Maurice Merleau-Ponty's words—built like detective stories with investigation as plot, a genre that Welty liked for the required participation of the reader (qtd. in Felski 104). Briefly summarized, the central investigation turns around the identity of Gloria the orphan in *Losing Battles*, on the truth of the tense relationship of Judge McKelva and his wife, Becky, in *The Optimist's Daughter*, and on the effects of education, parents, and community on the making of a writer in *One Writer's Beginnings*. I will briefly examine "moments of truth" in *Losing Battles* for their innovative techniques and role, then discuss mourning and creativity in *The Optimist's Daughter*, and finally assess the key qualities and emotional axes that define Welty's last period with *One Writer's Beginnings*.

For all its humor and insistence on comedy and farce with recurring characters on and off of the stage, *Losing Battles* is Welty's darkest work because of its contents—bitter social and economic and political issues, rampant racism, and cruel forms of tyranny and betrayal—and because of the experimental technique of a novel written in dialogue that works to reveal the pettiness, selfishness, and cruelty of the individual in society; nevertheless, some redeeming moments of truth bring out the beauty and generosity of the heart. The reader is placed in the position of a theatergoer alert to the least line, called to construct characters and situations as they are gradually exposed and to speculate on the unsaid, for the long form gives the writer free range to indirection. Throughout *Losing Battles*, Welty manipulates suspense with little said and much to be inferred about her characters' involvement and feelings. Hints, chance remarks, or conversations, never given in chronological order, are dropped to the reader as clues to reconstruct events, guess motives, and reveal the roots of passions. And because this is not a true detective story, the novel remains open-ended. What matters is the shared experience of "moments of truth." Welty's technique here is innovative and subversive: she pairs two moments of truth and diverts the pathos of the first into the indignation of the second, the better to denounce the human plight. This technique provides a dramatic frame that creates mystery and suspense and transforms the Vaughn-Beecham-Renfro reunion into a melodramatic family saga, whose exemplarity appeals to the general reader.

I will briefly present three such pairings which turn on love and death, and also on justice, which is specific to this novel; together they create the emotional tempo of the novel as in a piece of music or with a summer storm: first, the intimation of drama with Sam Dale's love letter followed by the watermelon fight; then, violence reaches a crescendo with the dramatization of the dysfunction of justice, with Jack unfairly victimized by Judge Moody, followed by Dearman's murder and the hanging of an innocent black man; finally, emotions subside into a form of peace with religious echoes, with Jack playing the part of a redeemer and endorsing the wisdom of King Solomon.

First pairing: the production of Sam Dale Beecham's love letter to Rachel Sojourner, who has been identified as Gloria's mother, leads to a watermelon fight. The evocation of Rachel dying alone and destitute after leaving her newborn baby on the porch of the home demonstration agent to be brought up in the orphanage suddenly creates pathos, which becomes all the more wrenching as Sam Dale's letter tells such a different story (*LB* 690–92). Welty diverts the double pathos of the dead soldier's letter that was never sent and of the love message unduly kept secret by Granny and Grandpa Vaughn onto the indignation caused by the murderous violence of the aunts against Gloria. Out of her Bible, granny produces a photograph of Sam Dale wearing a soldier's uniform with a barely legible letter scribbled on the back: "a present for our—baby save it for when he gets here. . . . Sincerely your husband Sam Dale Beecham" (703–04). The photograph and a watch were sent to his grandparents after the young man's death in Georgia. The moving link between the two moments of truth—the undelivered letter and the ruthless watermelon fight—pivots on the use and abuse of justice, figuratively and literally. Sam Dale's letter evinces a superior sense of justice since he testifies to and redresses the injustice done to Rachel, and by claiming the child as his and Rachel as his wife, he cleanses her of dishonor. In reverse, the Beecham aunts, who take the letter literally, practice a primitive form of justice. Gloria's vehement refusal to *say* she is a Beecham leads to a dramatic watermelon fight as they force big chunks down Gloria's throat—the objective correlative of the identity they want to impose on her. Rather than a scene of rape, as critics have said, I see here the simulacrum of a ritualized execution, the reenactment of a very ancient form of justice: the sacrifice of a (usually innocent) scapegoat in order to save the community from the danger of chaos and disruption. If we follow the functioning of mimetic desire and of the scapegoat as developed by René Girard, we see how the wives of the Beecham brothers, who have surrendered to the mimetic desire and become Beecham themselves, see Gloria Short, the orphan, as the outsider who threatens the idealized image/myth of a strongly knit, loving family, whose symbol is the "reunion," when she refuses to be Beecham and say it. Gloria accepts her freely chosen status as Jack Renfro's wife—"I'm Renfro now"—and above all claims her self-built identity as an orphan who worked herself out of the orphanage and up through Normal thanks to Miss Julia Mortimer (692). Behind the violence of the scene, there lurks a worse violence, the crime of prevarication, an accusation thrown again and again at this family by

Miss Mortimer (739). A "prevaricator" is first, "one who evades or perverts the truth"; second, "one guilty of a breach of trust"; and third, "one guilty of collusion in a court of law." Granny and Grandpa Vaughn are prevaricators (first and second meanings) for keeping silent about Sam's letter and failing to take care of Rachel and her baby. Nathan is also a prevaricator (third meaning), as the reader will learn.

The next pairing, a dramatic expansion of the first, pivots again on differing notions of justice and concerns Jack Renfro, the eldest of the Renfro tribe, and his uncle Nathan, the eldest of the Beecham tribe. Although both men are guilty of having taken the law into their own hands, Jack remains the perfect hero for his family, while Nathan represents his dark counterpart. Jack's episode is treated at length as pure comedy in the picaresque vein when he tries to retrieve his grandmother's gold wedding ring, "stolen" by Curly Stovall, Banner storekeeper and elected official, in payment for debt. After exchanging blows, Jack inflicts all kinds of ludicrous misadventures on Stovall until he is arrested, tried by Judge Moody, and sentenced to two years' imprisonment at Parchman for "aggravated battery" (*LB* 487). What the family resents—unforgivable from one who grew up in those parts—is that the judge deliberately ignores their pathetic economic status: Jack, seventeen years old, is badly needed at home as head of a family of five young children with a disabled father on a very poor farm perpetually in debt and surviving on barter. Yet, and this is a deeply moving moment of truth, Jack's resentment of the sentence is overcome by gratitude and generosity when the Moodys risk their car up Banner Top to avoid running over Gloria and Lady May. To his mother's amazement and resentment, Jack invites and brings the stranded judge and his wife to the Vaughn reunion because they "saved my wife and baby" (557, 597, 633). As with Sam Dale's letter, the reader experiences "the brilliance and suffering of the world" (Barthes 346).

Conversely, the narration of Nathan Beecham playing the dispenser of justice is reduced to a few words that read like a police report and function like a blow to the reader's mind, the better to arouse his indignation and pity before the iniquity of justice. For the first time at the annual reunion, the enigmatic man of God publicly confesses his double murder in an agony of guilt and remorse: "Uncle Nathan moved; he turned his shaggy head toward Jack and spoke. 'Son, there's not but one bad thing either you or I or anybody else can do. And I already done it. That's kill a man. I killed Mr. Dearman with a stone to his head, and let 'em hang a sawmill n----- for it. After that, Jesus had to hold my hand'" (*LB* 784).

Nathan's story spans the whole range of human behavior from love, family loyalty and heroism, even fanaticism, to cowardice and racism, from self-sacrifice to self-abasement and punishment. Again, Welty denounces the use and abuse of justice figuratively and literally. Horror and pity are born from Nathan's literally taking justice into his own hands and literally inflicting upon himself a primitive punishment of cutting off his sinful right hand in a desperate act of atonement.

Figuratively, the theme of the scapegoat as a form of primitive justice takes on a dramatic evil resonance for its actuality. Far from the parodic watermelon fight with Gloria, the parody of justice that sacrifices an innocent man to restore order because he is black creates indignation in the reader's mind and opens up speculations as to the identity of Gloria's father. Welty's technique of indirection uses ninety-year-old Granny (who remembers and knows everything) to blurt out names and incidents and leaves the reader free to infer that Dearman is the girl's father. Nathan's taking the law into his own hands creates a double reaction: first, indignation, not for Dearman who was a rascal, but for the fate of the innocent African American victimized by racial prejudice when Nathan let racism and biased justice win and hang one of the African American employees Dearman had brought to North Mississippi; second, horror for the literal following of the Scriptures when he cut off his right hand. Pathos becomes sayable when Miss Mortimer's advice offers the possibility of redemption: "'Nathan, even when there's nothing left to hope for, you can start again from there, and go your way and be *good*.' He took her exactly at her word. He's seen the world," says Miss Beulah (*LB* 785). With Nathan's desperate attempt to redress wrongs and stop evil, and with Miss Mortimer restoring hope and self-respect, characters and readers are carried into the heart of humanity, darkness and goodness, suffering and hope, and are shown "the brilliance and suffering of the world," as Barthes said (346). This is *Losing Battles*' greatest "moment of truth," a fulguration "in which an overwhelming emotion is conjoined to a sense of truth, when the coincidence between what is written on the page and what is felt by the reading subject takes place on the level of sympathy and compassion" (about Barthes, Mathé 19). For a writer such as Welty, who lived through times of lynchings in the South and was active in the civil rights movement, the political importance of this episode should not be overlooked; as she told Charles T. Bunting, "There is [. . .] a very telling and essential incident in *Losing Battles* which is told about, that involves a Negro as such. Perhaps you remember" ("'The Interior'" 48).

Welty re-introduces ethics in the last pairing of moments of truth, a fitting end to her novel about the use and abuse of justice. What is at stake is Jack's and Gloria's enhanced vision of life and their new awareness of justice as a private concern—the experience they have gained with the events of the reunion. The time is just after Miss Mortimer's burial the next morning, when Jack and Gloria, alone for the first time and ready to step into their married life, try to express their most intimate vision of life: for Jack a commitment to other people with a chivalric sense of his responsibility, for Gloria a fierce belief in the individual's right to privacy: generosity versus self-centeredness. Brought up without love or family, educated to become a teacher, the orphan has built herself on her determination to be an independent individual refusing any form of domination unless freely chosen. Gloria's sense of a double betrayal has fostered resentment: her parents have betrayed her by abandoning her, yet she justifies her own betrayal of the high expectations and demanding care of Miss Mortimer, whose "dearest wish was to pass on the torch to me" (*LB* 679). That meant celibacy for women teachers in those days. Falling in love and marrying Jack Renfro during her first year of teaching forced Gloria to resign the job that gave her independence and to live and have her baby with the Renfros while Jack was at Parchman. "I'll just keep right on thinking about the future," she tells Jack as she presents her dream (877):

> "Look! We're to ourselves, Jack," said Gloria.
> He drew her close and led her a little distance away, toward the edge of the bank....
> "Oh, this is the way it could always be. It's what I've dreamed of," Gloria said, reaching both arms around Jack's neck. "I've got you all by myself, Jack Renfro. Nobody talking, nobody listening, nobody coming—nobody about to call you or walk in on us—there's nobody left but you and me, and nothing to be in our way."
> [...] "If we could stay this way always—build us a little two-room house, where nobody in the world could find us—" (873–74)

On the other hand, Jack's strength comes from the love of his family and a high moral sense of loyalty and responsibility as the eldest. His background experience is of the disfunction of the law and the inequity of judgment and penalty. Instead of despising Nathan for the murder of Dearman, also committed in defense of the family, Jack pities his uncle for his severe self-punishment (amputation of the right hand and solitude) and offers love and compassion in a Christ-like statement: by going to the pen when he did not deserve it, he, Jack, has redeemed Nathan.

The heroic theme of taking the place of another, dying for another, with many public and private instances in life and literature, is for twenty-first-century readers a great claim for their love of the book. Welty's control of pathos here is of the finest, as it is throughout the dialogue between husband and wife that follows, which further exposes the pathos of their differing visions. Jack's delicate kindness, he thinks, to his wife mourning the death of Miss Mortimer meets with her resentful brooding born of guilt when she explains Miss Mortimer's idealistic dream of education for Mississippi. The note of resentment, stubborn selfishness and narrowness of mind is unmistakable:

> "Miss Julia Mortimer didn't want anybody left in the dark, not about anything. She wanted everything brought out in the wide open, to see and be known. She wanted people to spread out their minds and their hearts to other people, so they could be read like books."
> "She sounds like Solomon," said Jack. "Like she ought to have been Solomon."
> "No, people don't want to be read like books." (875)

Jack's response comes later when he sees his beloved horse running in the pasture below. Jack is overjoyed to see the horse alive when his parents had told him Dan had to be sold and killed. When called, the horse does not seem to remember Jack:

> "He's fickle," Gloria told Jack. "Dan is fickle. And now he's Curly's horse and he's let you know it. Oh, Jack, I know you'd rather he was rendered!"
> "No, I rather he's alive and fickle than all mine and sold for his hide and tallow," said Jack. (878)

This is a rewriting of King Solomon's judgment (I Kings 3:16–28), textually prepared by Jack's previous remark about Miss Mortimer. Gloria speaks like the mother of the dead child, whereas Jack speaks like the mother of the living one. The blinding truth moves the reader to compassion for Gloria for if she lives by revenge and resentment and has no heart, it is because her life as an orphan has maimed her. To open eyes, heart, and mind, love is necessary just as love and respect of the Other are necessary to a fair sense of justice that sees in every individual of all races and standings a human person whose rights must be enforced. Jack's new responsibility and battle is the education of Gloria's heart and mind—to help his wife put her indomitability to the service of others and justice and forget revenge and resentment.

With her last fiction, *The Optimist's Daughter*, Welty pursues her quest for the essence of creativity and her search for patterns. Sprung as a cathartic work, written out of intense grief after the deaths of her mother and brother,

Edward, within days of each other in January 1966, *The Optimist's Daughter* (draft completed in 1967, published as a story in the *New Yorker* in March 1969, then revised, expanded, and published as a novel in 1972) is unique in Welty's *oeuvre* because of her strong personal investment and her interruption of the writing of *Losing Battles* in order to create a story dramatizing mourning and the work of mourning; it also represents a shift towards ontological issues that require new technique. There is unmistakable kinship between *The Optimist's Daughter* and two major twentieth-century works noted for their avant-garde technique, a novel and a film, which also deal with the issues of dying and death, the difficult relationship between husband and wife, parents and children, and a reevaluation of life and the passing of time: Virginia Woolf's *To the Lighthouse* and Ingmar Bergman's *Wild Strawberries*. Welty had read and reread Woolf's novel written in similar circumstances by an artist obsessed with her parents (Woolf, *Diary* 208). Echoes in technique and theme make me think that Welty, "a constant moviegoer," may have seen *Wild Strawberries*, considered by many to be Bergman's masterpiece (Welty, "A Visit" 169). Visual memory may have inspired her writing as she explains to Bill Ferris, for instance, about film technique, so close to what Bergman does in *Wild Strawberries* ("A Visit" 168–69).

In *The Optimist's Daughter*, the dream of the confluence of the Ohio and Mississippi Rivers is aesthetically and philosophically the key episode, a view later corroborated by Welty herself in *One Writer's Beginnings*. Confluence includes past, present, and future and provides a pattern for her vision of the essence of creativity born of the tragic relationship human beings entertain with life and death within a community founded on antagonistic egos. Three "moments of truth" epitomize beauty, love, and suffering when, in the face of death and loss, the spiritual world of creation soars up and takes its flight. The first moment finds its roots in the very ancient tradition of carnival, the second in the lyricism of celebration, and the third in mourning the Dead.

The pathos of the Mardi Gras episode on the night Clint McKelva dies is born of the clash between the festive riotous atmosphere in New Orleans, which celebrates a very ancient propitiatory rite of life against death with great artistry, and Laurel's grieving and between Clint's death and Fay's frustration and inability to understand the meaning of what excites her longing and resentment—masked revelers dressed up as skeletons or white figures of death. "Death in its reality passed her right over," Laurel reflects (*OD* 963).

The second moment of truth celebrates spring in Mississippi, with Laurel's awareness that it is her farewell to the South. The loveliness of the scene in the garden after the burial, with delicate additions to the setting with light and sound effects, "the porcelain light of the dogwood" in bloom, the red cardinals flying at "their tantalized reflections," and the repeated song of the mockingbird, turn the acid gossip of the ladies into a last homage to Becky's garden (*OD* 947, 954). As Becky's friends comment on Fay, the Judge, and their marriage, and on the behavior of everybody at the funeral, "Laurel went on pulling weeds. Her mother's voice came back with each weed she reached for, and its name with it" (947). The garden has become a place of commemoration.

The third moment of truth is an illumination that brings together love and death at the end of a tempestuous night, the time for revelation; as Max Milner writes, beyond physical darkness and that which, in reverse, favors the burst of color, "darkness represents what keeps man's spirit open to those areas of the self which light alone cannot account for" (236). For the first time in years, Laurel realizes that her deepest grief is not for the death of her father and her mother, but for the death of the young man whose love taught her how to become herself—an artist.

> A flood of feeling descended on Laurel. She . . . wept in grief for love and for the dead. She lay there with all that was adamant in her yielding to this night, yielding at last. Now all she had found had found her. The deepest spring in her heart had uncovered itself, and it began to flow again.
> *If Phil could have lived—*
> But Phil was lost. Nothing of their life together remained except in her own memory; love was sealed away into its perfection and had remained there.
> *If Phil had lived—*(*OD* 977)

Grief is part of the flow of life, and the living must never stop crying in pity and love for those who died young, demanding their rightful tears. Overcome with grief and guilt, Laurel falls asleep and has a dream that restores her dead husband's legitimate place by her side, along with Phil's active and endless role in her life as an artist. Likewise, what she has learned and felt from her dead parents is forever an active and creative part of herself since the living and the dead all participate in that confluence that feeds and flows endlessly on the stream of life. The dream has restored the pattern of her life: two married couples *en vis à vis*, the parents, Clint and Becky, and the children, Laurel and Phil. Laurel feels pardoned and elated with the joy of creation that will be hers for the rest of her life. I would like to stress the similarity of Laurel's "moment of truth" to Lily Briscoe's "vision" at the end of *To the Lighthouse*. After the chaos of World War I and three deaths in the family, the young painter, unsure of her talent, returns to a portrait of the Ramsay family, a mother and child picture with James and Mrs. Ramsay, begun ten years earlier and left unfinished. Before her canvas, deeply grieving over the death of Mrs. Ramsey, Lily watches in the distance Mr. Ramsay sailing at last to the lighthouse with James and Cam, and as they reach the lighthouse, she sees how the father's benevolent trust has won the affection of the adolescents. In a flash, Lily Briscoe understands her mistake and her inability to finish the painting: because she had eliminated the figure of Mr. Ramsay, her picture could not be completed. A final red stroke across her painting links everyone, the picture is finished, and Lily Briscoe has become a good abstract painter—"I have had my vision," she thinks (209).

Laurel's dream of confluence is one symbol of what the cathartic writing of *The Optimist's Daughter* has meant for Welty as a bereaved person; it is also part of her self-discovery as a writer, for confluence is what feeds her imagination, the source of everything in her fiction. One more discovery is necessary to complete the work of mourning: detachment and the functioning of memory. With one of her finest moments of truth, the writer ends her novel. During their last confrontation in the house, which Laurel is about to leave forever to Fay, the two women oppose two conceptions of life: time, and memory. Facing the aggressive, arrogant, heartless widow, Laurel has the revelation of the true nature of the past and memory and their relations to objects. Objects are not the past. Laurel has no need for objects to remind her of the past, just as she had known she could *see* her mother's garden in Chicago:

> The past is like [Father], impervious, and can never be awakened. It is memory that is the somnambulist. [. . .] The memory can be hurt, time and again—but in that may lie its final mercy. As long as it's vulnerable to the living moment, it lives for us, and while it lives, and while we are able, we can give it up its due. [. . .] Memory lived not in initial possession but in the freed hands, pardoned and freed, and in the heart that can empty but fill again, in the patterns restored by dreams. (991–92)

The Optimist's Daughter marks a further step in Welty's conceptualization of the origins of a work of art, the necessary detachment from the material world, and a stepping up towards the abstract world of suffering and joy—the realm of memory as a creative power necessary to celebrate those we love, one function of the novel for Barthes.

What makes the artist so free and daring, Welty asks, with Virginia Woolf and others? Welty, who herself had lost her father, inspirer, and supporter, at twenty-one, says that the experience of mourning is that necessary step in the artist's development. Mourning for the loss of what is very close to the artist's heart, what he feels has nourished and shaped his sensibilities, imagination, and awareness of the Other produces the vision that he tries to make visible in his art. Be they writers, painters, dancers, sculptors, or musicians, the loss of loved ones, native land, or childhood and youth makes them feel the urge to recapture what has been lost through a search of forms, with words, sounds, colors, and shapes as tools, a search that in the twentieth century often led to the abstract.

One Writer's Beginnings dramatizes this search. In spite of its tone, humor, and apparent simplicity, the book addresses serious issues that invite the reader to probe under the surface and reflect on the South in the 1920s and '30s, on the American imagination, life, and literature. I propose to read this writer's autobiography of sorts as a loose rewriting of Plato's Allegory of the Cave, since the writer's aim is to reach the highest truth through perceptions of ordinary life. Section 10 of "Finding a Voice," the book's last part, gives a clue to what seems to be Welty's enterprise. It represents the stepping out of the cave and its illusions to enter the world of ideas. Here, the lofty conception of the writer's mission is indeed to help readers accede to superior vision, the vision of truth and living knowledge through a work of art: "Experiences too indefinite of outline in themselves to be recognized for themselves connect and are identified as a larger shape. And suddenly a light is thrown back, as when your train makes a curve, showing that there has been a mountain of meaning rising behind you on the way you've come, is rising there still, proven now through retrospect" (*OWB* 933).

The first two parts of the book, "Listening" and "Learning to See," with remembered sensations, events, and various memories of her life as a child with her parents and family, are like the shadows seen on a blank wall by the chained prisoners. They are insubstantial like shadows, mere illusions and not the things themselves. But when the writer starts discussing her fiction, when her creative power gives her text the truth, force, and reality of art, we are no longer inside the cave, but outside in the "real" world of ideas, "shapes." The vision of the writer delivers the reader from the fragmented and disconnected illusions of the world he lives in but does not understand and provides instead the enlightenment that creates order, connection, patterns, and meaning.

Before quoting the full text of Laurel's dream to end *One Writer's Beginnings*, Welty explains her discovery of "*confluence*, which of itself exists as a reality and a symbol in one. It is the only kind of symbol that for me as a writer has any weight, testifying to the pattern, one of the chief patterns, of human experience" (947). Confluence is the ultimate pattern, a reservoir where the writer finds her material, a wealth of feelings, that is to say human experience, where good and evil, death and life are inextricably linked and close, where memory plays the somnambulist to hurt again and again and provide patterns of life restored by dreams, where time represents the whole tragedy of human life through aporia; in the human experience there is the inexorability of time passing as part of the great flow of life, yet also time moving forward and backward, time arrested, time proclaiming the endless presence of an absence. This movement beautifully defines the role of literature in making the reader an active participant as he projects himself into the shared experience: "Each of us is moving, changing, with respect to others. As we discover, we remember; remembering, we discover; and most intensely do we experience this when our separate journeys converge. Our living experience at those meeting points is one of the charged dramatic fields of fiction" (*OWB* 946).

To explore the world of shapes and ideas which Welty's mind envisioned when traveling is the reader's and critic's task. Welty's fiction evidences a search for the form most appropriate to represent a specific moment of the human experience, and her description of the movement of her texts strangely brings to mind twentieth-century abstract painting: "It is our inward journey that leads us through time—forward or back, seldom in a straight line, most often spiraling" (*OWB* 946). At the same time, paradoxically, but true to Welty's deep humanism, this abstraction is beautifully enhanced by a touch of lyrical poetry, very present in her last period, with evocations of night, skies, and gardens. Yet if close reading of the intricate patterns and structures of her stories is required from readers and critics to discover their full meaning, Welty never carried her experimentation too far; her imagination colored her writing with generous humanism, and she was always aware that her aim was to move and instruct through laughter and indignation, fantasy and poetry. Her fiction affects the reader as Paul Klee affects the viewer. Never a cubist painter, Paul Klee favored a delicate palette, with poetic interplay of colors, a fanciful or humorous touch ("A Young Lady's Adventure," 1922), an occasional strong note ("Fire at Full Moon," 1933). In March 1930, there was a show of his work at the Museum of Modern Art, when Welty was in New York. Both artists continue to appeal to the deepest springs of the mind, heart, and imagination.

Losing Battles, *The Optimist's Daughter*, and *One Writer's Beginnings* constitute the crowning achievement of Welty's career as a writer and give her a well-deserved place in world literature. With the long form, her creative imagination could probe deeply and widely the many layers of humanity within her experience, and the detective novel, a literary genre whose popularity has never waned among readers from all backgrounds since the nineteenth century, was the appropriate choice of a youthful, unconventional writer to reach a wider audience with the fictionalization of what had become her major project: the construction on a larger scale of the world of the people that had fed her vision, emotions, and creative spirit—an act of celebration and commemoration. With this project, Welty reaches the very foundation of literature, the celebration of dead heroes, great or small, and she grasps the very essence of humanity, for what characterizes man is the commemoration of man. The texts of that last period reflect a widening in the scope of the writer's subject. In *Losing Battles*, Welty starts from a restricted group, the people remotest from her young experience who nevertheless triggered her writing spirit, and she centers her novel on family commemoration and celebration, with the annual Vaughn-Beecham-Renfro reunion. *The Optimist's Daughter* dramatizes a private experience shared by many readers, the death of loved relatives, "the feeling of the daughter who can't help, [...] who wants to understand and help," as she told Patricia Wheatley ("Eudora Welty" 139). *One Writer's Beginnings*, as I have argued elsewhere, focuses on the quintessential relationship Welty entertains with the political, and, paradoxically, defines and celebrates American mythologies rather than Welty's private ones, with an emphasis on the general and universal.[3] Here, Welty asserts that the function of the novel is transmission.

AFTERWORD

FRANÇOIS PITAVY

When staying in Charlottesville on a grant from the American Council of Learned Societies, I remember one day bringing back home, from the Alderman Library at the University of Virginia where I worked on Faulkner's papers, a Welty novel a UVA professor had recommended to me. Danièle not only took great pleasure reading it, but decided she would write her "thèse de Doctorat" on Welty. Which she did, beautifully, becoming the French specialist of Welty's fiction.

She asked Eudora whether she could meet her, which was graciously accepted. Staying in Jackson several times to work in the archives and meet people who knew Eudora, Danièle was also received at Welty's home, Eudora even suggesting a couple of times that I join them. I remember long friendly discussions they had, and one day Eudora invited us for dinner at an elegant restaurant she often patronized. I will never forget entering, Welty at my arm, everybody watching us. I was impressed, and proud, though I was just Danièle's husband for the occasion. Afterward, we had whisky and discussions at her home, and she even graciously inscribed a couple of her novels for me. She knew how to make one at ease in no time, loved to tell all sorts of stories, laughed generously at anecdotes, no different from the ones she tells in her fiction.

Over the years, Welty always expressed her appreciation of Danièle's work on her, which made for their easy relationship, which ended only with Welty's death.

This volume tells of Danièle's fine understanding and love of Eudora Welty's work. The only regret Danièle had was the lack of popular recognition of her fiction in France. It seems that Gallimard, the French editor of Faulkner and so many American novelists, appears not to acknowledge her in their prestigious Pléiade series, at least for a time, apparently for the lack of a French specialist.

NOTES

PREFACE

1. "On My First Becoming Acquainted with Eudora Welty and Her Work," p. 77.
2. "Eudora Welty's *Légion d'honneur* Award Ceremony," p. 3.
3. "Eudora Welty's *Légion d'honneur* Award Ceremony," pp. 3–5.
4. Chouard, p. 24.
5. Atwood, p. 229; Milton, p. 168.
6. "Thoughts upon Receiving the *Légion d'honneur* Award," p. 26.
7. "Words into Fiction," p. 134.
8. "Thoughts upon Receiving the *Légion d'honneur* Award," p. 28.

INTRODUCTION

1. Benvenuto Cellini, *Perseus with the Head of Medusa*, circa 1545–1554.
2. Citations of the stories of *A Curtain of Green*, *The Wide Net*, *The Golden Apples*, and *The Bride of the Innisfallen* follow the texts collected in *Stories, Essays, and Memoir*.

CHAPTER 1: TECHNIQUE AS MYTH: THE STRUCTURE OF *THE GOLDEN APPLES* (1979)

1. "Variations sur un sujet," p. 370: "You noticed, one does not write with light on a dark background; the alphabet of the stars, alone, is marked in this way, uncompleted or interrupted; man pursues black against white." All translations of French texts are by Pitavy-Souques.
2. When Charles T. Bunting asked Eudora Welty about the genesis of *The Golden Apples* and suggested that this book, like her novels, began as short stories, she made this fine point: "In *The Golden Apples* they exist on their own as short stories; they have independent lives. They don't have to be connected, but I think by being connected there's something additional coming from them as a group with a meaning of its own." Earlier in the same interview, she had said: "I mostly loved working on the connected stories, finding the way

things emerged in my mind and the way one thing led to another; the interconnections of the book fascinated me" ("'The Interior World'" 43).

3. For a discussion of the criticism, see Thomas L. McHaney, "Eudora Welty and the Multitudinous Golden Apples," *Mississippi Quarterly*, 26 (Fall 1973), pp. 589–624, especially n.3, pp. 590–91. For a discussion of mythology, see Harry C. Morris, "Eudora Welty's Use of Mythology," *Shenandoah*, 6 (Spring 1955), 34–40 and Thomas McHaney. [See also Rebecca Mark, *The Dragon's Blood: Feminist Intertextuality in Eudora Welty's* The Golden Apples, UP of Mississippi, 2013.]

4. In a conversation, 18 January 1978, Eudora Welty herself confirmed to me that "June Recital" was the nucleus of *The Golden Apples* and the story she had written first. [See also Polk, 372.]

5. This is part of the long note to the first poem of *The Wind among the Reeds* ["The Hosting of the Sidhe"]. Here, as in "The Song of Wandering Aengus," Yeats is speaking of the same "tribes of the Goddess Danu that are in the waters."

6. In the note on "The Song of Wandering Aengus," Yeats wrote: "The poem was suggested to me by a Greek folk song; but the folk belief of Greece is very like that of Ireland, and I certainly thought, when I wrote it, of Ireland, and of the spirits that are in Ireland" (806).

7. See Sartre, *L'Etre et le Néant*, pp. 310–64, 410.

8. Very significant is Welty's review of *A Haunted House and Other Short Stories*: "Mirrors for Reality," *New York Times Book Review*, 16 April 1944, p. 3. [Reprinted in *A Writer's Eye: Collected Book Reviews*, pp. 25–9.] Most of what Welty writes about reflections and dream effects in Virginia Woolf's stories could apply to her own fiction. Besides stressing the affinity between these two writers, the review shows how much aware of her own technical research Eudora Welty was early in her career.

CHAPTER 2: A BLAZING BUTTERFLY:
THE MODERNITY OF EUDORA WELTY (1987)

1. A shorter version of this essay was read in Jackson, Mississippi, at the 1984 Southern Literary Festival honoring the seventy-fifth birthday of Eudora Welty.

2. From "Le Dessous de Carte d'une Partie de Whist" in *Les Diaboliques* (1874), available at www.gutenberg.org ("Beneath the Cards in a Game of Whist," in *Diaboliques: Six Tales of Decadence*). "Are you making fun of us, sir, with such a story? Isn't there, madame, a kind of tulle called illusion tulle?"

3. The word *modernité* was coined in 1849 by Chateaubriand and used, despairingly, to oppose a romantic landscape with storm and gothic architecture to modern bureaucracy. A few years later, Baudelaire took up the word to praise Constantin Guys, "the painter of modern life," for his desire to record moments and scenes from contemporary life. He valued this painter's efforts to extract poetry from fashion, eternal beauty from transience. *Curiosités Esthétiques*, "De l'héroïsm de la vie modern," p. 194. See also Baudelaire, *The Painter of Modern Life*.

4. For detailed discussion of postmodernist fiction, see Couturier, *Representation and Performance*, especially in the first part of Courtier's explanation of the theory in his essay

"Presentation of the Topic" and Regis Durand's brilliant essay, "The Disposition of the Familiar." This essay is centered on Henry James and Walter Abish and started my own reflections on the unfamiliar in Welty.

5. Durand quotes from a typed version of Walter Abish's paper that was circulated at the Nice, France, conference on postmodern fiction, April 1982.

6. This is also Chester E. Eisinger's perceptive reading of the scene, although I think the scene too "framed" in the threatening sense of the word to be truly pastoral. See Eisinger, p. 10.

CHAPTER 3: A REREADING OF EUDORA WELTY'S "FLOWERS FOR MARJORIE" (2018)

1. Qtd. in *Cubism* by Edward F. Fry, Thames and Hudson, 1966, pp. 165–66.

2. Here in *Dragon's Blood*, Mark, is "following Kristeva's analyses" (15). See Mark's introduction for a discussion of intertextuality.

3. For a detailed analysis of *The Ponder Heart* as dystopia, see Danièle Pitavy-Souques, "'Blacks and Other Very Dark Colors': William Faulkner and Eudora Welty," *Faulkner and His Contemporaries: Faulkner and Yoknapatawpha*, edited by Joseph R. Urgo and Ann J. Abadie, UP of Mississippi, 2004, pp. 132–54.

4. Permission to quote from the manuscript of "Flowers for Marjorie" is granted by Eudora Welty, LLC.

5. Interestingly, Welty gave a clue in her interview "Fiction as Event" that this coming out of the subway between two mother figures was her only striking visual memory of the story (24).

CHAPTER 4: OF HUMAN, ANIMAL, AND CELESTIAL BODIES IN WELTY'S "CIRCE" (2005)

1. [An early version of "Circe," "Put Me in the Sky!" was published in *Accent*, Autumn 1949, while Welty was traveling in Europe on a Guggenheim Fellowship (14 Oct. 1949–June 1950). Welty significantly revised the story as "Circe" for the 1955 collection *The Bride of the Innisfallen*; this is the story that Pitavy-Souques analyzes. See Chengges, "Textual Variants in 'Put Me in the Sky!' and 'Circe,'" *Eudora Welty Newsletter*, vol. 23, no. 2, 1999, pp. 11–27, and Marrs, *One Writer's Imagination*, pp. 145–48.]

2. The very ambiguity of the episode suggests the word "frontier" as François Hartog explores it in connection with the mythical character of Ulysses; see *Mémoire d'Ulysse, Récits sur la frontière en Grèce ancienne*.

3. At the time I interviewed Eudora Welty about "Circe" (Easter 1987), *Welty: A Life in Literature* with Albert J. Devlin and Peggy Prenshaw's interview (22 September 1986) had not yet come out (Welty, "A Conversation"). Both times, Eudora Welty presented "Circe" with similar wording except for that one sentence in her conversation with me: "What is it like to be immortal?" With it she was moving from theme into technique; this is what started my reflection for this essay.

4. I borrow this neologism from Jean-Claude Beaune, whose essay on decreation, "De l'absence matérielle à l'abîme symbolique," helped me for this reading of "Circe."

5. Eudora Welty may have chosen the constellation of Cassiopeia for its link with the myth of Perseus, so central to her previous book, *The Golden Apples*. Cassiopeia is the proud mother of Andromeda, and her torment was to see her beloved daughter tied to a rock and be devoured by a sea monster. Fortunately, Perseus rescued her. Another reason, I suspect, is that the constellation is associated with the South and thus emphasizes the southern location of Circe's island.

CHAPTER 5: "THE FICTIONAL EYE": EUDORA WELTY'S RETRANSLATION OF THE SOUTH (2000)

1. Circa 1935. Welty bibliographer Noel Polk notes that although a version of this story was included in the preliminary collection of typescripts for her first collection, *A Curtain of Green*, Welty told him it was never intended for publication in that book. It is not included in *Collected Stories* or in *Stories, Essays, and Memoir*. See Polk, p. 376.

2. For further references to the fascism of language in Welty's fiction, see Pitavy-Souques's "A Blazing Butterfly," elsewhere in this volume.

3. See Pitavy-Souques, "Le Voyageur de l'humanunité: Eudora Welty photographe."

4. "Under the red dust that coated [Jack's shoes] the uppers were worn nearly through. Their soles were split. The strings hung heavy with dust and weeds and their own extra knots" (*Losing Battles* 505).

5. The cover of the 1983 Harvest paperback edition of *Collected Stories* shows a painting by Barry Moser of Welty's photograph of "Baby Bluebird, Bird Pageant," *OTOP*, 94.

6. [See also Plate 1. in *Photographs*.]

7. This piece, originally entitled "Poor Eyes," was heavily revised from its *New Yorker* version to become the novel with the same title published in 1972 by Random House.

8. [See in particular pp. xx and xxi and perhaps Plates 216–22 in *Photographs* (1989).]

CHAPTER 6: PRIVATE AND POLITICAL THOUGHTS IN *ONE WRITER'S BEGINNINGS* (2001)

1. [Pitavy-Souques may be referring to Bloom's *The Western Canon* (1994) where of the twenty-nine authors discussed, only Jane Austen, George Eliot, Emily Dickinson, and Virginia Woolf are included. Bloom's *How to Read and Why* (2001, the year this essay was first published) includes only Flannery O'Connor, Emily Dickinson, Emily Brontë, Jane Austen, and Toni Morrison of the forty-one authors.]

2. [First published in 2001, "Private and Political Thoughts in *One Writer's Beginnings*" reflects the contemporary critical concerns.]

3. Welty failed to convince Frank Lentricchia, at least, who called her "the Cumaean Sibyl of the new regionalism" as late as 1989 (qtd. in Brantley 120). For a discussion of Ruth Vande Kieft's defense of Welty, see also Brantley, ibid.

4. In *One Writer's Beginnings*, Eudora Welty says that she wrote out of anger just once, after the murder of Medgar Evers: "There was one story that anger certainly lit the fuse of" (882). Nevertheless, controlled indignation before injustice and prejudice has always been present in her work.

5. Harriet Pollack, "Photographic Convention and Story Composition: Eudora Welty's Use of Detail, Plot, Genre, and Expectation from 'A Worn Path' through *The Bride of the Innisfallen*" and "Eudora Welty's 'Too Far to Walk It': Out Farther Still? A Correction."

6. I am indebted to Françoise Palleau's excellent study of Cather in her unpublished dissertation (Paris III Sorbonne Nouvelle, 1995) for drawing my attention to Krauss.

7. [See, for example, Piet Mondrian, *Composition No. 10*, 1939–1942.]

8. With more emotion and at greater length, Ellen Glasgow acknowledges a similar debt. Yet her moving portrayal turns her black mammy into a fictional character as opposed to a real person, thus intimating the faintest touch of condescension (*The Woman Within*, p. 18).

9. Willa Cather in a letter to *Commonweal*, November 23, 1927. Deep affinities between the two writers rather than Cather's influence of Welty seem a more appropriate explanation for *One Writer's Beginnings*. From what she said to John Griffin Jones, Welty did not realize Cather's possible influence upon her work before she reread Cather's work for an essay she contributed to the Cather centennial celebration in 1974 ("Eudora Welty" 324). Welty later included this essay under the title "The House of Willa Cather" in *The Eye of the Story*.

10. Welty closely associates artistic pleasure, such as going to the theater or writing, with guilt. When her mother sent her along with her father to see *Blossom Time*, young Eudora experienced guilt in spite of all the excitement and wonder: "I could hardly bear my pleasure for my guilt" (*OWB* 861). Likewise, when as a twenty-something woman Welty left her mother at home and journeyed to New York in an effort to sell her stories, she felt guilt at "being the loved one gone" even as she experienced the "joy ... connected with writing" (*OWB* 937). Both experiences imply the guilt of severing ties with the mother; this theme recurs not only in *One Writer's Beginnings* but also in many Welty stories.

11. On Miss Eckhart in "June Recital" as an example of the experience of creativity, see my essay "Watchers and Watching."

12. From the Greek *kritein*, to discern, as in *secret* and *critic*, and also *crime, certitude*, and *crisis*—a whole semantic network that binds together the strange avenues of this unique book.

CHAPTER 7: EUDORA WELTY AND THE MERLIN PRINCIPLE:
ASPECTS OF STORY-TELLING IN *THE GOLDEN APPLES* (2009)

1. Qtd. in *Cubism* by Edward F. Fry, Thames and Hudson, 1966, pp. 165–66.

2. Just as Faulkner was influenced by American and European writers of the preceding generation (Conrad, Joyce, Proust, for instance) so was Welty, for she is heir to such great women writers as Edith Wharton, Willa Cather, Virginia Woolf, and to male writers such as Yeats, the Joyce of *Dubliners* and *Ulysses*, and the Kafka of *The Trial* (not to mention the

nineteenth century's Hawthorne, Poe, Whitman, Melville, Twain, and James). As Reynolds Price suggested, in her turn, Welty made it possible for such a great writer as Toni Morrison to write the way she writes ("A Form of Thanks" 125–26).

3. [Welty probably read the stories of Merlin the magician, Uthur Pendragon, Arthur, and Merlin's creation of the Round Table in volume 5, *Every Child's Story Book* of *Our Wonder World*, pp. 179–85.] The figure of Merlin has never ceased to be alive in Great Britain and Ireland together with Vivianne and Morgana—the Lady of the Lake—as nineteenth- and twentieth-century well-known poems, engravings and paintings attest. In the United States, the figure of Merlin appears in different guises in popular books, including Twain's *A Connecticut Yankee in King Arthur's Court*. Welty's visual mind may have remembered Gustave Doré's engraving "Merlin Advising King Arthur" [1867, for Tennyson's *Idylls of the King*]. Among more contemporary books that may have attracted Welty's attention (she was a great lover of detective novels) is Raymond Chandler's *The Lady in the Lake* (1943), which revolves around a set of mysterious deaths in the San Bernardino Mountains. Here, the symbolic Arthur, questing for the Grail of truth and adhering to his own chivalric code, is Chandler's hero Philip Marlowe. Between 1938 and 1958, T. H. White published five volumes featuring Merlin, revised and gathered in *The Once and Future King*. And just at the time Welty was beginning to write *The Golden Apples*, C. S. Lewis, the great Oxford professor of medieval literature, published the third book in his *Space Trilogy*, *That Hideous Strength* (1946), in which the figure of Merlin Abroisius appears.

4. The etymology of hideous (Webster) is the Old French *hide* meaning terror, and the word suggests 1. "offensive to the sight": ugly, frightening, monstrous, 2. "offensive to the mind of the moral sense": hateful, shocking, embarrassing, ludicrous, dismaying. In relation to King MacLain and the Spanish guitarist, the word represents fascination, that awful power of the Medusa at the heart of creation and the world.

5. For a detailed analysis, see "Technique as Myth" in this volume.

6. In *The Great Gatsby*, Nick Carraway says, "Gradually I became aware of the old island here that flowered once for Dutch sailors' eyes—a fresh, green breast of the new world" (156). See also Pitavy-Souques, "Private and Political Thoughts in *One Writer's Beginnings*" in this volume.

7. At that time of writing "Sir Rabbit," Welty and Robinson were drafting together a screenplay of *The Robber Bridegroom*. A letter from Robinson to Welty suggesting that they invite Cocteau to film their "collaborated" screenplay is illuminating in the present context. See Pollack, "Reading John Robinson," p. 179.

8. In a similar, much earlier, sculptor's invention, Eve is represented in a snake-like position as she reaches toward the apple, which suggests she has absorbed fascination and become temptress herself. Eudora Welty visited the Cathedral of Autun in Burgundy several times after 1949, but when writing "Sir Rabbit," she may have had in mind a photograph of this well-known low-relief, Gislebertus' *Temptation of Eve*, circa 1130.

9. Welty may have seen some of the Maillol exhibitions (with catalogue) before she wrote "Sir Rabbit": 1925, the first major exhibition of Maillol's sculptures and drawings in the USA, The Buffalo Fine Arts Academy Albright Gallery, Buffalo, NY; in 1927, Memorial Art Gallery, Rochester, NY; January–February 1933, *Sculptures by Maillol*, Brummer Gallery, New York; 1939, *Exhibition Aristide Maillol*, Buchholz Gallery, New York; December 1940,

Aristide Maillol, The Arts Club of Chicago; January 1942, *Aristide Maillol: prints, sculpture*, Weihe Gallery, New York; 1945, *Aristide Maillol*, The Buffalo Fine Arts, Albright Arts Gallery, NY and in June, Buchholz Gallery, New York.

10. Brancusi first exhibited at *The Armory Show*, New York, 1913. The statue of *Leda* on her revolving pedestal [1926] is part of the second and highly successful exhibition of Brancusi's work at the Brummer Gallery, New York, 1933. *Leda* was exhibited again in *Cubism and Abstract Art*, Museum of Modern Art, New York, 1936.

11. Through Marcel Duchamp, already living in New York, Brancusi was acquainted with Calder's experiments with mobiles.

12. Cocteau's latest film then was *Beauty and the Beast*, released in October 1946 in France and in September 1947 in the USA. John Robinson must have felt the artistic and political kinship between Cocteau's filmic technique and Welty's technique in *The Robber Bridegroom* and in her recent stories: similarities in themes, even setting, in the use of illusions, disguise, mirror effects, daydreaming as well as exploitation and fascination. No doubt Robinson appreciated also Jean Marais's playing three roles: the Beast with magnificent makeup, then the Prince, and Avenant, the handsome treacherous suitor of Beauty. In his enchanting adaptation in black and white of an eighteenth-century fairy tale, Cocteau captivated his audience with surreal and visually striking effects, his use of poetic imagery and atmospheric sets, intended to evoke the illustrations and engravings of Gustave Doré and in the farmhouse scenes the paintings of Jan Vermeer.

13. See Pitavy-Souques, "'Shower of Gold' ou les ambiguïtés de la narration."

CHAPTER 8: "THE INSPIRED CHILD OF [HER] TIMES": EUDORA WELTY AS A TWENTIETH-CENTURY ARTIST (2010)

1. For an extended discussion of "Old Mr Marblehall" and "Kin," see "'A Blazing Butterfly'" in this volume.

2. The *structure en abyme* is appropriate here because of its well-known connection with the visual arts since André Gide's note in his *Journal*, in reference to the famous Van Eyck painting "Giovanni Arnolfini and His Bride" 1434, National Gallery, London (1395–1441). The subjects are standing, the bride has placed her hand in her husband's, behind them above a bed a convex mirror reflects the guests, that is to say, the witnesses, those who testify to the truth of the event; they are not shown directly but as reflections in a mirror. As twenty-first-century viewers standing where the witnesses stand, we too testify. By choosing appearances, artificiality, and the absurdly false, the living perpetuate an illusion. Yet, true values are seen, true courage exists. By rejecting false romanticism, Welty says, people can live authentically: the beauty and idealism of the South are all there. In this respect, "Kin" is a plea for the South, this South, which in a purely postmodern reading may amount to traces only.

3. For an extended analysis of "Flowers for Marjorie," see "A Re-reading" of the story in this volume.

4. "Circe" was first published under the title "Put Me in the Sky." During her stay in Europe and after she came back, Welty must have had time to think about Circe, her evil

power, and "what it is like to be immortal," as she told me in 1987, and thus be able to polish to perfection that short masterpiece that "Circe" is for *The Bride of the Innisfallen and Other Stories*. For a longer analysis of the story, see "Of Human, Animal, and Celestial Bodies in Welty's 'Circe'" in this volume.

5. We are indebted to Pearl McHaney for judiciously (and fortunately for us devoted readers) including it in *Eudora Welty as Photographer* (51) after selecting it for the tenth-anniversary issue of *Five Points* with a fine commentary ([96], [80]).

CHAPTER 9: "MOMENTS OF TRUTH": EUDORA WELTY'S HUMANISM (2014)

1. The Eudora Welty Society international conference was held at Texas A&M University April 4–7, 2013, directed by Sarah Ford and David McWhirter.

2. "Where Is the Voice Coming From?," "The Demonstrators," and "One Time, One Place."

3. See "Private and Political Thoughts in *One Writer's Beginnings*" in this volume.

WORKS CITED

Abish, Walter. "On Aspects of the Familiar World." Nice, France, unpublished, 1982.
Apollinaire, Guillaume. *L'enchanteur pourrissant*, 1909. Gallimard, 1972.
Atkinson, Saye. "Frames of Reference: Remarks on Eudora Welty and Sir Arthur Eddington." *Eudora Welty Newsletter*, vol. 32, no. 1, 2008, pp. 7–11.
Atwood, Margaret. *Surfacing*. Ballentine, 1972.
Barbey d'Aurévilly, Jule Amedée. "Le Dessous de Cartes d'une Partie de Whist," *Les Diaboliques* (1874). www/gutenberg.org. 2004. Accessed 30 June 2020.
Baris, Sharon Deykin, "Judgments in *The Ponder Heart*, Welty's Trials of the 1950s." *Eudora Welty and Politics*, edited by Suzanne Marrs and Harriet Pollack. Louisiana State UP, 2001, pp. 179–202.
Barthes, Roland. *La Chambre Claire*. Paris: Gallimard Le Seuil, 1980.
Barthes, Roland. "Lecture in Inauguration of the Chair of Literary Semiology, Collège De France, January 7, 1977." Translated by Richard Howard. *October*, vol. 8, 1979, pp. 3–16.
Barthes, Roland. "L'Étrangère." *La Quinzaine Littéraire*, vol. 94, May 1–15, 1970, pp. 19–20.
Barthes, Roland. "Longtemps je me suis couché de bonne heure." *Le Bruissement de la Langue, Essais Critiques IV*. Paris: Point Seuil, 1984, pp. 333–46.
Baudelaire, Charles. "De l'héroïsme de la vie moderne," *Curiostités Esthétiques*. Paris: M. Levy, 1868, pp. 193–98.
Baudelaire, Charles. "Eugène Delacroix." *Curiostités Esthétiques*. Paris: M. Levy, 1868, pp. 114–15.
Baudelaire, Charles. *The Painter of the Modern Life*. Translated by Jonathon Mayne. Phaidon, 1965.
Beaujour, Michel. *Miroirs d'encre: Rhétorique de l'autoportrait*. Translated by Françoise Lionnet. Paris: Seuil, 1980.
Beaune, Jean-Claude. "De l'absence matérielle à l'abîme symbolique." *Ecriture du corps*, no. 3, 1988, pp. 3–23.
Bercovitch, Sacvan. *The Rites of Assent: Transformations in the Symbolic Construction of America*. Routledge, 1993.
Bergman, Ingmar, director. *Wild Strawberries*. Ekelund, 1957.
Berman, Antoine. *L'Epreuve de l'étranger*. Paris: Gallimard, 1984.
Birat, Kathie. "'Pockets of Light': Rediscovering America in Paul Auster's *Moon Palace*." *Moon Palace de Paul Auster: Lectures d'une Oeuvre*, edited by Françoise Gallix. Paris: Éditions du Temps, 1996, pp. 131–45.

Bloch, Howard. *Etymologies and Genealogies: A Literary Anthropology of the French Middle Ages*. U of Chicago P, 1983.
Bloom, Harold. *The Western Canon: The Books and Schools of the Ages*. Houghton Mifflin, Harcourt, 1994.
Bourdieu, Pierre. *Méditations pascaliennes*. Paris: Seuil, 1997.
Bourke-White, Margaret, and Erskine Caldwell. *You Have Seen Their Faces*. Viking P, 1937.
Brantley, Will. *Feminine Sense in Southern Memoir*. Jackson: UP of Mississippi, 1993.
Brodhead, Richard. "Two Writers' Beginnings: Eudora Welty in the Neighborhood of Richard Wright." *Yale Review*, vol. 84, no. 2, 1996, pp. 1–21; rpt. in *The Good of This Place: Values and Challenges in College Education*. Yale UP, 2004, pp. 104–26.
Buñuel, Luis, director. *Last Breath*. Virgin, 1983.
Buñuel, Luis, director. *Un chien andalou*. France, 1929.
Buñuel, Luis, and Salvador Dali. "Un chien andalou." *La Révolution Surrealiste*, no. 12, 1929, pp. 34–37.
Carr, Emily. *Klee Wyck*. 1941. Fitzhenry and Whiteside, 2003.
Carroll, Lewis. *The Annotated Alice, Alice's Adventures in Wonderland and Through the Looking Glass*. Intro. and Notes by Martin Gardner, illus. by John Tenniel. Random House, 1960.
Cather, Willa. *Later Novels*. Library of America, 1990.
Cather, Willa. *Stories, Poems, and Other Writings*. Library of America, 1992.
Chekhov, Anton. "Panic Fears." *The School Mistress and Other Tales*, from *The Tales of Chekhov*, vol. 19. www.gutenberg.org. Accessed 20 May 2021.
Chengges, Catherine. "Textual Variants in 'Put Me in the Sky!' and 'Circe.'" *Eudora Welty Newsletter*, vol. 23, no. 2, 1999, pp. 11–27.
Chouard, Géraldine. "Phoenix and Légion d'honneur Awards for Danièle Pitavy-Souques." *Eudora Welty Newsletter*, vol. 27, no. 1, 2003, pp. 24–25.
Cixous, Hélène, Madeleine Gagnon, and Annie Leclerc. *La Venue à la l'écriture*. Paris: Union générale d'éditions, 1977.
Claxton, Mae Miller, "'Untamable texts': The Art of Georgia O'Keeffe and Eudora Welty." *Mississippi Quarterly*, vol. 56, no. 2, 2003, pp. 315–30.
Cocteau, Jean, director. *Beauty and the Beast/La belle et la bête*. France, 1946.
Cocteau, Jean, director. *The Blood of the Poet/Le sang d'un poète*. France, 1930.
Cole, Hunter McKelva. "The Novels of Eudora Welty." Unpublished conference paper, Universities of Uppsala and Odense, Denmark, July 1995.
Compagnon, Antoine. *La littérature, pour quoi faire?* Leçon inaugurale du Collège de France. Paris: Collège de France, 2007. Web. 26 June 2014.
Couturier, Maurice. "Presentation of the Topic." *Representation and Performance in Postmodern Fiction*, edited by Maurice Couturier. Delta, Montpelier, France: Université Paul Valéry, 1983, pp. 3–8.
Couturier, Maurice, editor. *Representation and Performance in Postmodern Fiction*. Delta, Montpelier, France: Université Paul Valéry, 1983.
de Man, Paul. "Literary History and Literary Modernity." *Dædalus*, vol. 99, no. 2, 1970, pp. 384–404.

Durand, Regis. "The Disposition of the Familiar." *Representation and Performance in Postmodern Fiction*, edited by Maurice Couturier. *Delta*, Montpelier, France: Université Paul Valéry, 1983, pp. 73–84.
Eisinger, Chester E. "Traditionalism and Modernism in Eudora Welty. *Eudora Welty: Critical Essays*, edited by Peggy W. Prenshaw. UP of Mississippi, 1979, pp. 3–25.
Elger, Dietmar. *L'Expressionnisme*. Köln: Taschen, 2004.
Eliot, T. S. "*Ulysses*, Order, and Myth." *Selected Prose of T. S. Eliot*, edited by Frank Kermode. Harvest, 1975, pp. 175–78.
Felski, Rita. *Uses of Literature*. Malden, MA: Blackwell, 2008.
Fitzgerald, F. Scott. *The Great Gatsby*. Scribner Classic, 1996.
Flam, Jack D., editor. *Matisse on Art*. 1973. Oxford: Phaidon, 1990.
Foucault, Michel. *Les mots et les choses*. Gallimard, 1966.
Freud, Sigmund. "The Uncanny." *On Creativity and the Unconscious*. New York: Harper, 1958, pp. 122–61.
Fry, Edward F. *Cubism*. McGraw-Hill, 1966.
Gass, William. *Fiction and the Figures of Life*. Boston: Nonpareil Books, 1971.
Genette, Gérard. *Figures III*. Édition de Seuil, 1972.
Gide, André. *The Journals of André Gide 1889–1949*. Translated by J. O'Brien. Vintage Books, 1956.
Giedon-Welcker, Carola. *Constantin Brancusi*. Neuchâtel: Éditions du Griffon, 1958.
Girard, René. *Le Bouc Emissaire*. Paris: Grasset, 1982.
Glasgow, Ellen. *The Woman Within*. Harcourt Brace, 1954.
Hartog, François. *Mémoire d'Ulysse, Récits sur la frontière en Grèce ancienne*. Paris: Gallimard, 1996.
Hassan, Ihab. "II. Wars of Desires, Politics of the World." *Salmagundi*, vol. 55, no. 4, 1982, pp. 110–18.
Heidegger, Martin. *Being and Time*. Harper Perennial, 1962.
Heidegger, Martin. *Poetry, Language, Thought*. Harper and Row, 1971.
Hurston, Zora Neale. *Dust Tracks on a Road*. 1942. Harper Perennial, 1996.
James, Henry. *Wings of the Dove*. 1902. Penguin Classics, 2008.
Kandinsky, Vassily. *Du spirituel dans l'art, et dans la peinture in particulier*. 1911. Paris: Denoël Folio Essais, 1989.
Kandinsky, Vassily. *Kandinsky*. Éditions du Centre Pompidou, 2009.
Kendig, Daun. "Realities in 'Sir Rabbit': A Frame Analysis." *Eudora Welty: Eye of the Storyteller*, edited by Dawn Trouard. Kent State UP, 1989, pp. 119–32.
Klee, Paul. *Paul Klee Making Visible*. EY Exhibition. London: Tate Modern, 2013.
Krauss, Rosalind E. *The Optical Unconscious*. Cambridge: MIT P, 1983.
Kreyling, Michael. *Author and Agent: Eudora Welty and Diarmuid Russell*. Farrar Strauss Giroux, 1991.
Kristeva, Julia. "Approches de l'abjection." *Pouvoirs de l'horreur: Essai sur l'abjection*. Paris: Seuil, 1980, pp. 9–39.
Kristeva, Julia. *Desire in Language*. Edited by Leon S. Rouidez. [Paris: Seuil 1977], Columbia UP, 1980.

Leclaire, Serge. *Rompre des charmes: recueil pour des enchantés de la psychoanalyse.* InterÉditions, 1981.

Lemny, Doïna, "Leda entre mythe et réalité." *Leda, Les carnets de l'Atelier Brancusi.* Paris: Éditions du Centre Georges Pompidou, 1998, pp. 35–44.

Lévi-Strauss, Claude. *Saudades do Brasil.* Paris: Gallimard, 1995.

Lévi-Strauss, Claude. *Tristes Tropiques.* 1955. Paris: Plon, 1973.

Lionnet, Françoise. *Autobiographical Voices: Race, Gender, Self-Portraiture.* Cornell UP, 1989.

Lorquin, Bertrand. "The Art of Maillol," *Aristide Maillol,* edited by Dina Verny. Perpignan: Editions Benteli, 2000, pp. 12–24.

MacNeil, Robert. *Eudora Welty: Seeing Black and White.* UP of Mississippi, 1990.

Mallarmé, Stéphane. "Variations sur un sujet/Quant au Livre/L'action restraint," *Divagations* (1897), *Oeuvres Complètes,* edited by Henri Mondor and G. Jean-Aubry. Pleiade, Gallimard, 1945.

Malraux, André. *Sanctuaire* by William Faulkner, translated by Malraux. Gallimard, Le Livre de Poche, 1949.

Mark, Rebecca. *The Dragon's Blood: Feminist Intertextuality in Eudora Welty's* The Golden Apples. UP of Mississippi, 1994.

Marrs, Suzanne. *Eudora Welty: A Biography.* New York: Harcourt Brace, 2006.

Marrs, Suzanne. "'The Huge Fateful Stage of the Outside World': Eudora Welty's Life in Politics." *Eudora Welty and Politics: Did the Writer Crusade?,* edited by Harriet Pollack and Suzanne Marrs. Louisiana State UP, 2001, pp. 69–87.

Marrs, Suzanne. *One Writer's Imagination: The Fiction of Eudora Welty.* Louisiana State UP, 2002.

Marrs, Suzanne. *The Welty Collection: A Guide to the Eudora Welty Manuscripts and Documents at the Mississippi Department of Archives and History.* UP of Mississippi, 1989.

Mathé, Sylvia. "The Death of Ralph: The 'Moment of Truth' in *The Portrait of a Lady.*" *Que peut la littérature?,* edited by Sylvie Mathé. *Revue Française d'Études Américaines,* vol. 130, no. 4, 2011, pp. 19–31. Web. 26 June 2014.

McHaney, Pearl Amelia. "Line and Shadow: Photographs by Eudora Welty." *Five Points,* vol. 10, nos. 1 & 2, 2009, pp. 80–97.

McHaney, Pearl Amelia, editor. *Eudora Welty as Photographer.* UP of Mississippi, 2009.

McHaney, Thomas L. "Eudora Welty and the Multitudinous Golden Apples." *Mississippi Quarterly,* vol. 26, no. 3, 1973, pp. 589–624.

McHaney, Thomas L. "Falling into Cycles: *The Golden Apples,*" *Eudora Welty: Eye of the Storyteller,* edited by Dawn Trouard. Kent State UP, 1989, pp. 173–89.

Milner, Max. *L'Evners du visible, Essai sur l'ombre.* Paris: Seuil, 2005.

Milton, John. "Sonnet XIX." *Complete Poems and Prose,* edited by Merrit Y. Hughes. Odyssey P, 1957, p. 168.

Mississippi: A Guide to the Magnolia State. American Guide Series. Federal Writers' Project of the Works Progress Administration. Viking P, 1938.

Morris, Harry C. "Eudora Welty's Use of Mythology." *Shenandoah,* vol. 6, no. 2, 1955, pp. 34–40.

Natanson, Nicholas. *The Black Image in the New Deal: The Politics of FSA Photography.* U of Tennessee P, 1992.
Nissen, Axel. "Queer Welty, Camp Welty." *Mississippi Quarterly*, vol. 56, no. 2, 2003, pp. 209–29.
Paleolog, V. G. *C. Brancusi.* Bucharest: Forum, 1947.
Paz, Octavio. *On Poets and Others.* H. Holt, 1986.
Pitavy-Souques, Danièle. "'Blacks and Other Very Dark Colors': William Faulkner and Eudora Welty." *Faulkner and His Contemporaries: Faulkner and Yoknapatawpha*, edited by Joseph R. Urgo and Ann J. Abadie. UP of Mississippi, 2004, pp. 132–54.
Pitavy-Souques, Danièle. "A Blazing Butterfly: The Modernity of Eudora Welty." *Welty: A Life in Literature*, edited by Albert J. Devlin. UP of Mississippi, 1987, pp. 113–38. Rpt. in *The Eye That Is Language*, 2022, pp. 17–35.
Pitavy-Souques, Danièle. Conversation with Eudora Welty. Jackson, Mississippi, 1987.
Pitavy-Souques, Danièle. Conversation with Eudora Welty. Jackson, Mississippi, November 1993.
Pitavy-Souques, Danièle. Conversation with Eudora Welty. Jackson, Mississippi, April 1994.
Pitavy-Souques, Danièle. Conversation with Eudora Welty, Jackson, Mississippi, April 13, 1997.
Pitavy-Souques, Danièle. "Eudora Welty and the Merlin Principle: Aspects of Story-Telling in *The Golden Apples*—'The Whole World Knows' and 'Sir Rabbit,'" *Mississippi Quarterly: Eudora Welty Centennial Supplement*, April 2009, pp. 101–23. Rpt. in *The Eye That Is Language*, 2022, pp. 90–106.
Pitavy-Souques, Danièle. "Eudora Welty et l'espace chamanique: relecture de la nouvelle 'A Curtain of Green.'" *L'espace du Sud au féminin*, edited by Brigitte Zaugg and Gérald Preher. Metz: Centre Écriture / Université Paul Verlaine, Littératures des mondes contemporains, Série Amériques, 2011, pp. 199–214.
Pitavy-Souques, Danièle. "Eudora Welty's *Légion d'honneur* Award Ceremony." *Eudora Welty Newsletter*, vol. 21, no. 1, 1997, pp. 2–5.
Pitavy-Souques, Danièle. "'The Fictional Eye': Eudora Welty's Retranslation of the South," *South Atlantic Review*, vol. 65, no. 4, 2000, pp. 90–113. Rpt. in *The Eye That Is Language*, 2022, pp. 57–74.
Pitavy-Souques, Danièle. "The Inspired Child of [Her] Times: Eudora Welty as a Twentieth-Century Artist," *Eudora Welty Review*, vol. 2, 2010, pp. 69–92. Rpt. in *The Eye That Is Language*, 2022, pp. 107–26.
Pitavy-Souques, Danièle. "'Moments of Truth': Eudora Welty's Humanism." *Eudora Welty Review*, vol. 6, 2014, pp. 9–26. Rpt. in *The Eye That Is Language*, 2022, pp. 127–41.
Pitavy-Souques, Danièle. "Of Human, Animal, and Celestial Bodies in Welty's 'Circe.'" *Eudora Welty and The Poetics of the Body*, Etudes Faulknériennes, edited by Géraldine Chouard and Danièle Pitavy-Souques, PUR, 2005, pp. 167–73. Rpt. in *The Eye That Is Language*, 2022, pp. 46–56.
Pitavy-Souques, Danièle. "On My First Becoming Acquainted with Eudora Welty and Her Work." *Eudora Welty: Writers' Reflections upon First Reading Welty*, edited by Pearl Amelia McHaney. Athens, GA, Hill Street P, 1999, pp. 77–84. U South Carolina P, 2010, pp. 77–84.

Pitavy-Souques, Danièle. "Poétique/politique de la Piste des Natchez chez Eudora Welty." *Lieux d'Amériques*, edited by Michel Granger. Lyon: Presses Universitaires, 2010, pp. 151–72.

Pitavy-Souques, Danièle. "Private and Political Thoughts in *One Writer's Beginnings*." *Eudora Welty and Politics: Did the Writer Crusade?*, edited by Harriet Pollack and Suzanne Marrs. Louisiana State UP, 2001, pp. 203–21. Rpt. in *The Eye That Is Language*, 2022, pp. 75–89.

Pitavy-Souques, Danièle. "'Shower of Gold' ou les ambiguïtés de la narration." *Eudora Welty, Delta*, no. 5, 1977, pp. 63–81.

Pitavy-Souques, Danièle. "Technique as Myth: The Structure of *The Golden Apples*." *Eudora Welty: Critical Essays*, edited by Peggy Whitman Prenshaw. UP of Mississippi, 1979, pp. 258–68. Rpt. in *Eudora Welty: Thirteen Essays*, edited by Peggy Whitman Prenshaw. UP of Mississippi, 1983, pp. 146–56. Rpt. in *Modern Critical Views: Eudora Welty*, edited by Harold Bloom. Chelsea House, 1986, pp. 109–18. Rpt. in *The Eye That Is Language*, 2022, pp. 7–16.

Pitavy-Souques, Danièle. "Thoughts upon Receiving the *Légion d'honneur* Award." *Eudora Welty Newsletter*, vol. 27, no. 1, 2003, pp. 25–28.

Pitavy-Souques, Danièle. "Le voyageur de l'humanité: Eudora Welty photographe." *Interfaces*, no. 7, 1995, Dijon: Presses de l'Université de Bourgogne, pp. 99–112; Rpt. in *Eudora Welty* by Pitavy-Souques, Paris: Belin, 1999, pp. 29–42.

Pitavy-Souques, Danièle. "Watchers and Watching: Point of View in Welty's 'June Recital.'" *Southern Review*, vol. 19, no. 3, 1983, pp. 483–509.

Plato. *Republic*. Cambridge, MA: Hackett, 1992.

Polcari, Stephen. "L'aboutissement: le *dripping* ou l'image de l'invisible." *Jackson Pollock et le chamanisme*, edited by Marc Restellini. Pinacothèque de Paris, 2008, pp. 72–92.

Polcari, Stephen. "L'idée du chamanisme de Jackson Pollock." *Jackson Pollock et le chamanisme*, edited by Marc Restellini. Pinacothèque de Paris, 2008, pp. 24–37.

Polk, Noel. *Eudora Welty: A Bibliography of Her Work*. UP of Mississippi, 1994.

Pollack, Harriet. "Eudora Welty's 'Too Far to Walk It': Out Farther Still? A Correction." *South Central Review*, vol. 14, no. 3, 1997, pp. 114–16.

Pollack, Harriet. "Photographic Convention and Story Composition: Eudora Welty's Use of Detail, Plot, Genre, and Expectation from 'A Worn Path' through *The Bride of the Innisfallen*." *South Central Review*, vol. 14, no. 2, 1997, pp. 15–34.

Pollack, Harriet. "Reading John Robinson." *Mississippi Quarterly*, vol. 56, no. 2, 2003, pp. 175–208.

Pollack, Harriet, and Suzanne Marrs. "Seeing Welty's Political Vision in Her Photographs." *Eudora Welty and Politics*, pp. 223–51.

Pollack, Harriet, and Suzanne Marrs, editors. *Eudora Welty and Politics: Did the Writer Crusade?* Louisiana State UP, 2001.

Price, Reynolds. "Dodging Apples." *Things Themselves: Essays & Scenes*. Atheneum, 1972, pp. 7–12.

Price, Reynolds. "A Form of Thanks." *A Form of Thanks*, edited by Louis Dollarhide and Ann J. Abadie. UP of Mississippi, 1979, pp. 123–28.

Proust, Marcel. *Remembrance of Things Past*, 1913–1927, translated by C. K. Scott Moncrieff Random House, 1934.
Ricardo, Jean. *Problémes du nouveau roman*. Paris: Seuil, 1967.
Richard, Claude. "Causality and Mimesis in Contemporary Fiction." *SubStance*, vol. 12, no. 3, iss. 40: Determinism, 1983, pp. 84–93.
Ricoeur, Paul. *La Critique et la Conviction*. Calmann-Levy, 1995.
Sartre, Jean Paul. *L'Etre et le Néant*. Paris: Gallimard, 1943.
Sartre, Jean Paul. *L'Imaginaire, Psychologie phénoménologique de l'imagination*. Paris: Gallimard, 1940.
Sartre, Jean Paul. *L'Imagination*. Paris: PUF, 1981.
Schama, Simon. *Landscape and Memory*. Knopf, 1995.
Scholes, Robert. *The Fabulators*. Oxford UP, 1967.
Simon, Claude. *Les Georgiques* (*The Georgics*). Les Éditions de Minuit, 1981.
Sollers, Philippe. *Le Paradis de Cézanne*. Paris: Gallimard, 1995.
Spencer, Elizabeth. "An Abundance of Angels." *Country Churchyards*, by Eudora Welty. UP of Mississippi, 2000, pp. 13–20.
Tanner, Tony. "Frames and Sentences." *Representation and Performance in Postmodern Fiction*, edited by Maurice Couturier. *Delta*, Montpelier, France: Université Paul Valéry, 1983, pp. 21–32.
Travers, Martin, editor. *European Literature from Romanticism to Postmodernism: A Reader in Aesthetic Practice*. Columbian International Publishing, 2001.
Vadé, Yves. *Pour un tombeau de Merlin: Du barde celte à la poésie moderne*. Paris: José Corti, 2008.
Vande Kieft, Ruth M. *Eudora Welty*. Twayne, 1962.
Verny, Dina, editor. *Aristide Maillol*. Perpgnan: Editions Benteli, 2000.
Vitrac, Roger. "Preface," *Brancusi, November 13-January 13*. Brummer Gallery, New York, 1933, pp. [1–3].
Warren, Robert Penn. "The Love and Separateness in Miss Welty." *Kenyon Review*, vol. 6, no. 2, 1944, pp. 246–59.
Welty, Eudora. "Acrobats in a Park" [1935]. *Delta*, No. 5, 1977, pp. 3–11; rpt. *Occasions: Selected Writings*, edited by Pearl Amelia McHaney. UP of Mississippi, 2009, pp. 3–13.
Welty, Eudora. "The Art of Fiction XLVII: Eudora Welty," Interview with Linda Kuehl. *Conversations*, pp. 74–91.
Welty, Eudora. "Asphodel." *Stories*, pp. 241–51.
Welty, Eudora. "The Bride of the Innisfallen." *Stories*, pp. 596–624.
Welty, Eudora. "Circe." *Stories*, pp. 639–46.
Welty, Eudora. *Collected Stories*. Harvest, 1983.
Welty, Eudora. *Complete Novels*. Library of America, 1998.
Welty, Eudora. "A Conversation with Eudora Welty," Interview with Albert J. Devlin and Peggy Whitman Prenshaw. *Welty: A Life in Literature*, edited by Albert J. Devlin. UP of Mississippi, 1987, pp. 3–26, rpt. in *Conversations*, pp. 100–19.
Welty, Eudora. *Conversations with Eudora Welty*, edited by Peggy W. Prenshaw. UP of Mississippi, 1984.

Welty, Eudora. "A Curtain of Green." *Stories*, pp. 130–36.
Welty, Eudora. "Death of a Traveling Salesman." *Stories*, pp. 144–57.
Welty, Eudora. *Delta Wedding. Complete Novels*, pp. 89–336.
Welty, Eudora. "The Demonstrators." *Stories*, pp. 733–50.
Welty, Eudora. "Eudora Welty," Interview with John Griffin Jones. *Conversations*, pp. 316–41.
Welty, Eudora. *Eudora Welty as Photographer*. UP of Mississippi, 2009.
Welty, Eudora. "Eudora Welty: 'I Worry over My Stories,'" Interview with Don Lee Keith. *Conversations*, pp. 141–53.
Welty, Eudora. "Eudora Welty: A Writer's Beginnings," Interview with Patricia Wheatley. *More Conversations with Eudora Welty*, edited by Peggy Whitman Prenshaw. UP of Mississippi, 1996, pp. 120–45.
Welty, Eudora. *The Eye of the Story: Selected Essays and Reviews*. Random House, 1979.
Welty, Eudora. "Fiction as Event: An Interview with Eudora Welty," Interview with Jeanne Rolfe Nostrandt. *More Conversations with Eudora Welty*, edited by Peggy Whitman Prenshaw. UP of Mississippi, 1996, pp. 14–30.
Welty, Eudora. "Flowers for Marjorie." Manuscript, Series 2. *A Curtain of Green*, 1941, Eudora Welty Collection. Jackson: Mississippi Department of Archives and History.
Welty, Eudora. "Flowers for Marjorie." *Stories*, pp. 119–29.
Welty, Eudora. "Golden Apples." *Harper's Bazaar*, Sept. 1947, pp. 216–17, +.
Welty, Eudora. *The Golden Apples. Stories*, pp. 313–556.
Welty, Eudora. "The House of Willa Cather." *Eye of the* Story, pp. 41–60.
Welty, Eudora. "How I Write." *Virginia Quarterly Review*, vol. 31, no. 2, 1955, pp. 240–51.
Welty, Eudora. "'The Interior World': An Interview with Eudora Welty," Interview with Charles T. Bunting. *Conversations*, pp. 40–63.
Welty, Eudora. "Is Phoenix Jackson's Grandson Really Dead?" *Stories*, pp. 815–18.
Welty, Eudora. "Keela, the Outcast Indian Maiden." *Stories*, pp. 48–56.
Welty, Eudora. "The Key." *Stories*, pp. 37–47.
Welty, Eudora. "Kin." *Stories*, pp. 647–81.
Welty, Eudora. "Ladies in Spring." *Stories*, pp. 625–38.
Welty, Eudora. "Lily Daw and the Three Ladies." *Stories*, pp. 5–15.
Welty, Eudora. "Livvie." *Stories*, pp. 276–90.
Welty, Eudora. *Losing Battles. Complete Novels*, pp. 425–879.
Welty, Eudora. "A Memory." *Stories*, pp. 92–98.
Welty, Eudora. "Moon Lake." *Stories*, pp. 412–50.
Welty, Eudora. "Music from Spain," *Stories*, pp. 473–514.
Welty, Eudora. "Must the Novelist Crusade?" *Stories*, pp. 803–14.
Welty, Eudora. "Old Mr Marblehall." *Stories*, pp. 111–18.
Welty, Eudora. "One Time, One Place." *Eye of the Story*, pp. 349–55.
Welty, Eudora. *One Time, One Place: Mississippi in the Depression, A Snapshot Album*. New York: Random, 1971. Rev. ed. Jackson: UP of Mississippi, 1996.
Welty, Eudora. *One Writer's Beginnings. Stories*, pp. [831]–948.
Welty, Eudora. "The Optimist's Daughter." *The New Yorker*, vol. 45, 15 Mar. 1969, pp. 37–46, +.
Welty, Eudora. *The Optimist's Daughter. Complete Novels*, pp. [881]–992.
Welty, Eudora. *Photographs*. UP of Mississippi, 1989.

Welty, Eudora. "A Piece of News." *Stories*, pp. 16–21.
Welty, Eudora. "Place in Fiction." *Stories*, pp. 781–96.
Welty, Eudora. *The Ponder Heart. Complete Novels*, pp. 337–424.
Welty, Eudora. "Powerhouse." *Stories*, pp. 158–70.
Welty, Eudora. "Put Me in the Sky!" *Accent*, vol. 10, no. 4, 1949, pp. 3–10.
Welty, Eudora. Review of *The Collected Stories of Elizabeth Bowen. A Writer's Eye*, pp. 231–36.
Welty, Eudora. Review of *A Haunted House and Other Short Stories* by Virginia Woolf. *A Writer's Eye*, pp. 25–29.
Welty, Eudora. Review of *Martha Graham: Portrait of the Lady as an Artist* by Leroy Leatherman. *A Writer's Eye*, pp. 141–45.
Welty, Eudora. *The Robber Bridegroom. Complete Novels*, pp. [1]–88.
Welty, Eudora. "Sir Rabbit." *Stories*, pp. 400–11.
Welty, Eudora. "Some Notes on Time in Fiction." *Eye of the Story*, pp. 163–73.
Welty, Eudora. "A Still Moment." *Stories*, pp. 228–40.
Welty, Eudora. *Stories, Essays and Memoir*. Library of America, 1998.
Welty, Eudora. "A Visit with Eudora Welty," Interview with Bill Ferris. *Conversations*, pp. 154–71.
Welty, Eudora. "The Wanderers." *Stories*, pp. 515–56.
Welty, Eudora. "Where Is the Voice Coming From?" *Stories*, pp. 727–32.
Welty, Eudora. "The Whole World Knows." *Stories*, pp. 451–72.
Welty, Eudora. "Words into Fiction." *Eye of the Story*, pp. 134–45.
Welty, Eudora. *A Writer's Eye: Collected Book Reviews*, edited by Pearl Amelia McHaney. UP of Mississippi, 1994.
Welty, Eudora. "Writing and Analyzing a Story." *Stories*, pp. 776–80.
Wenders, Wim, director and co-producer. *On the Wings of Desire*. Road Movies, 1987.
Wiebe, Rudy Henry. "Unearthing Language: An Interview with Rudy Wiebe and Robert Kroetsch" with Shirley Neuman. *A Voice in the Land: Essays by and about Rudy Wiebe*, edited by W. J. Keith, Western Canadian Literary Documents Series, no. 2. Edmonton: NeWest Press, 1981, pp. 226–47.
Woolf, Virginia. *The Diary of Virginia Woolf, Vol. 3: 1925–1930*. Harcourt Brace/Harvest, 1981.
Woolf, Virginia. *To the Lighthouse*. 1927. Harcourt Brace Jovanovich, 1981.
Wright, Richard. *Black Boy*. 1945. Library Classics of the United States, 1993.
Yaeger, Patricia S. "Eudora Welty and the Dialogic Imagination." *Welty: A Life in Literature*, edited by Albert J. Devlin. UP of Mississippi, 1987, pp. 139–67.
Yeats, W. B. *The Variorum Edition of the Poems of W. B. Yeats*, edited by Peter Allt and Russell Alspach. New York: Macmillan, 1957.

ADDITIONAL PUBLICATIONS BY DANIÈLE PITAVY-SOUQUES

BOOKS

La Mort de Méduse: L'art de nouvelle chez Eudora Welty. Lyons: Universitaires de Lyon, 1991.

Eudora Welty, Les sortilèges du conteur. Voix Américaines series. Paris: Belin, 1999.

L'homme et la Steppe, edited Maryvonne Perrot and Danièle Pitavy. Dijon: Édition Universitaires de Dijon, 1999.

Femmes et ècriture au Canada, edited by Danièle Pitavy-Souques. Dijon: Édition Universitaires de Dijon, 2002.

ADDITIONAL ESSAYS ON WELTY

"'Shower of Gold' ou les ambiguïtés de la narration." *Eudora Welty, Delta V,* 1977, pp. 63–81.

"Watchers and Watching: Point of View in Welty's 'June Recital,'" *Southern Review,* vol. 19, no. 3, July 1983, pp. 483–509.

"Of Suffering and Joy: Aspects of Storytelling in Welty's Short Fiction," *Eudora Welty: Eye of the Storyteller,* edited by Dawn Trouard, Kent State UP, 1989, pp. 142–50.

"Eudora Welty's *Légion d'honneur* Award Ceremony." *Eudora Welty Newsletter,* vol. 21, no. 1, 1997, pp. 2–5.

"Le voyageur de l'humanité: Eudora Welty photographe." *Interfaces,* no. 7, 1995, Dijon: Presses de l'Université de Bourgogne, pp. 99–112; Rpt. in *Eudora Welty* by Pitavy-Souques, Paris: Belin, 1999, pp. 29–42.

"'Blacks and Other Very Dark Colors': William Faulkner and Eudora Welty," *Faulkner and His Contemporaries,* Faulkner and Yoknapatawpha, 2002, edited by Joseph Urgo and Ann J. Abadie, UP of Mississippi, pp. 132–54.

"Thoughts upon Receiving the *Légion d'honneur* Award." *Eudora Welty Newsletter,* vol. 27, no. 1, 2003, pp. 25–28.

"Eudora Welty in France: *Delta V* [1977], *Eudora Welty Newsletter* 1979, *Eudora Welty Review,* vol. 1, no. 1, 2009, 217–20.

"On My First Becoming Acquainted with Eudora Welty and Her Work," *Eudora Welty: Writers' Reflections upon First Reading Welty*, edited by Pearl Amelia McHaney, Hill Street P, 1999. U South Carolina P, 2010, pp. 77–84.

"Poétique/politique de la Piste des Natchez chez Eudora Welty." *Lieux d'Amériques*, edited by Michel Granger. Lyon: Presses Universitaires, 2010, pp. 151–72.

"Eudora Welty et l'espace chamanique: relecture de la nouvelle 'A Curtain of Green.'" *L'espace du Sud au féminin*, edited by Brigitte Zaugg and Gérald Preher. Metz: Centre Écriture/Université Paul Verlaine, Littératures des mondes contemporains, Série Amériques, 2011, pp. 199–214.

ADDITIONAL ESSAYS ON THE SOUTH AND OTHER WRITERS

"America Discovered in Reverse: The Feminine in O'Neill's *Desire under the Elms* and Williams's *A Streetcar Named Desire*." *The American Columbiad*, edited by M. Materassi and M. I. Ramalho de Sousa Santos. Amsterdam: VU University P. 1996, pp. 367–83.

"Dire la femme nouvelle: quelques stratégies narratives chez Ellen Glasgow, Kate Chopin et Willa Cather." *Revue Française d'Etudes Américaines*, no. 89, 1996, pp. 67–76.

"Femmes écrivains au tournant du siècle." *Revue Française d'Etudes Américaines*, no. 89, 1996, pp. 3–18.

"L'Arcadie de Josephine Humphreys." *Europe, USA: Voix nouvelles du Sud*, 1997, pp. 164–74.

"Le politique dans l'autobiographie: une relecture de Zora Neale Hurston et Eudora Welty", *Des Mots pour s'écrire*, edited by Sylvie Crinquand. Éditions Universitaires de Dijon, 1997, pp. 121–34.

"Dancers and Angels: Communication in the Fiction of Josephine Humphreys." *The Southern State of Mind*, edited by Jan Nordby Gretlund. U of South Carolina P, 1999, pp. 185–200.

"Enfant Inspiré de son siècle: Esthétique du Territoire chez Willa Cather." *Les Débuts de siècles*, edited by Terence McCarthy. Éditions Universitaires de Dijon, 2000, pp. 475–88.

"Fabric of Dreams—Fabrication of Dreams: A Bolt of White Cloth." *White Gloves of the Doorman: The Works of Leon Rooke*, edited by Branko Gorjup. Toronto: Exile Editions, 2004, pp. 139–50.

"'A Negotiation Between Familiarity and Strangeness': History in Kaye Gibbons and Jane Urquhart." *Intercultural America*, edited by Alfred Hornung in collaboration with Winfried Herget and Klaus Lubbers. Universitätsverlag, Winter Heidelberg, 2007, pp. 175–86.

"Emily Carr, Forest, British Columbia (circa 1931)" *Textes d'Amérique, Ecrivains et artistes américains entre américanité et originalité*, edited by Rédouane Abouddahab. Presses Universitaires de Lyon, 2008, pp. 43–51.

INDEX

Aaron, Daniel, 76
Abish, Walter, 22, 24, 25
"Abundance of Angels, An" (Spencer), 69
"Acrobats in a Park," 60
African Americans, 62, 63, 64, 70, 71, 72, 80–81, 88, 111–12, 122, 132, 133
Agrarians, 59
Alice's Adventures in Wonderland (Carroll), 97, 100
America, 88–89, 107, 108, 119, 124
American Book Award, 128
American Dream, 41, 87, 88, 89, 100
Andromeda, 9
animism, 4, 120
Apollinaire, Guillaume, 93
Arcadia, 59–63, 93
Arp, Jean, 103
art: abstract, 114; African, 112; avant-garde, 93, 120; emotion expressed in, 111, 112–13; immortality of, 16; philosophy of, 111. *See also* vision
Arthurian legends, 92
artist, 10, 15–16, 26, 84, 109, 110, 120, 121–22, 123, 125, 138–49; avant-garde, 4; as character, 26; surreal, 4; territory of, 5. *See also* Welty, Eudora: "A Still Moment"
Atkinson, Saye, 124
Atwood, Margaret, ix, x, 38, 145n5
Augustine of Hippo, 78
Author and Agent (Kreyling), 4, 94, 123
Autun, France, ix, 113, 150n8
avant-garde, 109, 125

Bakhtin, Mikail, 91, 93
ballet, 109
Balzac, Honoré de, 31
Baris, Sharon Deykin, 94, 119
baroque technique, viii, 117
Barthes, Roland, 22, 23, 59, 60, 68, 127–29, 133, 138
Baudelaire, Charles, 19–20, 146n3 (chap. 2)
Beaujour, Michel, 77
Beaune, Jean Claude, 148n4 (chap. 4)
Beauty and the Beast (Cocteau), 151n12
Beckmann, Max, 44, 118
Belhaven College, 58
Bercovitch, Sacvan, 87–88
Bergson, Henri, 103
Berman, Ingmar, 136
Bible, the, 23, 28, 84
Bible Belt, 61
Birat, Kathie, 87
Black Boy (Wright), 84
Block, Howard, 92
Bloom, Harold, 76, 148n1 (chap. 6)
body, 11, 41, 43, 44–45, 47–48, 49, 52, 53, 55–56, 60, 68, 69, 95–96, 99, 102, 103, 105, 112, 121, 129
Bourdieu, Pierre, 69
Bourke-White, Margaret, 65
Bowen, Elizabeth, 110
Brancusi, Constantin, 92, 112, 151n10
Brantley, Will, 77, 78, 80, 86
Brave New World (Huxley), 38
Bridge, The (group), 38
Blue Rider, The (group), 38

165

INDEX

Brodhead, Richard, 77, 84
Buñel, Luis, 44
burlesque, viii

Caldwell, Erskine, 65
Carr, Emily, ix, 113
Carroll, Lewis, 97, 100
Cassiopeia, 51, 55, 148n5 (chap. 4)
Cather, Willa, 17–18, 36–37, 59, 75, 88, 90–91, 108, 149n2, 149n6, 149n9
Cellini, Benvenuto, 4
Cézanne, Paul, 71
Chandler, Raymond, 150n3
chaos, xi, 16, 120, 121
Charlottesville, VA, 143
Chartres Cathedral, ix, 113
Chateaubriand, François-René de, 87
Chekhov, Anton, 21, 43
Chengges, Catherine, 147n1 (chap. 4)
Chicago, IL, 110
Chien Andalou, Un (Buñel), 118
Chouard, Géraldine, vii
cinema, 37, 38, 39, 43, 44, 93, 94, 109, 110
Circe, 46–56
civil rights movement, 78, 83, 94, 118, 128, 133
Civil War, 82, 119
Cixous, Hélène, 85, 129
Claxton, Mae Miller, 110
Cocteau, Jean, 105, 112, 116, 150n7
Collected Stories (Bowen), 60
Columbia University, 37, 57, 58, 93, 108, 110
Columbus, MS, 83
comedy, viii, 32, 38, 39, 66, 97, 110, 117, 118, 119, 130, 132. See also humor
Compagnon, Antoine, 127
concentration camp, x, xi, 119. See also death camp
concerts, 37, 94
Confederacy, 82
Conrad, Joseph, 19, 149n2
Constitution, American, 86
Couturier, Maurice, 23, 146n4 (chap. 2)

Dali, Salvador, 44
D'Aurévilly, Barbery, 17

David, Jacques-Louis, 20
death, ix, x, xi, 11, 13, 15, 28, 52–53, 69, 72, 84, 93, 94, 95, 102, 106, 111–12, 119, 120, 121, 125, 127, 128, 129, 135–40. See also concentration camp; death camp
death camp, 61, 119
Death Comes for the Archbishop (Cather), 81
deconstruction, 26, 31, 111, 115, 120, 121, 124, 125
Delacroix, Eugène, 20
de Man, Paul, 34
Derrida, Jacques, 23
Doré, Gustav, 150n3, 151n12
Dragon's Blood, The (Mark), 95, 146n3 (chap. 1)
Duchamp, Marcel, 151n11
Durand, Regis, 21–22, 23, 24, 146n4 (chap. 2)
Dust Tracks on a Road (Hurston), 77, 84–85
dystopia, xi, 38, 41, 42, 92, 119

Eddington, Sir Arthur, 123–24
Edschmid, Kasimir, 41
Einstein, Albert, 107, 123
Eisenhower, Dwight, 119
Eisinger, Chester E., 147n6
Eliot, T. S., 8, 10
Emerson, Ralph Waldo, 123
Ensor, James, 97
epiphany, 114
Ernst, Max, 44, 98, 118
Eudora Welty and Politics (Pollack and Marrs), 38, 94
Europe, xi, 37, 38, 50, 59, 93, 94, 110, 119
Evers, Medgar, 78
expressionism, xi, 10, 38, 39, 40–44, 92, 109, 117, 118

Fanon, Frantz, 81
Farm Security Administration (FSA), 65
fascination, xi, 11–15, 18, 49, 69, 94, 95, 101, 102, 103, 105, 117, 150n4, 150n8, 150n12. See also death
fascism, 61, 109; of language, 23
Faulkner, William, viii, 12, 70, 76, 91, 95, 143, 149n2

fiction, 37; avant-garde, 29–30; characters in, 30–31; defined, 20; frame in, 22–24, 62; shape of, 3, 29; vision, 29
Fitzgerald, F. Scott, 88, 97, 99–100, 150n6
Florence, Italy, 4
Ford, Sarah, 152n1
Foucault, Michel, 126
France, vii, viii, ix, 4, 52, 79, 93, 109, 143
Franklin, Benjamin, 79
Freud, Sigmund, 25, 109, 120; "uncanny," 24
frontier, American, 84, 85, 86, 147n2 (chap. 4)
Fulbright grant, x
futurism, 109

Gablik, Suzi, 20–21
Gallimard, 143
Gass, William, 19, 30
Gaugin, Paul, 38
gaze, 11–12, 19, 27, 41, 70, 94, 95, 125
Genette, Gérard, 30
Germany, 37
Gide, André, 32, 151n2
Giovanni Arnolfini and His Bride (Van Eyck), 32, 151n2
Girard, René, 131
Gislebertus, 150n8
Glasgow, Ellen, 77, 86, 149n8
Gold Medal for Fiction of the National Institute of Arts and Letters, 128
Gorgo, 11
gothic, viii, 112
Graham, Martha, 112
Grand Gulf, MS, 63
Great Depression, 39–40, 42–44, 58, 59, 73, 79, 118, 120, 122
Great Gatsby, The (Fitzgerald), 88, 97, 99–100, 150n6
grief, 9, 47, 52–53, 54–56, 69, 122, 128–29, 135, 137
grotesque (art form), viii, 112
Guggenheim Fellowship, 58
Guys, Constantin, 146n3 (chap. 2)

Handmaid's Tale, The (Atwood), 8
Hassan, Ihab, 20–21

Haunted House and Other Stories, A (Woolf), 93, 96–97
Hawkes, John, 29
Hawthorne, Nathaniel, 39, 82, 149n2
Heidegger, Martin, 23
Heracles, 12
Hermes, 62
Homer: Homeric tradition, 50; *The Odyssey*, 46–56
humanism, 129–30, 140
humanity, x, xi, 45, 49, 50, 53–55, 57, 118
humor, 50, 101, 130, 139. *See also* comedy
Hurston, Zora Neale, 81, 85
Huxley, Aldous, 38

impressionism, 80
influenza, 83
Ingres, Jean-Auguste-Dominique, 20

Jackson, MS, viii, 59, 73, 77, 79, 80, 143
James, Henry, 19, 22, 28, 149n2
jazz, 81, 110, 111–12
Joyce, James, 10, 19, 95, 114, 149n2
Jung, Carl, 120

Kafka, Franz, 149n2
Kandinsky, Wassily, 38, 107, 113, 114
Keats, John, vii
Kendig, Dawn, 100
King Solomon's judgment, 135
Klee, Paul, 85, 140
Klimt, Gustav, 112
Krauss, Rosalind, 63–64, 80, 98, 149n6
Kreyling, Michael, 4, 120
Kristeva, Julia, 29, 47, 53–54, 60, 91, 96

Ladd, Barbara, 94
Lamar Life Insurance Company, 86
language, xi–xii, 3, 23, 54, 57, 59, 62, 64, 67, 77, 79, 82, 109, 110, 113, 119. *See also* fascism
Leatherman, LeRoy, 112
Leclaire, Serge, 25
Leda (Brancusi), 102–5, 106, 117
Leda (Maillol), 102–4

"Leda and the Swan" (Yeats), 8, 92, 101–4, 105
Legion of Honor, viii, ix–x, xi–xii
Lentricchia, Frank, 148n3 (chap. 6)
Lévi-Strauss, Claude, 57, 67, 126
Lewis, C. S., 150n3
Lionnet, Françoise, 77, 81
"Lord Randall," 97
Lorrain, Claude, 26
Lyell, Frank, 58

MacNeil, Robert, 64, 65
Maillol, Aristide, 92, 150n9
Malevich, Kazimir, 38
Mallarmé, Stéphane, 7, 16
Malraux, André, 12
Manifest Destiny, 87
Mansfield, Katherine, 75
Marais, Jean, 151n12
Mark, Rebecca, 36, 95, 99, 102
Marrs, Suzanne, 38, 39, 78
mask, xi, 4, 19, 111, 136; African, 112
Mathé, Sylvia, 127, 129, 133
Matisse, Henri, 67–68, 73, 103, 126
McCarthyism, 119
McHaney, Thomas, 95
McWhirter, David, 152n1
Medusa, xi, 9, 11, 12, 14–15, 17, 18, 19, 25, 67, 72, 84, 95, 105, 121, 124, 125
Melville, Herman, 149n2
memory, 16, 26, 28, 31, 53, 71, 129, 136, 138, 140. *See also* Welty, Eudora: "A Memory"
Mencken, H. L., 83
Merleau-Ponty, Maurice, 130
Merlin, 91–93, 94, 150n3; Merlin principle, 91–93, 94, 101, 102, 105
Midsummer Night's Dream, A (Shakespeare), 117
Millsaps College, 58
Milner, Max, 137
Milton, John, x
mimesis, Aristotelian, 20
Minerva, 70–71
Minotaur, 110
mirror, xi, 11, 13, 14–15, 26, 27, 28, 32, 33, 95–96, 100, 105; mirror effect, 14, 19, 80, 84, 116–17, 129; mirror-shield, 4, 11, 67, 72, 125
mise en abyme, 41
Mississippi, 40, 41, 45, 58, 72, 118
Mississippi: A Guide to the Magnolia State, 63
Mississippi State College for Women, 58, 83
modernism, xi, 40, 44, 63–64, 108, 116, 118, 125, 138
modernity, 17–35, 57, 92, 93, 103, 108, 112, 119, 123, 126, 146n1
Mondrian, Piet, 38, 73, 80, 98, 110, 149n7
Monet, Claude, 32, 116
Montaigne, Michel, 78
Moreau, Gustave, 67
Morgana, 14, 27, 94
Morris, Henry C., 146n3 (chap. 1)
Morrison, Toni, 148n1 (chap. 6), 149n2
Moser, Barry, 148n5 (chap. 5)
Munch, Edvard, 38
Murdoch, Iris, 114
Murnau, F. W., 38
Museum of Modern Art, 104, 140, 151n10
musicals, 37, 110
"My Kinsman, Major Molineux" (Hawthorne), 39
mystery, ix, 3; of human heart, 67; southern, xi. *See also* Circe
mythical method, 8
mythology, 8, 29, 70, 125; Celtic, 7, 10, 92–93, 95; Greek, 7, 8, 9, 10, 92. *See also* Circe; "Leda and the Swan"; Medusa; Perseus; *individual mythic characters*

Natanson, Nathan, 65
Natchez, MS, 62
Natchez Trace, 63, 124
National Book Critics Circle Award, 128
nature, 4, 47, 49, 50, 54, 55, 59, 92, 119, 120, 121, 123. *See also* Arcadia
Nature of the Physical World, The (Eddington), 123–24
New Orleans, LA, 50, 73, 79, 110, 136
New York City, NY, 4, 37, 40, 41, 43, 44, 45, 57, 58, 60, 63, 73, 79, 93, 110, 118, 140; Union Square, 39–40, 73

New Yorker, 136
Niagara Falls, 86
Nietzsche, Friedrich, viii
1984 (Orwell), 38
Nissen, Axel, 93
North, the, 32, 40, 83, 118
nouveau roman, 31
novel, 112, 114–15, 128–30, 136, 141; form of, 29; modernist, 19, 22, 29; myth in, 29; pattern in, 29; postmodernist, 22

O'Connor, Flannery, 78
Odyssey, The (Homer), 46–56
Ohio, 86
O'Keefe, Georgia, 110
One Writer's Imagination (Marrs), 37, 94
On the Wings of Desire (Wenders), 70
operas, 37, 94
Orpheus, 92
Orwell, George, 38
other/otherness, 4, 5, 6, 11, 24–25, 27–28, 58, 61, 62, 64, 67, 81, 82, 95, 96, 99, 101, 122–23, 124, 126, 135, 139
Our Wonder World, 150n3

painters, xi; American, 120; avant-garde, 57–58; British, 120; Mexican, 120. *See also individual painters*
painting, 37, 38, 39, 41, 63–64, 94, 109, 110, 114; modern, 40, 44, 73, 80, 92, 97, 106, 121, 124
Paleolog, V. G., 104
Palleau, Françoise, 149n6
parody, viii
paternalism, 62
pattern, 29, 30
Paz, Octavio, 44
Penelope, 49
Persephone, 61
Perseus, xi, 4, 9–10, 11, 12, 13, 15, 18, 19, 26, 67, 72, 84, 95, 105, 125
photography, 6, 37, 58, 64–74, 88, 94, 109, 110
Piaget, Jean, 21
Picasso, Pablo, 36, 57, 90, 98, 110, 112
Pitavy, François, 143

Pitavy-Souques, Danièle, vii–xii, 143, 145n2 (chap. 1), 147n3 (chap. 3), 148n3 (chap. 5)
plantation, 62
Plato, Allegory of the Cave, 139
Poe, Edgar Allan, 19–20, 39, 52, 149n2
poetry, 20, 30, 37, 92, 94, 122, 140, 146n3 (chap. 2)
poets, 52, 53, 91, 109, 120
Polcari, Stephen, 120, 123
Polk, Noel, 94, 146n4 (chap. 1), 148n1 (chap. 5)
Pollack, Harriet, 38, 39, 79–80, 94, 149n5
Pollack, Jackson, 120, 123, 124
postmodernism, viii, xi, 19, 21, 22, 23, 29, 30, 34, 124–25, 146n4 (chap. 2), 147n5 (chap. 2), 151n2 (chap. 8)
Prenshaw, Peggy, 94
Price, Reynolds, 11, 12, 125, 149n2
Prometheus, 12, 55
Proust, Marcel, 22, 149n2
Pulitzer Prize, 128
Puritans, 82, 86, 87

race, 59, 65, 70, 78, 117, 135
racism, 80, 81, 82, 130, 132–33
rape, 69, 101, 102, 131
"Rappaccini's Daughter" (Hawthorne), 117
Ray, Man, 38
realism, 22–24, 25, 92
regionalism, 76, 78
Rembrandt, 88
Remembrance of Things Past (Proust), 127–29
representation, 20–22, 26. *See also* simulacrum
Ricardou, Jean, 15
Richard, Claude, 26
Ricoeur, Paul, 38
Robinson, John, 94, 104
Rodney, MS, 63
romanticism, 52
Rosenberg, Ethel and Julius, 119
Russell, Diarmuid, 96, 123
Russell, George William (A. E.), 4, 123

San Fransisco, CA, 58, 110
Sanctuary (Faulkner), 12

Sartre, Jean Paul, 11, 21, 95, 96, 99, 105
Saudades do Brasil (Lévi-Strauss), 66–67
Schama, Simon, 59, 62, 92–93
Scholes, Robert, 29, 114
sculpture, xi, 37, 94, 109, 110; modern, 103–4, 106
segregation, 59
Shakespeare, William, 117
shamanism, xi, 4, 5, 39, 52, 120–23, 124
Sicily, 46
Simon, Claude, 29
simulacrum, xi, 49, 52, 53, 55, 121, 131
slavery, xi, 59, 61, 62, 82, 119
Sollers, Philippe, 71
"Song of Wandering Aengus, The" (Yeats), 8, 146nn5–6
Sound and the Fury, The (Faulkner), 99
South, the, viii, 4–5, 19–20, 30, 31, 32, 33–34, 40, 50, 57–74, 75, 76, 77, 78, 80, 81, 82, 83, 115, 116, 118, 128, 137, 139, 151n2; modern, 63; women writers, 75, 78
Southern Literary Festival, 146n1
Southern Review, 4, 120
Spencer, Elizabeth, 69
Stevenson, Adlai, 78
structure en abyme, 116, 151n2
Surfacing (Atwood), x
surrealism, 38, 39, 40–44, 92, 98, 106, 109, 116, 117, 118, 119, 120

Tanner, Tony, 23
technique: displacement, 111–12; myth, 7–16; narrative, xi, 3, 7–16; transformation, 111, 112
Temptation of Eve (Gislebertus), 150n8
theater, 37, 94, 110; catoptric, 117
time, ix, 16, 32, 38, 44, 46, 47, 55, 75, 84, 88, 100. *See also* Welty, Eudora: "Circe"; "A Still Moment"
Tolstoy, Leo, 127
Tombigbee River, 83
Torcello, Italy, 113
totalitarianism, 61, 120
To the Lighthouse (Woolf), 114, 136, 137–38
transcendentalism, 123

Twain, Mark, 17–18, 36–37, 90–91, 108, 149n2, 150n3

Ulysses (Joyce), 7, 147n2 (chap. 4)
United States, 59, 93, 94
University of Burgundy, viii, x
University of Virginia, 143
University of Wisconsin, 58, 91, 108
"Upon Looking into Chapman's Homer" (Keats), vii

Vadé, Yves, 91, 92, 93
Vande Kieft, Ruth, 20, 21, 148n3 (chap. 6)
Van Eyck, Jan, 32, 151n2
Van Gogh, Vincent, 38
vaunting, xi, 12, 17–19, 37, 90, 108
Vermeer, Jan, 151n2
violence, viii, 24, 38–44, 54, 75, 79, 92, 94, 109, 117, 118, 130–31
Virginia, 81–82
vision, 13, 23, 26, 29, 31, 53, 57, 88, 92, 95, 100, 101, 114, 118, 124, 126, 137–38, 141; in art, 3–4, 16, 71–72, 111–12, 139; of life, 3, 58, 67, 85, 96, 105, 133–35; of South, 58, 60–61. *See also* Welty, Eudora: "Flowers for Marjorie"; "A Still Moment"
Vitrac, Roger, 106
Vuillard, Édouard, 32, 116

Waller, Thomas (Fats), 111
War and Peace (Tolstoy), 127
Warren, Robert Penn, 20
Welty, Edward, 129, 135–36
Welty, Eudora: "Acrobats in a Park," 60; Americanness of, 78; "The Bride of the Innisfallen," 18, 69; *The Bride of the Innisfallen and Other Stories*, 46, 116, 128; brother (Walter), 129; "Circe," 46–56, 147n1 (chap. 4), 147n3 (chap. 4), 151n4; *Collected Stories*, 71, 148n5 (chap. 5); *Country Churchyards*, 69; "A Curtain of Green," 4–6, 15, 44, 120–23, 124, 125; *A Curtain of Green and Other Stories*, 4, 21, 39, 70, 94, 115, 124; "Death of a Traveling Salesman," 21, 82, 114; *Delta Wedding*, 117;

"The Demonstrators," 82, 94, 118, 152n2; father (Christian), 86, 87, 107; "Flowers for Marjorie," 21, 36–45, 94, 110, 117, 118–19, 147n5 (chap. 3); "The Golden Apples," 8; *The Golden Apples*, viii, 7–16, 17, 27, 70, 72, 88–89, 90–106, 125, 126, 150n4; "The House of Willa Cather," 17–18, 36–37, 90–91, 108, 149n9; "How I Write," 3; "Is Phoenix Jackson's Grandson Really Dead?," 100, 111; "June Recital," 8, 10, 12, 13, 14–15, 17, 72, 85, 99, 107; "Keela, the Outcast Indian Maiden," 70; "The Key," 19, 87; "Kin," 30, 32–34, 112, 115, 116, 151n2; "Lily Daw and the Three Ladies," 69–70; "Livvie," 59, 61–63, 70, 119; *Losing Battles*, 15, 18, 63, 68, 69, 128–29, 130–35, 140–41, 148n4 (chap. 5); "A Memory," 21–25, 27, 57, 86, 97, 99; mother (Chestina), 83, 84, 86, 135; "Moon Lake," 9, 12, 13, 23, 27–28, 69, 103, 106; "Music from Spain," 12, 13, 60, 72, 110, 150n4; "Must the Novelist Crusade?," 36, 118; "No Place for You, My Love," 3; "Old Mr Grenada," 31; "Old Mr Marblehall," 17, 25, 30–32, 33, 112, 115–16; "One Time, One Place," 64, 66, 68, 72, 123, 152n2; *One Time, One Place*, 6, 60, 61, 66, 68, 69, 71, 128; *One Writer's Beginnings*, ix, 57, 75–89, 100, 107, 110, 113, 122, 128–30, 136, 139, 141, 149n4, 149n10; "The Optimist's Daughter," 72; *The Optimist's Daughter*, 15, 16, 18, 32, 63, 127, 128–30, 135–39, 140–41; parents, 59, 149n10; as photographer, 6, 39–40, 60, 64–74, 112, 124; *Photographs*, 148n8; photographs by, 39, 40, 61, 63, 68, 69, 71–72, 79, 124, 148n5 (chap. 4); "A Piece of News," 21, 69; "Place in Fiction," 67; *The Ponder Heart*, 39, 94, 118, 119; "Poor Eyes," 148n7; "Powerhouse," 21, 70, 72, 81, 111–12, 120; "Put Me in the Sky!," 51, 147n1 (chap. 4); *The Robber Bridegroom*, 19, 94, 101, 104, 105, 117, 118, 150n7, 151n12; "Shower of Gold," 8–9, 10, 11, 13–14, 96, 105, 106, 127; "Sir Rabbit," 12, 13, 90, 92, 96, 100–103, 105; "Some Notes on Time in Fiction," 46, 85; in *The Spectator*, 83; "A Still Moment," 12, 25–27, 61, 121, 124–25; "The Wanderers," 9, 11–12, 13, 15, 71, 88–89, 94–95, 96, 99, 104, 125, 126; "Where Is the Voice Coming From?," 94, 118, 149n4, 152n2; "The Whistle," 94; "The Whole World Knows," 12, 13, 90, 92, 96, 97–102, 105; *The Wide Net and Other Stories*, 25, 29, 121; "The Winds," 99; "Words into Fiction," 3, 23, 29, 60, 108, 113, 114–15, 116, 122; "A Worn Path," 70, 81; "Writing and Analyzing a Short Story," 3
Wenders, Wim, 70
West Virginia, 81–82, 84–86, 87
Wharton, Edith, 58, 149n2
Wheatley, Patricia, 141
White, T. H., 150n3
Whitman, Walt, 149n2
Wiebe, Rudy, 3, 57, 67
Wild Strawberries (Bergman), 136
William E. Massey Sr. Lectures in the History of American Civilization, 76, 78, 107
Winter, William, viii
women, ix, 28, 45, 46, 65, 69, 70, 97, 105, 112, 117, 119, 134, 138, 165; as writers, ix, 76, 85, 91, 149n2. *See also* South, the; *individual women writers*
Woodburn, John, 4, 5
Woolf, Virginia, 13, 19, 26, 97, 102, 114, 116, 125, 136, 138, 146n8, 149n2
WPA (Works Progress Administration), 6, 43, 58, 63, 73, 129
World War I, 37, 39, 109, 120, 137
World War II, 5, 120
Wright, Richard, 77

Yaeger, Patricia, 100
Yeats, W. B., 8, 10, 91, 146n5, 149n2
"Young Goodman Brown" (Hawthorne), 39, 44

ABOUT THE AUTHOR AND EDITOR

Danièle Pitavy-Souques (1937–2019), former professor emerita of the University of Burgundy, France, and recipient of the Eudora Welty Society Phoenix Award, was the European powerhouse of Welty studies. She is the author of two monographs and more than a dozen essays on Welty. A recipient of the French Legion of Honor for her work on international women's rights, she made major contributions to Southern and Canadian studies.

Pearl Amelia McHaney, Kenneth M. England Professor of Southern Literature emerita of Georgia State University, is also a recipient of the Eudora Welty Society Phoenix Award for outstanding achievement in Welty studies. She published *A Tyrannous Eye: Eudora Welty's Nonfiction and Photography* and edited *Eudora Welty as Photographer* (Eudora Welty Prize); *Occasions: Selected Writings by Eudora Welty*; *Eudora Welty: Contemporary Reviews*; and *A Writer's Eye: Collected Reviews by Eudora Welty*.

Printed by BoD in Norderstedt, Germany